LESSONS LEARNED

PRAISE FOR LESSONS LEARNED

Burke's essays speak to a multitude of audiences, reminding us that we are all both teachers and learners. I enjoyed the humor, honesty, and grit of his anecdotes, but I found myself wanting to speed to the end of some essays—where Burke reflects on what he learned—because that was (to me) the highest portion of the work. What did he learn and from whom? —Mr. Darren Pierre, Senior Lecturer, Office of Global Engineering Leadership, University of Maryland; author of *The Invitation to Love: Recognizing the Gift Despite Pain, Fear, and Resistance*; recipient of the 2021 Loyola University Chicago Transformative Educator Award

I cannot wait to buy this book for everyone I know: new teachers who would like a fast-track to hard-earned wisdom; veteran teachers who enjoy reminiscing and reflecting on their own practice; parents who want to raise strong, thoughtful children; anyone who loves to laugh out loud and then get choked up from a masterfully told story; and myself. I raced through my first read to discover how each anecdote would end and what the next anecdote would be about, but now I want to linger in the philosophy and keep pondering even after I close the cover. —Ms. Laura Johnson, English Teacher; master's in literature, Northwestern University; master's in writing and publishing, DePaul University

This book is not really, or at least not all, about teaching. It's about teaching. And it's not. It's about a man's quest to examine his life and to live it meaningfully. It's a model for how we can learn from the most painful and the most joyful moments of our lives and use these lessons to make us better teachers, coaches, leaders, and people. —Mr. Jacob Sweetow, Licensed Clinical Social Worker

These essays—and the discussion questions at the end—are ideal for education classes and professional development. Burke confronts issues both in and out of the classroom that are relevant to all teachers and prime for deliberation and debate.—Mr. Andrew Sharos, high school administrator, author of *All 4s and 5s: A Guide to Teaching and Leading Advanced Placement Programs* and *Finding Lifelines: A Practical Tale about Teachers and Mentors*

LESSONS LEARNED

A TEACHER AND COACH REFLECTS

MICHAEL F. BURKE, SR.

W. Brand Publishing

NASHVILLE, TENNESSEE

W. Brand Publishing is committed to publishing works of quality and integrity. In that spirit, we are proud to offer this book to our readers; however, the story, the experiences, and the words are the author's alone and portrayed to the best of their recollection. In some cases, names have been changed to protect the privacy of the people involved.

Copyright ©2025 Michael F. Burke, Sr.

All rights reserved. No part of this publication may be reproduced, distributed, or transmitted in any form or by any means, including photocopying, recording, or other electronic or mechanical methods, without the prior written permission of the publisher, except in the case of brief quotations embodied in critical reviews and certain other noncommercial uses permitted by copyright law. For permission requests, write to the publisher, addressed "Attention Permission Request" at the email below.

j.brand@wbrandpub.com
W. Brand Publishing
www.wbrandpub.com

Cover design by JuLee Brand / designchik

Lessons Learned / Michael F. Burke, Sr.–1st ed.

Available in Paperback, Kindle, and eBook formats.
Paperback: 979-8-89503-016-5
eBook: 979-8-89503-017-2
Library of Congress Control Number: 2025906452

CONTENTS

Chapter 1: Moonshine 1
Chapter 2: Seek Thyself 7
Chapter 3: Ethos and Titular Power 11
Chapter 4: Hot Lava 29
Chapter 5: Soldier's Work 41
Chapter 6: The Sneeze 63
Chapter 7: Love Taps 67
Chapter 8: A Recovery Run 87
Chapter 9: Escalation 105
Chapter 10: Righteous Indignation 123
Chapter 11: The Olive Tree 143
Chapter 12: Ought versus Actual: Clarissa 153
Chapter 13: The Double Bird 161
Chapter 14: Wrestling with an Existential Crisis 167
Chapter 15: Survival 191
Chapter 16: A Healthy Dose of Skepticism (x3) 213
Chapter 17: The Mask 235
Chapter 18: Why Wrestling 255
Chapter 19: Viewing Death 263
Chapter 20: Football and "The Scorpion and the Frog" .. 285
Chapter 21: Tough Love and Late Essays 313
Chapter 22: The Journey 325
Chapter 23: On Altruism 351
Chapter 24: Why Read Literature: Whitman, "Song of
    Myself, 52" 371
Chapter 25: Acknowledgments 383
Chapter 26: Discussion Questions: Lessons Learned 391
About the Author 397

The unexamined life is not worth living.
—Socrates

***

I too am not a bit tamed, I too am untranslatable,
I sound my barbaric yawp over the roofs of the world.
—Walt Whitman, from *Song of Myself*, 52

***

People more frequently require to be reminded than informed.
—Samuel Johnson

***

Be a Filter, Not a Funnel
—M.F. Burke

CHAPTER 1

MOONSHINE

The end of all philosophy is absurdity.
—Anonymous

(1)

IN LATE FALL OF 1964, my parents went to visit a friend of my father from high school who was, at the time, a Trappist monk at the Abbey of Our Lady of Gethsemani in Bardstown, Kentucky. They stayed the weekend.

Sunday morning, after my parents attended mass with the monks at the Abbey, as they prepared to leave, Brother Steve gave my father a gift to help him "fight insomnia": a bottle of Kentucky moonshine. 190 proof. 95% alcohol. Strong enough to power their Plymouth station wagon should they run short of gasoline on the way home.

The clear, glass bottle had a cork stopper and contained a perfectly transparent liquid. The bottle had no actual label, though there were three black X's across the middle. These three X's, I later learned, meant the contents had been distilled three times. With each distillation, the alcohol content rose, and the taste smoothed. Brother Steve had gotten my father the good stuff.

When my parents returned from Kentucky Sunday evening, they bragged to my oldest siblings about this special gift. They opened the bottle that night, filled two shot glasses, toasted each other: "Sláinte!" and nipped the moonshine. Each assessed and shrugged. Though the alcohol content was evident, the moonshine had no real flavor. My parents preferred their Manhattans. They finished the shots—no need for waste—put the bottle in their liquor cabinet, and let it be.

The following weekend, my parents went to our neighbor's house to play bridge, their favorite card game. They left my oldest brother and oldest sister, 14 and 12 respectively, to babysit the rest of us. (I have seven total siblings: four older brothers, two older sisters, and one younger sister.)

After my parents left, the eight of us spread across the various chairs and couches of our family room—my infant sister in her playpen—to watch *Flipper*. Each time Flipper surfaced, some sibling would try to mimic the dolphin's kookaburra cackle. My parody apparently drew the most laughs, sounding somewhere between Elmer Fudd's giggle and the bray of a jackass. We stayed that way through thirty minutes of wholesome, family entertainment.

At the program break, before *The Adventures of Mr. Magoo* began, my brother popped up from the chair he stretched diagonally across and rushed from the room. No one took note—program breaks and bathroom visits often coincided—until he sauntered back into the room, his arms wrapped behind him, an impish smile on his face. He took center stage in front of the TV and paused, milking the audience, before drawing the bottle of moonshine from behind his back and holding it up before him. We all smiled. Mr. Magoo was entertaining, but this was naughty—one of my mom's oft-used words to describe our transgressions.

In a sing-song voice, my sister chimed, "You're gonna get in trouuuu-ble."

My brother leered at her, muttering, "Shut up." (In our house, "Shut up" was a curse.) She didn't flinch. Ignoring her, he raised the corked bottle to his lips and pretended to take a drink. Much to our amusement, he crossed his eyes, slanted his jaw far to the right, and began staggering around. We all laughed.

"Open it!" my sister dared, now an instigator. The price of poker just went up.

"Yeah!" another brother added. The younger of us began clapping in unison; the baby lifted her head to the disturbance.

My one sister, however, the middle one, the seven-year-old, protested. Drawing shallow breaths, dawning tears moistening her eyes, she cautioned, barely a whisper, "Don't!" She shook her head, pleading. She had reached the age of reason, made her first confession, and, just a few weeks earlier, received her first communion. She was trying to be good.

But she was outnumbered. Everyone else egged my brother on: Do It! He popped the cork. We sighed in awe. He slowly pulled the bottle to his nose and took a sniff. He puzzled, took a stronger whiff, frowned, and, skeptical of the lack of smell and color, moved the bottle away to check it at arm's length. What *was* in here?

My sister seized on his hesitancy. "Gimme it!" Now a conspirator, she snatched the bottle and drew it close. She kissed the rim with both lips, then let her tongue slip just inside. She began tilting the bottle so the moonshine slid toward her taste buds, but she too flinched and pulled back.

"Not me," she said, handing the bottle back and returning to her seat on the couch. My brother scanned the lot of us, probing for a victim. He had no volunteers. No one spoke up. My eyes, however, let slip my desire.

"Michael," he announced, pointing his right index finger heavenward. Everyone turned to me, the four-year-old. I sprang from the couch and stood square-shouldered, a dutiful private.

I should note that, for soon-to-be apparent reasons, I don't have a firsthand memory of this specific event. However, I do remember, throughout my childhood, being willing to do just about anything to gain the attention and approval of my older brothers and sisters. Plus, I was the perfect patsy: too young to understand what was happening meant too young to squeal.

My brother started to pass me the moonshine . . . and pulled it back. He thought for a second. There were risks here. He tapped the bottle with his forefinger, thinking this through. In short, the light bulb above him flickered to a blaze. Eureka! Another flash of inspiration. Not wanting to risk me chugging half the bottle, he pointed toward the kitchen and shared his revelation: "A shot glass!"

The seven of us adjourned to the kitchen, leaving the infant behind. My brother took down the shot glass and filled it seven-eighths full. He handed me the tiny glass—well-suited for my wee hand—and I held it up to the semi-circle of siblings now surrounding me.

Steady, I brought it to my lips, hesitated, and downed it with bravado.

I winced and shivered, but bravely held the glass out in front of me as if for another. One more tremble bubbled up, my breathing hitched, and I timbered like a pine tree and fell face first into the floor. They thought they killed me.

First comes the laughing, then comes the crying.

With siblings, horseplay almost always ends up with someone getting hurt. Under these circumstances, in our family, crying was disdained and tattling was anathema. Do the first, and you'll be teased mercilessly. Do the second, and you'll be ostracized from any future tomfoolery (another mom word). Cast out. Banished. The underlying principle is one of personal responsibility. You knew (or should have known) what we were getting into when this started, so no waterworks. And, should things go awry, we handle this ourselves. Leave mom and dad out of it.

They stood over me.

"Michael!" My brother called. I didn't move.

"Michael?" He repeated.

My sister inched forward and nudged me with her foot, "Michael?" Nothing. She kicked a little harder. No response. The younger siblings slid back a step.

A moment of silence.

And another epiphany. My brother and my sister looked at each other and shrugged. Palms up, saying nothing but reading each other's minds, they reached a simultaneous conclusion: None of this had ever happened!

They sent the others back to the family room and Mr. Magoo. Together in the kitchen, my brother took my shoulders, and my sister took my feet, and they carried my body upstairs. They changed me into my pajamas and tucked me comfortably into the white cotton sheets of my bed. They covered me with the crocheted blanket my aunt had gifted at my birth. For the pièce de résistance, they curled Mr. Cuddles (my teddy bear) into my arm.

They stood back. "He looks just like he's sleeping," my brother observed. My sister bowed serenely, then caught herself.

"He *is* sleeping," she insisted, and elbowed him in the ribs.

"Right."

They turned and left, closing the door behind them.

In the morning, when I was found dead, my parents would think I had mercifully passed during the night—not a bad way to go—and all would be buried.

(2)

All that is not tragedy is comedy

One advantage of looking back is appreciating that so much of what could have been tragedy ends up comedy.

As I mentioned, I don't remember this story. What I do remember is it being told so often because it was funny. They could have killed me, but they didn't. They had no malicious intent. Their decisions were purely pragmatic. And everything turned out okay.

Yes, learn from the experience—one reason to keep re-telling the story—but don't obsess over an outcome that didn't occur. Sometimes—most times—it's best to laugh and shake our heads at the absurdity of it all.

CHAPTER 2

SEEK THYSELF

(1)

I LOVED TEACHING AND coaching.
That's the catharsis of completing a marathon. Once it's over, you look back and think: That was . . . for the most part . . . *fun*. And then you head to the beer tent.
I had a long career. Four-plus decades in education. Though I felt the heat, I didn't burn out, and I never got fired. I finished with my sanity, my self-respect, and my sense-of-humor intact. I was also decent at what I did right through my final day. These things are important because I'm somewhat surprised I survived. I've always had an Oedipus Rex-ian fear of, excuse my language (and the pun), fucking things up:

Let every man in mankind's frailty consider his last day; and let none presume on his good fortune until he finds life, at his death, a memory without pain. —Sophocles, *Oedipus the King.*

But I didn't, and despite some adversity, I made it. I finished.
When I retired, I wanted to try writing (every English teacher's dream). I've always been intrigued by

Socrates' dictum, "The unexamined life is not worth living," so I decided to start there: an examined life. Or, to quote a sign hanging in my classroom, *Seek Thyself!*

I began by word-vomiting any story or experience or musing that came to mind, anything that seemed to matter from any point in my life. I had a lot in my head, but I didn't try to control or organize what came out. I figured that whatever fought its way to the top was worth putting down on paper (keying into the cloud?).

I did this for nine months—whatever gurgled up from whatever stage of my life—and ended up with over 150,000 words worth of "stuff." I took a month off and then re-read everything to determine what I had.

What I had was the good fortune of a memory without pain.[1] Trials and tribulations, for sure, some gut punches, but a lot of laughs, meaningful relationships, and notable lessons.

I started revising with a focus on what helped me be a better teacher, as in *a person who teaches*, not just the professional educator. I zeroed in on anecdotes and people and lessons. What did I learn and from whom? To use a writing metaphor, I went through and picked out the best bones and then set about piecing them together and adding the vital flesh essential to bringing it all to life.[2]

This collection is the result.

---

1   I like the word *fortune* in this context. I wasn't lucky; lucky things just happen. Fortune is, as a former colleague says, "Learned and Earned." They don't call the top businesses the Lucky 500, and the expression isn't "Luck favors the brave." *Fortune* 500 and *Fortune* favors the brave. Learned and Earned.

2   There is a certain Frankensteinian element to writing anecdotes: resurrecting and sewing together that which is dead and gone, and giving it new life.

I wrote these essays as a teacher for teachers (and students), including anyone who wants to teach well, in any role. That's all of us. I also wrote them for everyone working to be decent at what they do on their everyday human journey. In other words, me pursuing my better, most authentic self. Introspection, practical philosophy, critical thinking, and laughter. Four essentials.

(2)

ALL THE SIGNIFICANT EVENTS in these essays happened. For the most part, I wrote each experience the way I remembered it. I did, however, exercise discretion by changing names, amalgamating characters, and altering a few details. I also had fun writing.

Though these essays are meant to be read consecutively—I have put thought into the order—they are not chronological. Like Billy Pilgrim, they are unstuck in time.[3] I did this to honor some of the randomness of my original brainstorming. At the same time, I wanted to provide a navigable arc to my life and career. So, I jump around, but with some design. Everything should fit together by the end.

(3)

WHEN I FIRST STARTED teaching, my division head at Notre Dame High School, Mr. Vanden Busch, gave me some great advice. He said that the best teachers don't "instruct"; they share what they've learned. That's what I'm trying to do here, share the good stuff,

---

3   Kurt Vonnegut, *Slaughterhouse-Five*.

starting with a shot of triple distilled moonshine and ending with a *Yawp!*

Join me for a few good hours.

CHAPTER 3

ETHOS & TITULAR POWER

(1)

MY TEACHING CAREER BEGAN with a lie.

In the spring of 1982, shortly before graduating from the University of Notre Dame, I applied for a job teaching English at Fenwick High School in Oak Park, Illinois. Fenwick was, and still is, an elite Catholic institution run by members of the Dominican Order.

I had an inside connection. A friend of mine from Notre Dame who had graduated from Fenwick and remained in very high standing had called both the principal and the athletic director on my behalf. I wasn't surprised when the English Division Head, Father Uhrik, called to invite me in for an interview. We met at Fenwick on a Saturday afternoon and spent an hour or so walking the mostly empty halls of the building talking about literature, writing, and my student-teaching experience. Because we were walking and talking, the interview didn't feel like an interview, which made me more comfortable and more cautious.

Twice during our journey we stopped outside classrooms where teachers were instructing small groups of students. "Tutoring," Fr. Uhrik said, and I knew this was an unpaid expectation. There would be no "school day" at Fenwick.

My afternoon with Fr. Uhrik went well—I saw much of those I respected in him—and I was invited to meet the following Thursday with the principal, the assistant principal for curriculum, and the dean of students. For all intents and purposes, I had the job. This second interview was more to introduce Fenwick to me and prepare me for how things were done.

On the Tuesday before that meeting, I received a phone call from the Assistant Principal for Curriculum, Dr. Johnson. "Mike, we need you to teach one section of foreign language. How's your Spanish?"

Ummmm, "I had four years in high school."

"It's freshmen. Beginning Spanish. You'll be fine. This should be just a one year gig."

I assumed she had read my transcripts and knew I took Intermediate Spanish the first semester of my freshman year in college. However, unless she brought it up, I wasn't going to remind her that I got a "D" in the class or inform her that my near failing was mostly because I kept blowing off the live discussion sessions. Who in the hell schedules live discussion sessions on Thursday night, the first night of the weekend?

I also didn't tell her that my Honors Spanish teacher junior and senior year of high school had been much more into Spanish history and literature than the language itself. We learned a lot about Spain—a dozen of us even flew to Spain with him and a history teacher for a week during winter break of my senior year—we just didn't learn that much conversational Spanish.

"I'm not certified to teach Spanish. Is that a problem?" I have no idea why I said this. I needed a job. I should have been willing to teach AP Physics if that's what it took to get hired.

"Don't worry about it. We'll get a provisional." A provisional is a one-time exception from the Illinois State Board of Education that allows a non-certified teacher to fill an area of need.

"Great," I said. "I can handle it. I'll do whatever you need."

She paused.

"The head of Foreign Languages is kind of a stickler though, so he's going to interview you as well. He'll do his interview in Spanish. Any problem with that?"

I immediately regretted all those missed Thursday night live discussion sessions. "No problema."

I didn't really say that.

"No, Ma'am," is what I said.

"Good. Monday morning. 8 a.m. You'll meet with the administrative team first and then interview with Father Francisco. See you Monday."

"Thanks," I said. I hung up the phone. An interview, in Spanish. I nodded toward my reflection in the kitchen window, muttering a catchphrase from the old Laurel and Hardy movies: Well, here's another nice mess you've gotten me into!

(2)

MY INTERVIEW WITH THE administrative team went well.

My interview with Fr. Francisco[4] began well. We started in English, talking about my general education background, the Spanish classes I had taken, even the trip to Spain during my senior year of high school.

"Now let's continue in Spanish," he said, and we did. I would love to record here some of the questions he asked in Spanish, but I still have no idea what he was saying.

I leaned closer, as if proximity—along with scrunching my cheeks and tilting my head to get a better angle on the sounds—might help my understanding. I could pick out a few words and phrases, but stringing it all together into some discernible question, let alone then formulating a coherent response to that question, was impossible.

I kept repeating, "Mas despacio, por favor." In English: *Please, slow down!*

Each time I said it he cringed. I felt like a fool.

After just five minutes of futility, he gave up. His eyes fell to the desk, and he palmed his forehead in his right hand and whispered, "Ay, Dios mío!" I knew what that meant.

I thought I was finished, but Fr. Francisco regrouped and changed tack. Neither one of us wanted to be in this position, but he was stuck with one extra section of Freshman Spanish to fill, and the administration was not about to hire a part-time teacher. I was his only option.

In clear, definitive English, slow and deliberate, he told me, "You seem like a good kid."

---

4   Those familiar with Fr. Francisco called him "Fr. Pancho." However, that familiarity—and the mutual respect it entailed—had to be earned from and bestowed by Fr. Francisco. He decided when you could use this more informal and amicable moniker.

He reached to a table behind him and grabbed a copy of the text I'd be teaching from. "Read the first few chapters and then we'll talk about how to construct your lesson plans. Teaching a foreign language is not the same as teaching English. We'll work it out."

I nodded, ready to leave, but he planted his elbow on the table, pointed his index finger at me, and, looking straight down the barrel, added, "No more bullshit. I'm not going to look over your shoulder every minute, but if you get lost or are unsure of anything, you come to me immediately. We'll work it out."

We stood and shook hands, but he held on a little too long, unable to resist a jab at my incompetence.

"Mas despacio," he chaffed, shaking his head. I shrugged and smiled.

I got the job, contingent on my taking a class called *Conversational Spanish* that summer at Oakton Community College.

(3)

FENWICK'S NICKNAME IS THE Friars. The school's colors are black and white. Literally, black and white.

In most years, 100% of its 250+ graduates go on to attend a four-year college. Highly selective. Academics are paramount. Fenwick now is co-ed; at the time, it was all-boys.

The students and the male lay faculty, at that time, all wore dress pants: preferably black; a long sleeve dress shirt: preferably white; and a tie: preferably red. The female faculty members preferred skirts and long sleeve blouses.

The religious members of the faculty and administrative team preferred the Blackfriar habit of the Dominican order: a white tunic, scapular, and capuce covered with a black cappa and capuce. In other words, a white tunic, shoulder cape, and hood, covered by a black shoulder cape and hood. The ensemble was secured by a leather belt from which hung a palm-sized wooden rosary, always visible and in reach.

There were few disciplinary issues.

The most rebellious behavior I witnessed during my year at Fenwick was the occasional senior unbuttoning the top button of his dress shirt and allowing his tie to hang slack around his neck. If I passed such a student in the hall, all I had to do was point and say, "Fix it."

The student always obliged, because he should, and because if he didn't, he'd be on his way to see the Dean of Students, Father Hell.

Corporal punishment was still very much in vogue at Fenwick in the early 1980's. Father Hell—a nickname I doubt he resented; his actual name was Father Heilmann—paced the halls of the high school with his left arm folded behind his back and his right hand gently covering his heart. The fingers of this right hand were spread in an El Greco "W," the middle and ring fingers together, the index and pinky each spread slightly. He was rumored to have elastic digits, fingers that gumbied several inches as that right hand took flight, adding considerably to the whip of his justice. A smack upside the head or across the cheek, expedient and emphatic, corrected all indiscretions. With Father Hell as the alternative, students—even seniors who were only four years my junior—obeyed me.

Father Heilmann administered his most personal form of counsel with Machiavellian discretion, maintaining fear, but never provoking hatred. To be fair, only once did I see Father Hell actually strike a student: a slap across the face for a delinquency I did not witness. When it happened, I averted my eyes and kept moving, as did all the other students and staff passing in the hallway.

Most often, he paced the halls with a stately gait, nodding and smiling as he passed students and staff; polite, but distant. His presence and potential were enough to ensure that students—and staff—complied with norms.

Fenwick students had fun; there were clubs and plays and sports and band and even a spring variety show. They just knew boundaries, and the consequence of violating those boundaries.

(4)

THE INSTANT I WAS hired at Fenwick I had credibility. My title, *Mr.* Burke, meant I had authority, power. I was the teacher. After a lifetime of being the student, I had flipped sides. I loved it.

I had four sections of freshman English, three regular and one honors. No problem there. I had gotten good advice at Notre Dame and supplemented the normal variety of literature classes most English majors take with courses in rhetoric, linguistics, and advanced grammar construction. The freshmen I taught didn't see me as a rookie; they saw me as an adult, a professional, mostly because I knew so much more than they did.

My one Spanish class kept me busy, but I managed to stay the requisite one-chapter-ahead of the students. I went to Fr. Francisco for advice, always when I needed it and sometimes when I didn't. He kept his vow as well and allowed me space to figure out most things for myself.

In English, I thrived. In Spanish, I survived.

(5)

Fenwick's parent-teacher conferences were held six weeks into each semester. The conferences took place in the gym in what I realize now was an absurd, but perhaps purposeful arrangement.

Fifty-some teachers lined up around the outside perimeter of the gym, about ten feet apart. Each teacher stood behind a small strip of masking tape designating his or her spot. In front of each teacher, ten feet into the center of the gym, was another strip of masking tape. This is where parents desiring a conference would line up and wait their turn. When I first arrived, just the teachers and staff were in the gym, milling about, talking, laughing. Then we got our cue from Fr. Heilmann, and we receded to our spots, silent for a moment of reflection until the main doors of the gym swung outward and a throng of parents herded en masse to the open center of the gym. It was chaos.

To have a conference, parents had to find one of their child's teachers (we were grouped alphabetically by department) and then stand in line for twenty minutes for a three-minute discussion where little could be accomplished. There were no chairs, minimal privacy, and a nauseating buzz of white noise.

The whole rigmarole had an air of condescension. The Dominican Order is known for its emphasis on wholistic education. Fenwick has been a premier college preparatory school since 1929. "We know what we are doing, we are the experts," the chaos suggested, "but since you (the parents) insist on Parent-Teacher conferences, here you go."

The night of fall conferences, I shaved close, spruced up with some Old Spice cologne, perfectly parted my hair, donned my only suit: a pinstripe navy blue three-piece with a starched white dress shirt and a red-over-white houndstooth tie, and felt mature.

Twenty-two-year-old me, the Teacher, was set to preside over the common folk. I stood on my spot in the gym and regally waved forward whoever had moved to the front of the line.

"What is your son's name?" I'd ask. I'd page through my grade book and tell the parents what a great kid they had if he had an A. I told them what a good kid they had if he had a B and how he could move up to an A if he put in more time and effort.

I had few C's, and fewer of these parents showed up. If they did, I lowered my voice when advising that their son needed to step up. More time. More focus. More effort.

I didn't have any D's or F's.

In pressure situations, I have a propensity for both poise and perspiration. Keep calm and sweat. I trace these antithetical abilities to my many nights losing weight as a high school wrestler: Two pounds to go, don't stress, take a few deep breaths, and get back in the sauna.

Which is what, ninety minutes in, the gym now resembled. Warm, moist air puffed out with every spoken word. Kinetic shuffling. Anxious fidgeting. The gym had no air conditioning, and I'm pretty sure the ventilation system was turned off. Conferences were winding down, and for a moment, I had no one waiting. Perhaps that's why I suddenly became aware of my own dampness. My crotch, my armpits, my sternum. Everything was swampy, but, fortunately, hidden by the various layers of that navy blue suit. Only my face was exposed.

I reached to the inside pocket of my suit jacket and withdrew my handkerchief. I dabbed my forehead and my upper lip and took a deep breath. A momentary respite. Almost done, and, if I might say, *well* done. I tucked the handkerchief into my back pants pocket, took another breath, looked up, and smiled at the parent now waiting. Come forward.

(6)

Sergio's mom.

When his mom introduced herself, I felt an excitement, as if I had bragging rights to her son's performance in my class. *I* was proud of him. I raved about what a great student Sergio was. "He has the highest grade in my Spanish class, a near perfect A." She smiled, and nodded, dropping her eyes modestly. There wasn't much more to say, he was excellent, so I prepared to dismiss her.

Instead, she violated protocol.

She pulled a sheet of paper from her purse and politely asked a question in deliberate English, "Mr. Burke, el professor, Sergio showed me this quiz. He does not understand why his answers were incorrect." She handed me the quiz.

The quiz was a simple *Days of the Week* fill-in-the-blanks. Next to Monday, the students were to write "Lunes"; next to Tuesday, "Martes"; and so on.

Sergio, however, had added the article next to each day of the week: *el* Lunes, *el* Martes, et cetera.

The Monday, *The* Tuesday? Out of 30 in the class, his was the only quiz that added articles.

I remembered the quiz and his answer sheet. It had stood out to me as I sat in my townhouse sipping a Guinness, watching the White Sox, and doing some evening grading.

"He didn't know any better?" I assumed, feeling a little sorry for Sergio. I used a red pen to slash out each of the articles on the paper but deducted only one point overall. He did, after all, get the days correct.

Later, after I had handed back the quizzes, I asked Fr. Francisco about days of the week and articles and learned that, yes, the article should be included except in certain circumstances. I learned something, but pride prevented me from telling Sergio and giving him back his point.

I was the teacher; I wasn't about to debase myself to a student, especially a freshman. He didn't need that point anyhow.

When Sergio's mom handed me the quiz, I never considered being honest. I took one look at it, knew fully well what had happened, and coughed up bullshit so fast and so ingenious that I'm still impressed with myself.

"Where are you from?" I asked.

"Madrid, Spain. My husband and I moved here with Sergio a few years ago."

"That explains it," I reassured her. "My college professor was from Cuba, and in Cuba, they don't use articles with days of the week."

A college professor from Cuba? Malebolge, the eighth circle of Dante's Hell, awaits me[5].

She took it, gladly. She clapped her hands together beneath her chin and pursed her lips in a deep sigh. Tears welled in her eyes and the tension fell from her shoulders. She cried—I am not exaggerating. She was so relieved. Sergio had not been wrong; and, more important, the teacher had not been wrong.

"From now on," she said, "I will tell Sergio to follow whatever you teach."

From now on, I thought to myself, *I will use Sergio's answer sheet as the key.*

She reached out and took my right hand with both of hers, lowering her eyes in welcome supplication.

"Gracias, Profesor," she said, "Gracias."

(7)

AM I PROUD OF what I did?

---

5 In his *Inferno*, part one of *The Divine Comedy,* Dante imagines nine circles of hell, each reserved for a specific type of sinner. The deeper the circle (the first circle, reserved for the unbaptized, is at the top), the more grave the sin and extreme the punishment. Malebolge, the eighth circle, is for deceivers. The circle is divided into ten pits, each reserved for a specific variety of fraud. Had I dropped dead at that moment, I would have awoken in pit eight for those who use their position of influence to deceive others for personal benefit. I would have spent eternity burning in a tongue of flame, my consequence for having mocked the Holy Spirit. I hope I have since atoned for deceiving Sergio's mom.

At the time, I impressed myself with how quickly and convincingly I lied. I duped this lady so easily. I knew instantly that I could "Sell," especially the idea of me as teacher, as *El Profesor*! I could make people believe me, even if what I was saying was total bullshit. That's a valuable asset.

Did I learn from what I did?

Absolutely. Sergio's mom made me a better teacher which is why, forty years later, her story still matters. For several nights after parent-teacher conferences, I lay awake thinking about Sergio's mom and the tears in her eyes. I literally tossed and turned in bed, pounding a fist into my pillow with each flip, left side right side, catching glimpses of the digital clock at my bedside eating away needed sleep. She haunted me. Because it worked didn't make my lying right. At the same time, we both needed that lie.

Sergio's mom's tears demonstrated a relief bordering on spirituality. She needed to believe that the teacher knew what was right. She needed to believe that the Catholic institution she had put her faith in was just.

The honest answer, "Well, I'm just an English major who got forced to teach a Spanish class where I am barely staying one chapter ahead of the students; so, I fucked up" might have destroyed her faith in me: the teacher, and in Fenwick: the institution. She needed to believe that this prestigious Catholic high school on which she and her husband had pinned all hopes for her son achieving the American Dream was everything she had prayed and paid for.

Should I have destroyed her illusions?

No. For her, in that situation, she was better off with the lie. So was I.

(8)

Ethos and Titular Power

IN ARISTOTELIAN RHETORIC, ETHOS refers to the credibility of the speaker. The more credible the speaker—the more we can believe and trust that individual—the more persuasive the argument.

There are five common ways to establish ethos: titular power (the power of a title), practical experience, associative credibility (linking yourself to someone or something that is already credible), virtue (establishing yourself as a good person), and disinterest (acting for the greater good rather than personal interest).

The weakest of these is titular power; the strongest are practical experience and virtue. The best leaders I've met—Fr. Francisco[6], for example—possess all five.

At that time, at that age, I didn't know how to play the humble sage, the venerable professor who can admit his mistakes and gain credibility by doing so. Later in my career, I had a sign hanging in my classroom: "Challenge me to be a better teacher." I invited contention. I could afford to be honest and vulnerable because

---

6   I only taught one year at Fenwick. At my final evaluation, Fr. Francisco gave me some very constructive criticism about what it means to be a teacher. He pointed out the strengths I possessed, suggested some areas for improvement, and anticipated the benefits these adaptations would bring. When I said goodbye: "Fr. Francisco, thank you," he took my hand and benignly nodded, giving me permission to call him Father Pancho. I had earned his respect. I couldn't do it, though. I choked up, teared up, bowed reverently, and left.

I had ethos in a variety of ways. But at Fenwick, I had only titular power.

Sergio's mom taught me the power and potentially malignant impunity of anchoring my character to a title.

Sergio's mom believed in the mystique of my title and ignored the reality of the fallible person standing in front of her. Or maybe she didn't. Maybe she was more intuitive than I realized. I hope what she witnessed and trusted, what affirmed her faith, was my heart, and not my words, not my lie. I really did care about my students. I cared about Sergio, and I vowed to work on living up to the expectations of my being *el profesor*.

Titular power is the weakest form of credibility. Putting faith in a title—my own or anyone else's—without a healthy dose of skepticism, without acknowledging human fallibility, without requiring a more comprehensive exhibition of ethos, is dangerous.

Teacher. Lawyer. Doctor. Principal. President. Priest. They're just titles. I needed to remember that.

(9)

Bonus Content: On Walking and Talking

FATHER UHRIK WAS THE first, but not the only administrator to take me on a "walk and talk" interview.

Years later I applied for a job at Glenbard South High School in Glen Ellyn, Illinois. Unlike previous schools I had applied at where the interviews were spread over multiple days, this was to be a one-day, two-part experience, beginning with a casual building tour—while school was in session—and followed by an intense panel discussion. The tour would be given by the principal. In the interest of shared decision-making, the discussion panel was made up of several English teachers, the English and Fine Arts division head, her administrative assistant, the dean of students, the band director, a tennis coach/math teacher, and the athletic director.

The building tour was a fascinating study in psychology. The principal was a master.

We started walking and talking in empty halls, and he asked me generic questions about my teaching experience and coaching background, soft tosses to get me comfortable. He already knew the answers to everything he asked based on the résumé I had submitted. He wanted to hear how I would answer, not what.

The bell rang for the passing period, and as students filled and filed through the halls for the next five minutes the questions got tougher, questions about how I handled disciplinary issues and academic dishonesty, and how I planned to balance family, teaching, coaching, and pursuing another graduate degree. Did I worry about burn-out?

I answered his questions honestly and yet knew that the answers to his questions were only part of what he was studying. He took us down the busiest hallways and while I talked, he casually observed how I interacted with the students: Did my eyes scoff at the boy with the leather jacket and blue hair? Did they ogle the girl with the short skirt and brimming cleavage? Did I slip and weave to minimize contact with students rushing absentmindedly to class or did I plow on through? When a student smiled at the principal and said, "Hello!"—interrupting me—did I pause and smile or was I annoyed? Each encounter was a test, the principal continually critiquing my nonverbals.

The bell rang to end the passing period. Our tour was coming to a close. We turned down a long, vacant hallway that led to the conference room where phase two would take place. At the end of the hall, to the left of the door to the conference room, was a trash can. As we entered the hallway, the principal turned, as closure, and shook my hand, apparently about to reverse direction and head off on his own. However, in finest Detective Colombo fashion[7], he hesitated and dropped another question, one that just seemed to pop into his head at that moment. "Oh, one more thing... You're coming from a school, Proviso East, that is predominately minority and low income, to a school, Glenbard South, that is overwhelmingly white and affluent. How are you going to manage that transition?"

I slowed as we continued down the hall together, me thinking about the question, him waiting. I didn't want to rush a response. As we got to the end, I saw a crumple of paper on the floor to my right. Without breaking stride, I scooped and picked it up and banked it off the wall, underhand, into the trash can.

I stopped in front of the conference room door, turned to face him, and started to answer his question, "I think teaching, in general, is more about . . ." He cut me off.

---

7 *Columbo* was a crime drama in the 1970s starring Peter Falk as a disheveled, unassuming, and apparently muddle-headed detective. He was known for asking a series of rhetorical questions as he interviewed suspects, and then dropping one zinger as he left the room, not expecting an answer, but looking for a nonverbal reaction, a tell.

"Never mind," he said. He opened the door for me and gave me a light pat on the shoulder, guiding me through. I went inside.

I had the job. As long as I didn't do anything rash during the panel discussion, my interview had been completed.

A few months after I was hired, I learned that the crumpled-paper test was a staple of this principal's process. He didn't not hire you if you didn't pick it up; but if you did pick it up, the probability of your being hired increased dramatically. The correct answer to his last question had nothing to do with words. He wanted to see if I would take the time to think through a sensitive issue, not be flustered, remain aware of my surroundings, and do the little things that help make a school successful. I passed.

CHAPTER 4

HOT LAVA

He who spares his rod hates his son, but he who loves him disciplines him promptly.
—Proverbs 13:24 (KJV)

(1)

RELATIVE TO THE 1960s, I grew up in a pretty normal Irish Catholic family. My dad owned a blue-collar business, and my mom was a housewife. She bore seven children in ten years then added a caboose (unexpecting) four years later.

We ate our dinners as a family. We went to church every Sunday, filling half a pew. We grew up together.

Our house was a two-story rectangle, similar, proportionately, to a box of Barnum's Animal Crackers: the width one-third the length, the length twice the height. All five bedrooms were all on the second floor, laid out in a two-one-two pattern.

Though we all slept on that second floor, most of my siblings had it easy. My parents' master bedroom was in the northeast corner of the house. Two of my sisters were in the carpeted bedroom in the northwest corner. They could detonate explosives, and as long as my parents were not yet in bed, no one would hear. My oldest sister had a tiny, carpeted bedroom of her own in the southwest corner; she played 45s on her modest portable phonograph and kept quiet. My two oldest brothers shared a carpeted bedroom in the southeast corner. From early adolescence on, they tolerated each other, so silence was the natural order in their room.

My two other brothers and I were set up for failure. We had the largest bedroom in the house, that middle room, even larger than my parents' bedroom. We had a hardwood floor. We had the only bedroom with three occupants. Those occupants were pre-adolescent boys. And, our bedroom was situated directly above the family room where my parents watched TV each night.

When the incident described below occurred, my two brothers and I were, respectively, 9, 8, and 6 years old. The 9-year-old and I slept in bunk beds; he on the bottom, I on the top. The other, the 8-year-old, slept in his own twin bed on the opposite side of the room.

Even though he was the younger of the two, that brother got his own bed for two disparate reasons: (1) the bunk bed was by the windows and the 9-year-old wanted to be closer to fresh air: three boys together in one room expel a plethora of cacophonous odors; and (2) the 8-year-old needed more space because he had an imaginary friend. Not that the imaginary friend took up any space, we just thought it prudent to give a little more room to someone who occasionally shut himself in the bedroom closet to have an extended conversation with a phantom.

At the time, I found my brother's behavior a little disconcerting. No one else I knew had an imaginary friend. Turns out that—based on a 2004 study by psychologists from the University of Washington and the

University of Oregon—65% of children, by the age of 7, have had an imaginary friend at some point in their lives, and that school age children are more likely than preschoolers to engage in such behavior.

Considering that my "other" brother aligned with the 65%, he was the normal one.

On a typical school night, around 8:30, my parents would send all the kids to bed at once. We would line up by age, youngest to oldest, behind the couch upon which my parents sat side-by-side. One at a time, we'd step forward, ping pong a kiss off my mother's right cheek followed by one off my father's left cheek, and proclaim, each on our own, the family mantra: "Love you and God bless you." Eight times my parents, in unison and with mastered sincerity, echoed the sentiment, "Love you and God bless you, too."

We'd then disperse to our various upstairs rooms with the expectation that, while we didn't have to go to sleep, we better damn well be quiet. Mom and Dad would then mix a couple more Manhattans and settle themselves on the couch to drink, chain-smoke, and watch TV in peace. Sunday was the only exception to this routine. On Sundays, my three oldest siblings were allowed up until 9:00 to watch the end of *The Ed Sullivan Show*.

Our TV, a Magnavox Color Stereo Theatre combo (with record player!), was backed against the outer wall of the family room, directly below our bunk bed. In my bed, some nights, I'd lie awake with my hand on the wall reading the vibrations—mostly bass accents—that skittered beneath its surface. On Tuesday nights, though I couldn't hear any actual dialogue, I'd fall asleep to the laugh track of *The Red Skelton Show*, punctuated by occasional guffaws from my father. I enjoyed that laughter.

(2)

Most nights my two brothers and I conformed to expectations. We read, or talked quietly, or just went to sleep. We knew to stay off the floor because sound traveled, and once we children had been sent off to bed, my father expected his well-earned respite undisturbed.

Still, human beings are fallible, and, as Edgar Allan Poe explained, the young are especially susceptible to what he called the Imp of the Perverse: the need to stretch boundaries and dabble in impropriety. In other words, occasionally, we screwed around. I need to note here that our youthful impropriety was not the deliberate, rebellious, and at times malicious, "fuck you" of teenagers. That's a different Imp. Our behavior was spontaneous and self-absorbed. Kids being kids.

My two brothers and I didn't screw around often, but when we did, my father followed a protocol to address our indiscretions.

First Warning. If we made any noise, my father, at a commercial break, would get up from his chair, stride or shuffle—depending—over to the closet in the family room, and grab the broom. He'd sit back down and listen. If silence didn't resound from above, he'd grab the broom by its base and whack the ceiling three times.[8]

---

[8] Looking back now, I don't understand how he could strike the ceiling so aggressively and not leave dents imbedded above the couch. How there were no marks, at least as far as I remember? A puzzlement.

We had been warned.

The problem with first warnings is they are completely useless for American children who grow up playing the national pastime. In baseball, you get three strikes; every kid knows this. The first one is a freebie, almost an expectation. You're supposed to take a rip.

Second Warning. Now things were getting serious, especially if this were a Thursday night when my father, the former FBI agent, watched *Ironside*. The second warning started with the same three-whack broom-on-the-ceiling, then added, "God Dammit! Shut up!" followed by a single whack, and finally, "Go to Bed!"

Strike two.

In this game, the logical response to strike two was to put your bat down and head back to the bench. What could possibly be gained by taking a wild swing at a pitcher you knew you couldn't possibly hit? Strike three would not be a warning; strike three meant you're out. My father would lumber up the short flight of stairs to the kitchen, cut across to the dining room, and then loop through the living room to the main stairs. Up those stairs he'd step one at a time using the banister for balance and support. The final leg was the short left down the back hallway to our bedroom door.

He took his time on this journey, a long trip for a man who had worked a good day and deserved time to watch TV, smoke his Pall Malls, and drink his Manhattans. He always paused a moment before entering our room. Two streaks of shadow broadcast his presence from beneath the door. Inside the room we felt the air stiffen, a potential gathering.

If the alcohol wasn't fueled by need—if his drinking that night was just habit—he'd burst through the door and holler at us. We'd cower beneath our covers, apologize and apologize and apologize, and that would be the end of it.

However, if downstairs while he drank, if his fingers white-knuckled his lowball glass, if the ice cubes clinked and spasmed when he raised it to his lips, if nothing inside that glass could be enough, on those nights, he'd open the door slow, and one of us would get dragged out into the hallway where the beating, though not eye-witnessed, could be viscerally imagined by the others.

This was the protocol, the normal cause and effect, action and reaction, of events we three boys were especially aware of. The full progression—all the way to strike three—rarely happened. We knew better.

But it did happen.

On this night, I must have been exhausted because I slept soundly—a rarity for me—out cold on my top bunk through everything but the very end of this episode.

The full Imp must have seized my brothers that night because they decided to play "Hot Lava," an excellent daytime game, but the most dangerous nighttime game, the one with the highest risk (strike three) and the sweetest reward (whimsical noncompliance with impunity).

The goal of "Hot Lava" is to move around the bedroom without touching the hardwood floor, the "lava." The bunk bed, the twin bed, the three dressers, the desk, the desk chair, and the ancient deep-purple wingback chair wedged into the corner by the closet served as primary terra firma. Pillows strategically tossed from our beds to crisscross the floor as rocks-in-the-lava provided additional, though hazardous, base points to manage our 14' by 16' room.

The game began.

At first, my two brothers circled stealthily, mirroring each other on opposite sides of the room like two boxers, neither willing to risk the center of the ring. Around they went, speeding and slowing, changing direction, as first one then the other dictated. So far, so good. Not a toe in the lava. Not a sound made.

Time to raise the stakes.

Instead of mirroring, the 8-year-old fell in step behind the 9-year-old, and the goal became to navigate the room in figure-eight patterns, rounding to the edges and then cutting across diagonally upon the pillows. This necessitated hopping to cover long stretches of open lava. As the boys sped their routes, the furniture squeaked, and the hops became leaps. On one leap, the pillow he sought for safety shot out from under his foot and my brother crunched elbows and ass into the floor.

BOOM. BOOM. BOOM. Strike one.

My brothers froze, and I remained asleep.

After seconds seeming like minutes to let the situation remedy, they resumed, slow and again stealthy, at first, but, as kids, soon quickening.

It didn't take long. My father was attuned now to the distinctive stir of their play. What before he had overlooked as the normal white noise of a large house: a few creaks and settles, now incensed him because the behavior that had been innocent, in his estimation, had become defiant. My brothers were taunting him.

BOOM. BOOM. BOOM. "GOD DAMMIT! SHUT UP!" *BOOM.* "GO TO SLEEP!"

My brothers knew to cease and desist. They tip-toe gathered their pillows and returned to their beds.

Soon, however, like laughter at a funeral, they began exchanging giggles. It just couldn't be helped. They laughed at nothing. They laughed at each other laughing at nothing. The volume and the frequency accelerated until they sensed his presence outside the door. He had been standing out there listening to them laugh, laugh at him.

A moment of silence.

My dad burst through the door, and my brothers' primal instincts kicked in, serving them well: when facing an irrational, ferocious predator set on tearing you to pieces, play dead. They both acted like they were asleep.

Unfortunately, I *had* been asleep, and when the door exploded, I sat up in bed and screamed out, "HEY!"

I had no idea who or what I was screaming at. I was just sounding an alarm, and I drew the attention of the Beast. He charged across the room. I snapped awake, recognizing this scenario, and did what kids in bed do for survival. I pulled the covers up over my head and curled into fetal position. My father threw a few quick punches—tight punishing hooks—at the swaddled creature I was, then seized the whole bundle and threw me to the floor. In the four-foot fall to the hardwood, my right arm sprang free—a catch—and my face was uncovered. He grabbed my loosed wrist and yanked. My right shoulder popped out and then back in as I pivoted to my stomach and reached across with my left arm to secure my right against the strain. I rasped out a drool of blood and spittle (I'd bitten through my tongue; I didn't know if from the fall or a blow[9]).

My father began dragging me out of the room and into the hall.

Thank God. Thank God. My brothers had a flash of conscience.

"It wasn't him!" the 8-year-old screamed.

"It wasn't him!" the 9-year-old confirmed. "It was us! He was asleep!" he added.

"It was US! It wasn't HIM!" They shouted in unison.

My father stopped, still stretching me by the arm.

He looked back and forth at both of them, each cowering in the farthest nooks of their beds. He looked down at me and I up at him. I was dazed, but I'd like to believe my eyes were as righteous as a 6-year-old's could be. I had done nothing wrong!

He understood, after a few breaths, but there would be no apology. Instead, he flung my arm back to me, jabbed his finger at my face, and bellowed, "That's for the next time... when I *don't* catch you!"

He swung his head across the room, turned, and left, slamming the door behind him.

(3)

"REMEMBER THE TIME DAD beat Michael up for doing nothing, and then told him, 'That's for the next time, when I don't catch you!'"

Everyone laughs. There is no need to retell the whole story; the punchline is enough.

---

[9] The scar is still there, having stretched over time into a small gully.

We are sitting, all the siblings, around a table at Lou Malnati's Pizzeria in Lincolnwood, a northern suburb of Chicago. The remnants of a deep-dish sausage-and-onion and a deep-dish pepperoni-and-black-olive dirty our plates. Five pitchers of Old Style are emptied into our glasses and our bellies; my youngest sister drinks a Coke. It's around 11 o'clock at night. My dad's wake ended at 9.

My father died of an aneurism that left him, for a few weeks, conscious, but oblivious to his surroundings. He sat in his hospital bed, I kid not, puffing on imaginary Pall Malls and sipping imaginary Manhattans. I was 22 years old then, and I can't speak for my mother or my siblings, but I know that, on the few occasions I visited, he didn't recognize me.

He was 58.

That story and this night, the night of his wake—the last we are eight of us together—are part of our family legacy.

I'm 62 now, at this writing, and though he has been dead for decades, both the story and the night still resonate.

(4)

Comedy and Tragedy

God is a comedian playing to an audience too afraid to laugh. —Voltaire

What if there is malicious intent? What if what happened was bad?[10] Can I laugh this off just because I survived?

---

10   My father was a beast, and the violence inflicted on me in this anecdote is nothing compared to what my older siblings went through.

Maybe. Life is some crazy shit, and if I survive that shit, often, the best thing I can do is sit back and laugh. I mean, what else? I'm sure as hell not going to figure it out, not this shit.

Maybe that's the key to survival: to listen to Voltaire, to not question God. Just point a finger up in the air and say, "Oh you crazy dude. You almost got me that time, LOL. You are one funny motherfucker." And then get up, dust yourself off, and keep going.

Maybe.

CHAPTER 5

SOLDIER'S WORK

Judge not, that ye be not judged. For with what judgment ye judge, ye shall be judged: and with what measure ye mete, it shall be measured to you again. And why beholdest thou the mote that is in thy brother's eye, but considerest not the beam that is in thine own eye? Or how wilt thou say to thy brother, Let me pull out the mote out of thine eye; and, behold, a beam is in thine own eye? Thou hypocrite, first cast out the beam out of thine own eye; and then shalt thou see clearly to cast out the mote out of thy brother's eye.
—Matthew 7: 1-5 (KJV)

(1)

MY FATHER OWNED A roofing company. Each summer, beginning after my senior year of high school and continuing until after I graduated college, he assigned me to one of the crews under his employ and set me to work. I appreciated this; I got paid well to work outdoors, do physical labor, and learn what I could.

The summer before my junior year of college, I worked a pitch tear-off on a ten-story building at the Water Tower campus of Loyola University. On a tear-off, as the name suggests, the old roof is torn off and discarded before applying the new one. This process is simple and messy. The old pea-gravel ballast is shoveled up, loaded into wheelbarrows, and emptied into a flat trash pan that is lowered into a dumpster on the ground via a hydraulic-powered hoist and swing beam.

The remaining built up roof is then cut into 2' x 2' squares using a machine called a Roof Cutter. (Roofers can be succinct.) These squares are then popped loose with a spade, picked up by hand, stacked in wheelbarrows, carted to the edge of the roof, lifted from the wheelbarrows, and re-stacked in that flat trash pan. Each load is then hoisted from the roof and lowered into a dumpster on the ground.

The roof we tore off that early '80's summer in Chicago had been applied in the 1950's. Old tar, like old paper or old anything, holds its shape as long as it is not disturbed. Unsettle it, and it crumbles and disintegrates. Every step of this process—the shoveling, loading, emptying, cutting, popping, picking, stacking, carting, lifting, and re-stacking—yields dust, coal tar pitch dust. With even the subtlest movement, it rose around us, puffed and expired like secondhand smoke, ubiquitous and invasive like sand on a windy beach.

However, unlike beach sand that merely irritates when it skulks into a crack or crevice where it is unwanted, coal tar pitch dust stinks and burns. It reddens and tears the eyes. It leeches onto the skin, worming into the pores. By the end of each day, I felt as if I had been slathered with a malignant strain of Bengay.

To minimize exposure, I wore high boots, long pants, a short sleeve T-shirt, and a long sleeve button-down work shirt over that. My hands were protected by gloves, the back of my neck and forehead by a baseball cap wedged over a T-shirt secured around my head like a durag, the short sleeves tied together at the base of my skull, the body draping down my back.

This was July, and in the Chicago heat and humidity, ten stories up, I soaked through my outer layers only an hour onto the roof. Through the morning, my sweat formed a shield catching all the dust like a gas mask. By afternoon, all had merged, and at quitting time, I wore a wetsuit of cloth, sweat, and pitch dust.

At the end of each day, I peeled off my clothes—stripped to my tighty-whities right on Pearson Street—and threw on a pair of shorts and a fresh T-shirt. I dumped the dirties in the trunk of my car.

I confess, I wore the same outer clothes every day of the tear-off. I never washed roofing clothes. I wore them until I could no longer stand them, then I threw them out. Only my skivvies—the underpants and short sleeve undershirt—got changed each day.

The tear-off took five days. They were good days: hard, physical labor that beat my body but refreshed my soul. I am not being needlessly philosophic here. These were five cathartic days, different from the other jobs we worked that summer. For whatever reason, the rest of the crew chose this week to work with purpose and not just for a paycheck. From the moment we stepped on that roof the first day, they resolved to knock out the tear-off phase of the job by that Friday, to not let it roll over into the next week. (The lay-up phase—putting down insulation, tarring down a base sheet and three plies of felt, and then weighing it all down with new pea-gravel ballast—was easy money compared to the tear-off.)

I should note that on most tear-offs, on most days in general, we let the job dictate how long it took. If, for example, the roof wasn't coming up easy or the day was unusually hot or a piece of machinery broke down, we simply slowed down and took an extra day or two to finish the job. We rarely had specific goals, and we rarely pushed ourselves.

I say we, but I mean they. I, after all, was a college student doing this as a summer job. To me, roofing was a novelty. These, however, were blue-collar men, some with families, some living solely out of motels. This was life to them, daily life. They rarely pushed themselves because they'll be doing this for the next thirty years and construction beats a person up. My brother taught me before I ever stepped on a roof to follow their lead, to work at their pace, to never show off. Respect these men.

This week they chose to push it, so I did as well. Each day we worked to be sure at least another fifth or more had been removed, that we were keeping on or ahead of pace. There were no cheerleaders, no inspirational speeches, no outward emotion. Just do that day's fucking job.

There was no extra pay for working extra hard. The reward was beer. That week, each day after work, seven of our eight crew members trudged around the corner to McGourty's Irish Pub on Rush Street. Cool air and cold beer in a shady bar at 2:30 in the afternoon following a tear-off. Three or four Miller Lites before heading home just in front of rush hour traffic.

Heaven.

The alcohol buzzed away some of the pitch burn and opened the pores just enough to let the poison start to flush out.

Out of courtesy, when we entered the bar, the seven of us tried to gather as far away from the other patrons as possible. Most days this was easy; there were not many mid-afternoon summertime collegiate drinkers.

On Thursday, however, the day we had pushed hardest to be sure we could finish Friday, conflict was unavoidable. Two Loyola students were sitting too close to our now "regular" spot by the front window. As we gathered, pushing a couple of smaller tables together and rearranging the chairs, these ladies popped from their seats like jack-in-the-box. The first lowered her forehead like a bull and rammed through a momentary opening that allowed her to get outside our group without any contact. The second was not so fortunate. The shifting of tables and chairs left her a maze to navigate. She sidled past one of my colleagues. However, as she tried to round another, she was cut off into repulsively close quarters with me. She had her head down and her books clutched to her chest, but she looked up as we didn't quite touch. She grimaced. I ignored the affront. She was my height, with warm vanilla skin, soft black hair, and bright blue eyes, a long-legged Galway girl in a pastel summer dress. Those eyes, with an enchanting brush of green around the irises. I tumbled into those eyes, smiling dumbly, thinking only of what we had in common: we were the same age, and I, too, was a college student. I backed up to let her pass, bowing as a gentleman does, trying at the same time to reach her somehow.

In response to my affability, as she stole past, part apology and part accusation, she informed me, sotto voce, "I'm sorry, but . . . you . . . *smell*."

I felt stoned, and as I processed what she said, time seemed to stretch like a gigantic soap bubble undulating in the wind before popping me back into reality: she saw me as a roofer, which I was.

Later, I imagined having delivered a witty retort: "No, my lady, you *smell*, I *stink*. Your nose is right, but your diction is wrong."

I didn't though. I had little response. She was honest. So, I gave her an emasculated grin and a subtle shrug to say, "I know."

(2)

During those one-to-two hours together each afternoon at the pub, loosened by beer and release from labor, I got to know more about the crew I worked with. I did this by doing something I rarely did. We had little in common, the six of them and I, other than our stench, so I kept my mouth shut, resisting the urge to contribute to the conversation somehow, to force my way in. Instead, I listened. That's the best way to be part of a group, especially if you're an outsider, which I was.

Three of them, I learned, were Vietnam combat veterans. Harold, Fred, and Henry.

Harold smoked dope before work, at lunch, and probably on the way home. He's the one who didn't come to the pub with us. Harold never talked much, just did his job. Most lunches—if the wind wasn't howling, if the dust was settled, and if the sun showed some mercy—we ate right on the roof. On these occasions, the average of us would drag over an unopened five-gallon bucket of roof cement or pile a short stack of insulation board to sit on. Harold chose to eat his homemade sandwich and munch from his bag of chips—Fritos one day, Doritos Nacho Cheese another—while straddling the two-foot-high parapet wall that ran around the perimeter of the building. He sat with his left foot planted firmly on the roof and his right leg dangling 100 feet in the air. If ever invited into the general conversation, he'd tune in just enough to shrug his shoulders and flash his Cool Hand Luke grin. To be among others but not obligated to interact, that was his preference.

After eating, he'd fire up a j and stare out along the ridge of the parapet wall, following it to the corner edge where the wall bent left. His gaze, however, stayed straight and lifted out into open space.

(3)

MANY, MANY YEARS LATER, I took a group of 11th Grade English students to the First Division Museum at Cantigny Park in Wheaton. I was an older teacher, close to retiring, and far removed from my roofing days. As I led my class through a section of the museum focusing on World War II, I rounded a corner and met a copy of Thomas Lea's painting, *The 2000 Yard Stare*. One soldier's face dominates the canvas. His skin is shaded by a thin layer of grime; his pupils are fully dilated; his thin jaw is slack.

Emotion often precedes memory. When I saw the painting, or, more accurately, when it confronted me, I started, and a profound mix of nostalgia and melancholy swept over me. I stood goose bumped and breathless, enveloped in a shiver of static electricity.

Lea's painting is beautiful, moving, poignant; but for me, there was something more, something else. It took a few seconds to make the connection.

My god, I thought, *that's Harold.*

(4)

THE SECOND COMBAT VETERAN, Fred, worked the hoist and swing beam that conveyed materials to and from the rooftop. During the tear-off phase, he was responsible for lowering each load of 2' by 2' squares into a 30-yard dumpster on the ground. During the lay-up phase, he kept us supplied with fresh 500-degree coal tar, aka "hot," pumped from a tanker on the ground into 55-gallon asphalt luggers that Fred raised onto the roof and that I then wheeled to wherever the rest of the crew was working. Hot tar sealed every layer of the new roof.

Fred liked working the hoist and swing beam because he was both alone and essential. He was very good at it, raising and lowering things. He had that feel for starting and stopping and speed. He, too, didn't mind the edge of the roof, watching over the side to monitor what was affixed to the rope.

One lunch, triggered by I-know-not-what, he went off. Fred started recounting how he and a bunch of his buddies in Vietnam had been sprayed with Agent

Orange, not by the enemy, but by our own government. We were eating on the ground that day, in a semi-circle spread out on a patch of lawn in the shade of the building.

"I got the Big C growing everywhere inside me," he bragged, adding a shivering cackle. He picked up a stick and began digging out quarter-sized wedges of dirt from the bare spots in the grass where he sat.

"Cancer," he clarified after a pause, his eyes still focused on the ground, "The Big C from the Big G: Uncle Sam."

At "Uncle Sam," he waved the stick in the air like a child at a parade. "Woo Hoo!" he cheered. He glanced up at our group. That's when Harold shot him a look.

Fred took it, chuckled, looked down, and gave one more dig at the dirt. Then he tossed the stick into a nearby bush, got up, and went to check the temperature of the tanker.

(5)

THE THIRD COMBAT VETERAN had dropped a lot of acid during his time in Vietnam.

I got to know him best.

The Saturday after we finished the tear-off—we finished on Friday; we got it done in five days—my car broke down. It wouldn't be fixed until Wednesday, at the earliest, depending on what was wrong. I asked my dad what I should do, and he told me, "Find a ride???" like I was an idiot, which, at this moment, I sort of was.

On Sunday afternoon, I got the number from my dad's Rolodex and called the only roofer I knew who lived in my direction. He answered the phone with an accusation: "Hello?"

I introduced myself, explained about my car, and asked if he wouldn't mind giving me a ride to work until I could get it fixed, which should be by Thursday. His response unsettled me. He chuckled, just like Fred had, though not nearly as loud. Then he said, "Sure," and he meant it. He wanted to help me. I drove to work with Henry for the next three days, Monday through Wednesday. He was married with a daughter and a son, but for now lived alone in a motel in Gages Lake.

He picked me up at 5:30 a.m. each day, a smile on his face and a beer already in hand. This was a routine I had to accept to be his passenger. In the back seat of his car was a full case (already three short) of Red, White, and Blue beer: *An Honest Beer at An Honest Price.* Next to the full case was an empty one, presumably from the day before. Over the course of each day, he methodically converted full cans to empties and transitioned them from the delivery case into the receptacle case.

Unlike Fred and Harold, Henry liked to talk, liked to tell stories about his current life. He shared anecdotes featuring his wife and kids, yet philosophized about how a little distance is at times good for every relationship.

He joked about how, at a recent physical (and I was gladdened to hear he had gone for a physical), his doctor had asked him how much beer he drank. He told the doc, "About a case." The doc, noting it on the record, echoed, "About a case . . . a week, that's not bad."

Henry laughed, "A case a week? A case a DAY, doc!" He told the story with a grin, proud of his timing and delivery. There was no hyperbole here.

I didn't laugh, didn't know if I should laugh. Instead, I feigned nonchalance, bobbing my head in acknowledgement of his story and in time with a song on the radio. He noticed.

"I'm a *functional* alcoholic," he extenuated, apparently having given this serious thought. Henry was neither stupid nor ignorant. "Just enough to keep me going." He toasted his beer toward me and took an obligatory swig.

Henry also told me he had dropped a lot of acid in Vietnam. He told me this on the drive home, our last together, late Wednesday morning, after he had had a flashback on the roof. He told me, in his post-flashback manic monologue, that the acid gets stored in the fat cells and when those fat cells get consumed—could be, as in this case, years later—you have a flashback. That's what had happened, he said. He explained this as we pulled onto the westbound lanes of the Dan Ryan Expressway, the pouring rain already behind us. He was okay now. He hadn't touched acid in years. Just a flashback, he repeated.

(6)

ROOFERS WATCH THE SKIES. Red sky at night, sailor's delight. Red sky in morning, sailor take warning.

When Henry picked me up just after dawn on Wednesday, the skies were streaked with crimson. By the time we got downtown, changed into our work clothes, and took the service elevator up to the tenth floor, they were apocalyptic.

On the eastern horizon, out over Lake Michigan, the sun had risen and the moisture that had created the earlier red sky had burned off. Everything was bright blue. A gentle breeze tempered the 80-degree heat.

Rising out of the west, however, was a bloated wall of black-grey thunderheads.

When we first pulled up to the job site, Henry was oddly silent. We parked, and he sat forward in the driver's seat, both hands on the steering wheel, vainly craning to see the sky through the obstruction of buildings hovering above us.

Then he looked pissed. He chugged the last of his beer, crunched the can, and fired it off the windshield. It clattered off the glass, deflected off the dashboard, and wound up in my lap. I picked it up two-fingered and set it in the receptacle case in back.

Henry got out of the car and, interspersing peeks at the sky, slammed his door shut, popped open the trunk, and fumbled abusively with his work gear. He stripped to underwear and socks, then transitioned to his work pants and a long sleeve shirt. He jammed his feet into his work boots. He started to wrap his work belt around his waist, eyed the sky again, and pitched it back into the trunk. No need. He took a large, black-and-white-over-red paisley patterned handkerchief from his pocket, shook it out, and, holding two corners, spun it into a headband. He tied this around his head, a widow's peak of fabric descending between his eyebrows.

Working from the same trunk, I had been mirroring his routine, stripping and dressing, while giving him plenty of space. I thought he was upset because we had driven here for nothing. We were sure to lose the day and a day's pay to the rain. But something else was triggering this.

Sweat bled through the back of his shirt, and we hadn't even hit the roof yet.

As we rode up to the top floor together in the service elevator, Henry said nothing.

To get onto the roof, we had to climb up an interior ladder and through a trap door that swung open like a hatch on a submarine. Henry let me go first. The hatch was already open, and from below I looked up at a depthless, luminescent square. I could imagine myself diving into that azure. The blue was dense and pure and tangible.

The view from a high-rise roof is always disorienting, especially, as with this one, when the roof is relatively small and there are no other similar height buildings near enough to add some perspective. The parapet wall around the perimeter is inconsequential, and despite standing in the middle of the roof, yards away from any edge, I imagine movement, as if on the deck of a ship, and that a tilt in any direction will start me tumbling, accelerating and inexorable, towards the edge and over and out into the vastness. I am not afraid of heights, but something about the open space of a roof terrifies me.

Each day I steeled myself against this anxiety. Before ascending this ladder, I sucked in a deep breath, exhaled in a slow silent five count blow, and started up the nine rungs to the roof. Like an actor who sheds his nerves his first step on stage, on most days, I felt fine once on the roof.

Not today.

The rest of the crew had already arrived, and I joined them, silent, staring to the west, awestruck. As roofers, we had seen dozens of morning storms, but the optics here were different. With no trees or other buildings to mitigate the view, the thunderheads looked alive. Never had I or have I since seen such a clean demarcation between clear blue sky and impending fury. Cumulus bulbs morphed together, their distinct curves accented by the rising sun. Lightning sparkled and the thunder belly-rumbled. All at a distance but rising and creeping closer.

Harold blew a long, low whistle from between his lips just as the wind shifted and the temperature dropped ten degrees. I shivered. We knew the day would be short. We were in the layup phase, so the roof was clean, except for rolls of felt and bundles of insulation. These had to be double-checked to be sure they were battened together so no gust could possibly tear pieces free. We had to hurry.

The foreman snapped us to work. "All right. Stop fucking staring. Let's get moving. Spread the fuck out and make sure everything is secure."

He turned to me, glanced around at what was obviously missing, and lifted his palms. "Where the fuck is Henry?"

I shrugged toward the hatch just as Henry began to emerge. He stopped, only his head and shoulders birthed, frozen. His hands gripped the top rung, eyes bulging toward that ominous western sky, an "oh oh oh oh" escaped his throat.

"Oh. Oh. Oh. Oh. Oh. Oh." He swept his chin slowly back and forth, the sound escaping in time, like the ticking of a metronome. He looked to me and then the foreman. He was crying, actual tears dribbling down his cheeks.

"What the fuck?" The foreman directed this comment to me, as if, because we rode together, I was somehow responsible for Henry. I shook my head.

Henry stopped and looked again at the darkness that marched on the city. I looked with him, now having to tilt my head back to take in the full expanse. Mountains of clouds towered toward us. Below those clouds, curtains of rain swept the landscape. Still, the sky directly above us remained that cloudless blue. This brought no comfort.

"It's the fucking end!" Henry yelled, laughing, and every part of him believed it could be true.

He started jerking back and forth, bouncing his chest off the top rung of the ladder, trying to rip it free and send himself tumbling back into the tiny maintenance room below.

The foreman lost it. "Get off the fucking ladder! Go down!" He stepped forward, into Henry's line of sight. "Henry, get the fuck *off* the ladder. Go back down!"

"Henry!" the foreman demanded. And for a moment, the spell was broken. Henry backed down the ladder.

We did what we could to prepare for the storm, dragging all the equipment and materials to the middle of the roof and binding everything together. Though no drop had yet fallen, the scent of rain was strong.

We exited the roof, the last man through, the foreman, securing the hatch behind him. We took the elevator down and left the building.

Between the street and the sidewalk, near where the cars were parked, Henry, still in his work clothes, was pacing—twelve steps up, twelve steps back—on a patch of grass beneath a young maple. His face locked on the terra firma beneath him, he lifted and planted each step with purposeful authority, taking control of his connection to solid ground. He muttered to himself, repetitive, unintelligible.

I moved toward him, but a quick shiver of his head told me to stay away.

The lightning was close and the thunder louder. The rest of the crew moved to their cars to change, but I had no choice but to wait on Henry. He had the keys.

One blinding bolt, the thunder detonating simultaneously, undid him (and jolted me: I felt a distinct, sentient potency rush past). Henry jumped up and grabbed a lower branch of the maple tree. Hanging with both arms extended, he lifted his weight in a pull-up, then sat down, lifted, sat, lifted and sat, until he ripped the branch free. He landed in a squat but stumbled sideways as he straightened, staggering a few steps before crashing shoulder first into the foreman's car parked by the curb.

"Henry, God Dammit!"

Henry bounced off and staggered upright, not noticing the foreman and never taking either hand off the branch. Enthralled that he had not fallen, he jigged in circles and pumped the bough over his head in savage ecstasy. That novelty, though, was short-lived, and the dance did little to diminish the angst this storm had provoked in him.

A curtain of rain moved up the block—fewer than one hundred feet away—and the first drops blown forward by the wind began to dampen us. Henry looked around for another diversion. He cast aside the branch and strode square-shouldered and barrel-chested toward the building, stopping in front of several stacks of insulation panels wrapped in plastic and awaiting our future use on the roof. Each stack was weighted down with several cinderblocks. Henry smiled. He grabbed a single cinder block off a stack and raised it above his head.

The rest of the crew, still changing clothes by the trunks of their respective cars, turned to watch what would unfold. All except Harold, who continued preparing to leave, whose stoic resilience had endured far worse.

Before any of us could intervene, Henry pulled down the cinderblock, *WHOMP WHOMP WHOMP*, trying to break it over his head. Three times, then he stopped, stunned. Frozen. He held the block above his head, out toward the sky. Blood soaked through his headband. A few tiny beads broke free and dripped across his temple, around the socket of his eye and down his cheek.

This was my ride home.

The cinder block helped. The old expression, "Knock some sense into him," has validity. Henry plopped the cinder block and himself onto the ground. The torrent arrived, and while the others slammed their trunks and scampered into the safety of their cars, I stood over Henry who sat splay-legged on the ground, limp like a Raggedy Andy.

Water revives. Henry turned his face up to the rain, squinting. He chuckled, much like he had when I first asked him for a ride to work. I reached out a hand to help, but he shrugged me off. He got himself up, and we hustled over to and into his car, still in our work clothes. He reached into the back seat for a Red, White, and Blue, and popped the top. Then he reached for another and tossed it into my lap. We drank in deafening silence, a waterfall of rain—gigantic, ridiculous drops—clanking off the hood, thumping on the windshield.

He finished his first and drank half a second before pushing the key into the ignition and starting us home. By then, the rain was subsiding, the storm passing. We inched away from the curb, Henry pulling a U-ey, heading in the opposite direction, toward clear skies. He said nothing for the first ten minutes of our drive.

As we pulled off Ogden Avenue and merged onto the expressway, he pointed an epiphanic finger up and then joggled it at me. Still thinking.

A few minutes later, he began his manic monologue to explain and rationalize what had just occurred. He was okay now, he insisted. Just a flashback. He was okay.

He was.

I made it home alive, as did he.

(7)

Why read literature?

I'VE NEVER BEEN IN combat, and I've never fought in war. I will never be able to grasp what it is to be a soldier. In this regard, I'm an outsider, and always will be.

And yet, I think I've learned some things about soldiers from reading and teaching literature: Whitman's "Specimen Days," Hemingway's "Soldier's Home," Vonnegut's *Slaughterhouse-Five*, and O'Brien's *The Things They Carried*.

Is it presumptuous of me, then, to think I *know* the things I've learned without ever having directly experienced them? Can I claim any understanding of or empathy with Harold or Fred or Henry just because I read a book?

This is a conundrum I've wrestled with since my junior year of high school when Mr. Vanden Busch first taught me to see literature as philosophy. One of the books we read in his class was Viktor E. Frankl's, *Man's Search for Meaning*. Early in the text, Frankl explains why former concentration camp prisoners don't talk about their experiences: "No explanations are needed for those who have been inside, and the others will understand neither how we felt then nor how we feel now." And yet, Frankl writes his book; his autobiographical account is called: "Experiences in a Concentration Camp."

Literature does allow me in, but to what extent and to what end?

(8)

HAROLD AND FRED AND Henry were average men who were drafted into war. I'm pretty sure each witnessed, in some manner, the unconscionable capacity of human beings to be horrific to one another. That experience changed each of them. I saw and felt, firsthand, elements of the disconnect each struggled with. I tried to understand without judging.

I don't see Harold and Fred and Henry as heroes. That's one of my semantic pet peeves: I don't think there are "heroes."[11] However, I do see their daily efforts to persist as heroic. It's heroic to die in the service of your country, but it's also heroic to try and live with what you've done for your country, and with what you've witnessed your country do. Literature taught me to respect these individuals.

There were times that summer, I admit, when I did judge them, when I condescended to their drinking, and smoking, and erratic behavior. This was a summer job, and I was going back to college in the fall to earn a degree and have a career. I had nothing in common with their desperate, manual-labor lives. I was not them. I was "better." But I also knew better.

(9)

I OPENED THIS ESSAY with the quote from Matthew because it highlights one challenge of being educated, of being well-read. I can read about things I've never experienced and be deceived into thinking I *know* something about how I would act in a given situation. That "knowing" can make me arrogant and judgmental. Pity and empathy are fraternal twins, very closely related, but not the same. When I allow myself to pity others, I assert my superiority. Not good.

---

11   There *are* heroic actions done by fallible individuals. Thus, each of us is capable of being heroic in a given moment. Heroic actions should be celebrated, not individuals.

My struggle is to keep learning all the while reminding myself, chastising myself, that I don't really *know* anything. This is especially true regarding other people and their experiences. To know is to judge, and I can never judge another person because, hell, I don't even *know* myself, at least not in every context.

I'm not being coy here. I have no idea who I would be if I had lived Henry's or Fred's or Harold's life. I have read about but never lived the absurdity that they have. I have no fucking idea how it would have changed me. To paraphrase Matthew, what "beams" would be in my eyes if I had walked a little in their shoes? I want to empathize, but I need to fight my human tendency to pity.

Acknowledging what I do not know and thus not judging, is a test of ego, and it is not easy.[12]

That being said, not judging doesn't mean not learning. I wasn't going to judge Henry—he needed to live his life as he saw fit—but I also wasn't going to keep driving to work with him. Fortunately, my car was ready that afternoon.

---

[12] I try to remind myself of this saying: "*I know* might be the most ignorant phrase in the English language."

CHAPTER 6

THE SNEEZE

(1)

EARLIER IN MY CAREER, while I am in my third year at Glenbard South High School, one random school day, I sneeze.

We are continuing our analysis of a few of "The Nick Adams Stories" by Ernest Hemingway, a collection of semi-autobiographic[13] stories about Nick's youth, adolescence, WWI experience, and post-war attempts to reconnect with life and find something worth living for. I stand in front of the class, scrambling notes on the chalkboard about Hemingway's "Iceberg Principle" and warming the class for our discussion of "The Big Two-Hearted River, Part Two."

I draw an iceberg, then slice it toward the top with a little wavy line to represent the surface level of the water. One-fifth of the iceberg is above this line, four-fifths below. Next to the area above the surface I write "Events" and "Details." Next to the area below the surface I write, "Memory," "Desire," "Fear," "Passion," "Guilt," "Need," and "Conscience."

---

13   All serious art is autobiographic. There is much of Hemingway in Nick Adams.

"Hemingway's Iceberg Principle," I explain, "suggests that, beneath the simplest details or the most mundane events—such as Nick's solitary fishing trip—there's often a whole bunch of stuff going on. We only see the tip of the iceberg; the bulk underneath needs to be inferred.

"See Beyond the Obvious[14]," I remind them. "Yea, sometimes white is just a color and water is just wet. But not always.

"A'ight," I say, "so what details or events from *this* story..." I pause to inhale; there's a tickle and a catch... catch... and I sneeze. This is not an uncommon occurrence in those days of powdery-dust clouds wafting around my head. I am a carver, one of those teachers who use chalk like an ice pick, stabbing each letter into the board and chipping off flecks and talc. With minimal interruption, I drift over to my desk, grab a Kleenex, give a little blow, wipe my nose, and continue, "... have meaning beyond just their surface level?"

We are on the cusp of a teachable moment. I know that my students get this "Iceberg Principle" and are close to applying it, not just to this story, but to life in general. Together we can share in a concept that transcends the classroom. Unfortunately, I see an awkwardness on their faces. The moment is slipping, and I become distinctly aware of being a teacher in front of a class, of being apart from them.

---

14   "See Beyond the Obvious" is one of my catchphrases; it prompts students to look beyond the literal and determine if there is any metaphorical meaning present. For example, white may just be a color, or it might suggest innocence; water might just be wet, or it might suggest rebirth. See Burke's website for more on the 4 Level Analysis/Individual Art Assignment.

Okay, don't overreact. What's up? Have I done or said something offensive? I begin my self-assessment. However, before I can fully process this situation, Jimmy McKay, second row, third seat, wiggles his hand for my attention. When I look, he gives a little finger-swipe gesture under his nose. Several students start bobbing their heads; a few cringe.

I turn to my desk, grab another Kleenex, give another swipe, and mouth to Jimmy, "Did I get it?"

He nods and smiles. I point back to the title on the board: "The Big Two-Hearted River, Part Two."

"Key details and events?" I repeat. "What's happening *beneath* the surface?"

"C'mon, Mr. Burke," Adrienne challenges, "nothing happens! This story is just 18 pages . . . 18 PAGES! . . . about FISHING!"

"Yep," I say, getting closer to landing that teachable moment. "But no, as well."

(2)

WHY DOES THIS MOMENT resonate from the poop-load of experiences in my four-decade teaching career?

I imagine all the ways teenagers could react to a teacher unaware that he has snot on his face. These students acknowledged the awkwardness—they needed me to address the problem—but they weren't embarrassed, nor did they seek to embarrass me. I too felt no call to be embarrassed. That is mutual respect.

My life is defined more by subtle gestures than by Hallmark moments. And this was one of the times in my career when I felt a connection with an entire class, an instant of solidarity, that said, "Yes, you are the teacher and we are the students, but we are in this together." In a minor, yet significant way, they had my back. On the surface, the moment was simple and seemingly insignificant, but the underlying message, the bulk of the iceberg, was profound. We had a meaningful relationship.

This was not every day, and the class and I didn't develop some magical, cathartic bond that stretched into a made-for-TV future.

But that day was good. It was a good day, and worth remembering.

CHAPTER 7

LOVE TAPS

(1)

MY FATHER AND MY older brother each had his preferred method of bestowing love taps.

My father followed a Catholic tradition of "smacking you upside the head." I'd fidget or twitch or let slip some subtle wit and my father's right hand would shoot up behind me and thwack the back of my head, with primary emphasis delivered by the ring and middle fingers.

I wasn't the only one getting whacked either. All five of us boys stayed on guard whenever my father was within an arm's length.

One older brother told me about a time when he was ten. My family, with me just an infant in my mother's arms, was leaving church: 10:00 a.m. mass every Sunday. My father ran into an old friend. Proud of his growing family, he turned to introduce his son. However, the instant my father's hand reached out, my brother slipped to the side and dipped back like a boxer avoiding a punch. He cowered, his eyes wide with fear, my father's outstretched fingers hanging empty. Not quite the message intended.

When he told me this story, many years later, my brother still had ember in his eyes and a smirk on his lips that insisted that though his initial action had been spontaneous, the overreaction—the cowering—had been deliberate just to embarrass my father.

I know it sounds insane to explain, but anyone who grew up in a family where violence was the expedient in matters of discipline knows there are three basic levels of correction: the love tap, the spanking, and the beating. I'm not going to deep dive into distinguishing between the three, other than to say that if you're using any of these on your loved ones (or anyone), you're fucking insane. If, on the other hand, you have no idea what I'm talking about, that's a good thing.

The love tap is meant to put one in their place, a quick reminder to keep in line, so to speak. I had a hard head, so they didn't hurt much, except when my father's class ring—an homage to one of his life's greatest achievements: having graduated with a degree in philosophy from the University of Notre Dame—nicked away a clip of flesh.

My father had to be careful with that Notre Dame ring. Hitting us with a soft hand, the slap primarily with the fingertips, sent a message but didn't leave a mark. Whacking with a stiff hand, however, the fingers arched slightly backwards to bring the ribbed shank of the ring into play, did both. Considering how often my father hit each of us and the fact that we all had crewcuts, if he didn't watch that ring, his sons would soon sport skulls mounded like warty gourds.

The majority of my love taps were collected at dinner time.

My family ate together in our kitchen at a laminated picnic table, complete with two detached benches. My father sat on a folding chair at one end, my mother on a folding chair at the other. My siblings and I lined up in designated spots four to a side (after my youngest sister had grown out of her highchair). For as long as we ten shared a table, we sat in the exact same places, with one exception. Originally, I sat closest to my mother, kitty-corner to my father. During my fifth year of existence, however, I got moved across the hypotenuse of the table within easy reach of my father. This move coincided with my developing a tongue.

I learned early that if I wanted to get a little attention or earn a little respect, I needed to do it with words. Though I obviously didn't know the technical terms then, I realize now I was dabbling in satire, attacking social conventions and human foibles, most often in a lighthearted Horatian manner, but sometimes with a more Juvenalian edge.[15] In short, I was a smart-ass. The older I got, the worse—or better—I got.

By the time I was eight, I watched the news and listened, trying to glean some material. I could do passable impressions of Richard Nixon, Spiro Agnew, and Walter Cronkite (and Jimmy Stewart). I mocked subjects I knew were incendiary but couldn't fully understand.

---

15   Satire relies primarily on irony, over-exaggeration (hyperbole), and gross understatement (litotes) for effect. Horatian satire is named for the Roman satirist Horatio and tends to be more witty, mild, and amicable. We laugh at ourselves. In contrast, Juvenalian satire is named for the Latin satirist Juvenal, a harsh critic of Roman society. Juvenalian satire is caustic and biting. We laugh more as a defense against the sting of its accusation. Jonathan Swift's "A Modest Proposal" is the classic example of Juvenalian satire. *The Simpsons* is a modern example of Horatian satire.

This did not include, however, the Vietnam War. My oldest brother was eighteen.

My father worshipped Nixon, and I got a laugh at the dinner table by asking for seconds while spoofing the eventually-impeached president: "Tricky DIC-Kuh would like two more scoops of mashed potatoes." I put extra emphasis on "Dick" and waggled two fingers of each hand in peace signs, my head tilted and tremoring slightly as I spoke.

I learned to judge my effectiveness—how far I had pushed that "line"—based on the response it elicited: a chuckle was good, a cringe was bad, a chuckle with a cringe was excellent, especially if my mother or my oldest sister called out, "Michael!" When this occurred, I knew I had nicked some truth.

The latter always got me smacked upside the head. I preferred these over the random smacks I received *"Just because!"* If I drew the contact, if I initiated the exchange, I was in control.

I remember our family dinners during those years, from the time I was five until the fall I turned nine, with great fondness. All ten of us huddled around one table, silverware clinking against porcelain plates, and a cold glass of whole milk in front of each of us kids.

By the time I turned ten, my family had started to splinter.

After I turned fifteen, we moved to a new, smaller house, and the old picnic table was left behind. We had been halved; only five of us were left. One older brother. My younger sister. My father. My mother. Myself. One brother was off to college. The rest had married and moved out or just moved out.

Over the years, as I got older, the physical smacks upside the head from my father became fewer and further between. But the impact increased.

Then they stopped.

It happened on a Saturday afternoon in December. I was seventeen. I got home from wrestling practice—a rarity on weekends since we usually had a tournament every Saturday—feeling weak and surly. I had lost a tough match the night before and had gone out with some friends afterwards and gorged my disgust with pizza. As a result, I left practice that afternoon still four pounds overweight, and we had a meet on Tuesday. Lettuce leaves and watered-down strawberry Jello, my diet for the next few days, awaited.

My father sat in his chair puffing on his Pall Malls and reading the newspaper when I entered the den through the side door that led to the garage. He was the only one home. "Nice job last night," he quipped. He ruffled the newspaper, not bothering to look at me. He had been at the meet last night—he came to all the meets—but I hadn't seen him because he didn't bother to talk to me afterward. He left early and was in bed by the time I got home.

Why? Why bring it up now? I already felt like shit. Why stick a finger in the wound?

I froze. I thought about turning and leaving, just getting back in the car and going, but I could hear the garage door rumbling closed behind me and knew that was not an option.

I was done.

"Fuck off." I told him, my words forceful and unburdened. I felt empowered.

I dropped my wrestling bag, kicking it to the side, and headed toward my room. He popped from his chair and took three quick strides from behind me to draw within reach. He cocked his arm, an open hand to smack me forcibly across the back of my skull, but before he could do it, I turned.

I was not a little kid anymore. I was growing, and I met him eye to eye. I don't remember saying anything, but we both understood that if he swung that hand, this time I would fight back. I would strike him, and I might not stop. The loss would be irredeemable.

He did nothing, and I didn't give him much time. No need to draw this out. I turned and went to my room.

(2)

THAT YEAR, 1977, THE British rock band The Alan Parsons Project released their album *I, Robot*. The lead single on the album is a song bluntly titled, "I Wouldn't Want to Be Like You." The lyrics are stark and concrete. The majority of the actual song has an upbeat, lively tempo, but the music I heard—the background score to many nights lying awake—was a low and melodious chant driven by a three-beat baseline and the tapping cymbal of a ticking time bomb. The title lyric played over and over and over in my mind, like a mantra.

(3)

MY OLDER BROTHER PREFERRED to backhand me in the solar plexus. He even called it a love tap. He'd shout, "Love Tap!" and follow with a *whump*.

When he was around, I got used to (a) having the air knocked out of me and (b) keeping my abs tight. Yes, I realize the order is backwards and an inversion might have prevented (a) from occurring. The problem was, he knew me too well and could sense when I started to drift into reverie, space out for whatever reason (as I was wont to do). When I relaxed, he pounced.

He'd call out to me as a warning, but that was only a tease, telling me what was coming, allowing me an instant—like Sisyphus turning to descend his hill—to contemplate my reality, but leaving me no option to do anything about it. The blow, like Sisyphus's waiting rock, was inevitable.

The solar plexus is a complex bundle of nerves located in the pit of the stomach and in front of the aorta. It is an essential part of the sympathetic nervous system. Our organs, everything from eyeballs to asshole, do not act independently. They behave in coordinated, rhythmic harmony. Relax, and they roll together like cool jazz. Under attack, a full fight or flight defense mechanism kicks in.

Sometimes the auto-response is to fight. Among other responses, pupils dilate, heart rate accelerates, sweat glands lube the body, peristalsis stops (no need to poop yourself), and the penis goes flaccid (no need to waste blood there).

Sometimes the auto-response is flight: bar the gates and lockdown all the valuables.

That's what happened each time I got hit in the solar plexus; each time he really caught me—when he attacked with his fist closed. My body reacted to a lethal threat. On impact, my diaphragm constricted, my organs locked up, and for the few moments it took to recover, my chest was paralyzed. Teary eyes and testicles retracted into my throat were the least of it. I was instantly convulsed, suffered to one knee in painful supplication. My fists clutched over my heart, my head bowed, and unable to suck in a breath, I could not have been more vulnerable.

However, also like Sisyphus, one must imagine me happy, because I chose my fate.[16] I knew the benefits and costs of being close to a brother who was a decade older. We couldn't be pals, too much separated us. But there was a mutual respect. He allowed me into a life I had no business sharing, not anything toxic, just moments and experiences, like sneaking out of school in eighth grade to hop on the Yellow Line and meet him downtown for a Cubs game or inviting me and my girlfriend to join him and his wife for the premiere of *Rocky*.

The love taps were a cost to be paid, a reminder, perhaps unnecessary, of a boundary. We could be close, but we were not equals. They were meant to keep me in my place. I was, after all, the younger brother, and so I masked the shame I felt each time it happened.

I did get him back once, sort of.

The summer after my freshman year of college, a few friends and I went to a Jackson Browne concert at Ravinia, a 36-acre outdoor music venue north of Chicago.

---

16 See Albert Camus, "The Myth of Sisyphus." Sisyphus is condemned by the gods to perpetual, furtive labor: rolling a rock to the top of a hill only to have it roll again back down. Camus argues that, despite his fate, one must imagine Sisyphus happy because this fate is his own; he chose to defy the gods knowing full well what the consequences would be. Each time he descends the hill to return to his rock, he doesn't regret what the gods have done to him; instead, he celebrates what he has forced the gods to do. He made a choice, not the gods.

No one sane goes to Ravinia to *watch* a concert; people go to listen to live music while they picnic, hang out, people watch, or just chill on a blanket spread out on the cool grass.

My friends and I went to meet girls. We also liked Jackson Browne's music.

By chance, we ran into my brother, there with his wife and some of their friends. He invited our group to join his for a few "Sneaky Pete's." A Sneaky Pete is beer mixed with sweet red wine, and it goes down easy. I've never reacted well to wine and was already buzzed on a few beers before we crashed his party, so it didn't take long for me to feel woozy. We talked with his friends and listened to a few songs, but I needed to walk around and sober up a little. My friends decided to leave en masse, so I went to say goodbye.

My brother was off to the side regaling some of his friends with a college story about how he got kicked out of school in spring of his senior year, a few weeks before graduation. He and a few friends were bored one afternoon, staring out their fifth-floor dorm window into the torrent of a thunderstorm, and thought it might be funny to take a BB gun and shoot some holes in the umbrellas of students scampering across campus. One of those students turned out to be the Dean of Students, and my brother and his friends were tracked down with great enthusiasm and promptly expelled.

I stood next to him, swaying slightly and waiting for the story I had heard many times to end. My brother's words and Jackson Browne's lyrics seemed harmonized, and I fell to wondering how this could be possible. I dazed.

Everyone laughed, so the story must have ended, and I smiled, stupid.

My brother turned to me and saw palpable vulnerability. Unable to pass such an easy mark and looking to augment his verbal humor with a little slapstick, he called out, "Love Tap!" and tried to backhand me in the solar plexus. My swaying moved the target, however, and he caught me square in the stomach instead.

I barked once and puked all over his pants and shoes, a very pretty lilac-shaded spray.

His wife and friends cringed and chuckled, a little grossed out, but more amused.

My brother and I stood frozen, assessing each other and the circumstances. I shrugged apology, and, after consideration, he shrugged acceptance. We were both equally culpable for this one.

(4)

I LIKED MATT. HE was an affable student with an easy smile and a benign wit.

I walked up and down the aisles of room 143 that day, leading a discussion on Whitman's poem, "Oh Me! Oh Life!" from among the students. I didn't like being the sage-on-the-stage behind a pulpit in front of class. I didn't want to lecture and tell the students what the poetry meant. The best teachers I knew drew the literature and the student closer together until they met on their own terms.

The best teachers don't deliver, they connect.

"Oh Me! Oh Life!" speaks to the despair we each face at seminal moments in our lives when we confront the existential questions: Who am I? and Why do I exist? The poem is about identity. Who do I want to be and how much control do I really have over that decision?

Matt and his classmates were juniors, and I was trying to get them to see that, within a year, when it came time to seriously think about life after high school, they too would face such a moment, an opportunity unlike any other in their lives so far to shape their identities, and that Whitman had some valuable advice to consider.

I was in my second year at Notre Dame High School. Only three years out of college, I wanted to make an impact. The best teachers I had, from grade school on up, had left a mark on me. I wanted to be like them.

I don't remember what exactly he said, I'm not sure I even fully heard it—it wasn't intended for me—but I know I was right behind Matt when he said it. The other kids chuckled, and I wasn't in on the joke. That meant either I or Mr. Whitman was being disrespected.

Without any thought, I shot my right hand forward and smacked Matt across the back of his head. Worse, I was wearing my Notre Dame college ring, and I felt the thick metal band nick into his scalp.

Matt bent over, his face to the tabletop, his fingers white knuckling the sides of his desk. He shuddered, but then lifted his head and bravely chuckled off the affront. His classmates bristled, but then feigned ignorance, a very Catholic-school thing to do. I barely broke stride and diverted attention from what I had just done by calling on another student to interpret some passage from the poem. This camouflaged my sudden shortness of breath and the heart now thumping spasmodically in my chest.

Violence at NDHS in the early 1980s was not uncommon. But I wasn't—or at least didn't want to be—one of those who did this. I had fucked up, royally. Worse, what I had done, my impulse to strike, had felt repulsively normal.

The next morning I had a message waiting in my mailbox, a call from Matt's father asking for a meeting. He didn't call my division head or my principal; he called me. I met with Matt, his father, and his mother that afternoon, after school, in my classroom. Matt's parents were kind, compassionate people. They weren't there to judge me. They were there to criticize my behavior.

Matt didn't speak at the meeting. He didn't want to be there. Instead, his parents presented the case, each speaking concisely, not belaboring any point. Matt was a good student, a quality person; he really liked my class and respected me as a teacher. He was hurt more by the fact that I had hit him, than by the actual blow itself. But the actual blow had been significant.

They asked me to feel the lump on the back of Matt's head, the welt left by my ring. I reached across my desk, Matt bowing his head, and stroked the nasty souvenir of where I had struck him.

"Understand the impact of what you do, Mr. Burke."

The double meaning of their diction was not lost on me; nor was their respect in referring to me as Mr. Burke, though I was two decades younger than they were.

I never worried about my job. Matt's parents weren't there to hurt me. Their compassion only aggravated my frustration and humiliation. Remembrance and regret tornadoed through me. I had been in Matt's place, I knew what he felt, but now I had done the damage. What the fuck is wrong with me? Goddammit! My conscience screamed: *You know better you know better you know better! You fucking idiot!*

I didn't try to justify any of what I had done. I apologized to Matt and his parents.[17] I thanked them. I promised them and swore to myself that I would work to fix this.

(5)

TWO YEARS LATER, THOUGH I still coached cross country at NDHS in the fall, I had quit teaching and joined two of my brothers at what had been my father's roofing company. He had died a few years earlier, and they had taken over the business. Under my father, the roofing company had been primarily commercial, focusing on flat-roof buildings—schools, factories, warehouses, apartment complexes—and tar-and-gravel construction.

My brothers wanted to expand into residential work: shingle roofs on single-family homes. They asked me to join them and help manage this new wing. I'd have an administrative job, giving estimates and supervising the crews doing the work.

---

17 If there are guardian angels that pop into our lives at certain seminal moments to help steer us toward our better selves, then this was one such miracle. I have never forgotten Matt's parents and the truly charitable manner in which they handled this situation.

I hated leaving teaching, but my wife and growing family needed the money. My salary at the roofing company would be ten grand more than what I had made teaching. I had to go, but I couldn't leave it all behind. With the proviso that, for one final fall season I could still coach cross country, I took the roofing job.

My older brother had joined my father at the roofing company immediately after not graduating college. However, like me, he had a passion for teaching and coaching. Had he graduated, he too might have gone into education, but that wasn't what fate had in mind. Destiny made him a roofer. Still, he volunteer-coached cross country at a local girls' school, a sister school of NDHS. Thus, he understood my need to finish what I had started, so he allowed me to bend my work schedule around cross country practices and meets. That meant putting in some late evening and weekend hours, but it was worth it. I felt connected to my runners, especially the seniors who had been with me for four years. I couldn't leave them to someone else.

We had two captains on that team. Both were seniors. Both led by example and by word. Yet, as often happens, they were foils to each other, especially in terms of talent. Len was easily the best runner on our team and ended up being the best in the state. Kevin barely made our top seven. They had an interesting, complementary relationship, the two of them. Both were intensely competitive, both were Alphas; yet, as mentioned, only one had talent.

What Kevin had was that blue collar, Irish Catholic diligence that borders on defiance. He worked his ass off and demanded everyone else do the same. He was envious of Len's talent and envious of the talent of the three underclassmen, two sophomores and freshman, who regularly beat him in workouts and races. However, instead of adopting the attitude of a coward who seeks to pull those ahead of him back, he turned his envy into righteous anger: I'm not going to waste what little ability I have and you sure as hell are not going to waste the wealth of talent you were given. If Len took it easy in a practice or a meet, Kevin gave him shit for coasting. And Len, to his credit, responded, though not without also giving Kevin shit for sucking.

They made each other better.

(6)

AT SOME POINT DURING that season, without reason, I started backslapping—a softer flick of just fingers—a few of the runners in the stomach. I didn't aim for the solar plexus, and my goal wasn't to debilitate. I did it for physical emphasis.[18]

I have never been an ass-slapper or a back-patter. I don't give shoulder squeezes, a handshake was too formal, and fist-bumps had not yet become ubiquitous. I am a tactile person, I like that physical connection, but I don't want to be intimate. A backhand to the gut seemed to fit my needs. At least, that was my rationalization.

The most common applications were during practices when we were running multiple repetitions. After a good rep, I might backhand a runner and say, "Well

---

18 I look back now and I think, how could I have been so stupid? How did I not realize that I was mimicking a behavior that, though I associated it with brotherhood, I also detested? And yet I was: stupid.

done! Keep it up." After a bad rep, "Hey," backhand, "pick it up."

Twice a week that season, I had the runners do a loose, five-mile run in the morning and then weightlifting—light upper body work—for half-an-hour before school started. I'd send them off and then go down to the weight room, a dungeon below the gym, to be sure all the equipment was in order.

That Wednesday, the boys, juiced by some competitive muse, sprinted the finish. They headed down the stairs to the weight room taxed and out of breath but still gabbing and jostling each other in amicable adolescent rivalry. I stood just inside the weight room door, arms folded, my back against the wall, relaxed and listening to their jabber. The younger runners came through first, and I picked up on snippets of an incident involving a tomato garden. I looked more closely and saw some orange stains on the shirts of the two sophomores and one freshman who typically finished as our 2nd, 3rd, and 4th best runners. They were laughing, so whatever had happened—most likely an ambush by the seniors—held no malice.

I waited for Kevin and Len, the last two down the steps, the captains. As they entered, without any word or warning, I backhanded Kevin. He wasn't ready. He was chattering with Len, exhaling, breathless, fatigued a little from the run. His walking quickly forward, having skipped down the final steps, added to the force of impact. I knocked him out. He crumpled toward the floor, landing on his knees, his elbows driving into his upper thighs, his head curling low chin to chest.

"Coach!" Len snapped, squatting and reaching to his teammate. "What the fuck?"

Miraculously, Kevin was only out for the fall itself. An instant after he hit the ground, he rolled onto his side and fought out of his fetal position. He pivoted back to his hands and knees and then popped, as best he could, back up to a standing position. He wobbled a second. Len steadied him. Still coming to, Kevin mumbled, "I must've passed out."

Then it hit him that I had hit him, that he had not just fainted. His look was more disappointment than anger, and I felt small and stupid, humiliated because I had put our mutual respect at risk. Everything had happened so fast that no one really noticed, other than Kevin and Len and me. My embarrassment was evident, and because I got it, and they got that I got it, they let me off with a shake of their heads before continuing into the weight room for some bench press.

I stopped the backhands.

Later that season, Kevin led us to victory over a conference rival that had more overall talent than we did but lacked our tenacity. "Led" is a relative term. Kevin never led the actual race; in fact, he never ran better than 5th place.

In cross country meets, each team enters seven runners. The top five finishers from that team are the scorers, and the sum of their places is the team score. Thus, if the top five runners finish 2nd, 4th, 5th, 8th, and 10th, the team score is 29. In cross country, the lowest team score wins.

During that meet, Len locked up 1st place early; he took off at the start and never looked back. The other team settled into 2nd, 3rd, and 4th. We needed to grab the next four places to win. Kevin willed us to those four spots. He and his three teammates formed a tight diamond with Kevin at the point. He led the attack on every hill and accelerated in and out of every tight turn. Eventually, over the three-mile course, he broke the other team's 4th and 5th runners.

As mentioned, Kevin didn't win the race; Len did. Kevin got passed by all three of his teammates, those two sophomores and the freshman, in the last 200 yards. They finished 5th, 6th, 7th, and Kevin, 8th, all within four seconds of each other and ten seconds ahead of any chasers. Kevin had led that diamond pack, had willed them together, for the first 2.9 miles of the race. His teammates had no trouble passing him at the finish, and though it frustrated him, he had no problem with them doing so.

We won the meet 27-28. The win earned us the conference championship.

After the race, I told Kevin this was his victory: he was our most valuable runner that day, and we hugged.

(7)

LIVING AN EXAMINED LIFE is essential to my well-being. I don't need to obsess, but I do need to be vigilant about making a conscious effort to pursue my better self. If not, I'll default or devolve into inbred or reflexive behaviors.

Human beings are by nature vicarious learners. We learn by the example of those around us, whether we want to or not. There is always information and patterns and behaviors being absorbed or recorded or picked up.

Monkey see, monkey do. The apple doesn't fall far from the tree. Stupid is as stupid does.

My father and my older brother were my role models growing up. I picked up some angels from them, some positive traits: my work ethic, my passion. But I caught a few demons as well. To change, I needed to make a conscious effort to be different, to remind myself to learn by both affirmation and negation: this is what I should do; this is what I should not do.

Regarding Matt and Kevin, I needed to be sure that what I had done—any action intended to degrade or belittle someone—remained a mistake and did not, through ignorance and stupidity, become a habit. I am a fallible being and a product of my upbringing, but that is no excuse. Intellect annuls fate,[19] but only through introspection and then action.

Matt forgave me and Kevin forgave me, partially because I had built equity before and I built more equity after to overcome the damage I had done, but mostly because I made it clear to them that I knew I was wrong. I fucked up, but I'm fortunate in both cases that I had the opportunity for reconciliation.

---

19   Ralph Waldo Emerson, "Fate"

CHAPTER 8

A RECOVERY RUN

(1)

ON NOVEMBER 8, 1986, Len Sitko, representing Notre Dame High School, won the Illinois High School Association (IHSA) Cross Country State Championship. He ran the 3-mile course around Detweiler Park in Peoria in 14:08.0. At the time, his was the seventh fastest time in IHSA history.

Len ended that fall season undefeated. No one had been close to him. He controlled every race from start to finish.

In track the following spring, during the regular season, Len again went undefeated. He won every individual race he ran.

In May, he qualified for the IHSA State Track meet in the 3200m run and the 1600m[20] run by winning both races at the Sectional meet, the qualifier. Each victory had been fairly easy, at least for Len. The competition was solid, but not elite. Winning both at the State meet, however, would be much more difficult.

The Double.

---

20 The metric equivalent of the 2 mile and the 1 mile. These are the two longest races of the IHSA State Track meet.

Sprinters often compete in more than one race in a track meet since their races are explosive, anaerobic events, all completed in under 60 seconds. Recovery from these events is usually pretty quick. Distance races, however, are extended, aerobic events that tax the body over a much longer period of time. Thus, more recovery time is needed.

If Len chose to run the Double, he would need to compete in three distance races in fewer than twenty-four hours. On Friday night, he would run the 1600m prelim. If he finished with one of the top 12 times (if???), he would qualify for the final on Saturday. On Saturday afternoon, he would run the 3200m and then, an hour later, the final of the 1600m. Few runners attempt the Double because adequate recovery between these races is unlikely, and full recovery is impossible.

Len's goal, however, wouldn't be to run the Double; it would be to win, to win all three races, to remain undefeated on the year. That was important to him, to finish his senior year undefeated in both Cross Country and Track. That would be a pretty memorable accomplishment. But it wouldn't be easy. Only three athletes had won the Double at the IHSA State Track Meet in the previous two decades.

So, the big question for us was whether to go for the Double, or, focus on just one event—either the 3200m or the 1600m—and look to dominate. After some discussion, I left the final decision up to Len. He flashed an easy smile and quipped, "Hey, I'm gonna be there either way. So, why run just one race when I can run three?"

We talked some more. Len wanted to win the Double, but his primary focus was on the 3200m. The state was stronger in 3200m runners, and for most of the competitors that would be their only race that weekend. "Win that," Len said, "and then I'll see what happens in the 1600m."

I knew Len's modest "see what happens in the 1600m" comment was a crock of shit; he wanted to win both races. Len was savvy, though. He didn't want to sound cocky, to me or to himself. He wanted the Double, but he knew to respect the athlete's maxim: Take one race at a time.

(2)

THE THURSDAY OF THE state meet, we drove the three-plus hours from Niles to Charleston, Illinois, home of Eastern Illinois University. We dropped our stuff off at the hotel, Len changed into his sweats, and we headed to the track.

Our goal was more mental than physical. Simple acclimation. Len had been here, had run in the state meet the previous two years. He was very familiar with this track and these surroundings. But this was different. For the first time, he was here as a favorite. Reporters interviewed him, some for downstate newspapers from towns he had never heard of. Other coaches and athletes—not just distance runners, but sprinters and throwers too—pointed him out. He was "That Kid," the one who had kicked ass in cross country and might look to Double in track. Eyes followed him. He needed to get used to this celebrity status so he could block it out. Nod and smile—you don't want to be standoffish and thus cast as arrogant—but keep your focus on the task at hand.

Len jogged some laps, did a few strides and sprints, and plopped down in different locations around the stadium for a lot of stretching.

Heraclitus[21] stated that a man never steps in the same river twice. Everything is in constant flux, and each moment the river and the man are changing. We are always becoming something new. Though I may have run a hundred races, today's race, *this* race, in minor or major ways, is new. I need to acknowledge and embrace this reality. To prepare for what might be unexpected.

Len needed to warm-up and acclimate himself, mentally and emotionally, to this new experience. He needed to visualize himself running, see himself in his uniform surrounded by the other runners, rounding this turn, accelerating on that straightaway, relaxed, under control, before exploding across the finish line. He needed to win each race before he ever ran it. That's why he sat down and did some stretching at different spots on the track: to visualize success from different perspectives.

As Len was doing his thing, I talked with some of the other coaches, scouting the competition. Most of the top runners in the state, like Len, had qualified in both the 3200m and 1600m races. However, his top two competitors in the 3200m, including the runner who finished second to Len in the IHSA Cross Country Championship, had withdrawn from the 1600m.

---

[21] Greek philosopher active around 500 B.C.

In addition, the best 1600m runners had withdrawn from the 3200m. Each of these runners had chosen to focus on one event. Only Len and one other top athlete would be doubling.

That was fine. Bring it on.

On Friday night, Len won his 1600m prelim in 4:16.4. He remained undefeated.

Saturday, the day of the State Finals, was a typical Central Illinois meteorological nightmare. The morning started with overcast skies, unseasonable coolness, and strong winds. Len loosened up in full sweats. The meet began.

In 1987, the IHSA State Track meet featured two classes, small schools in Class A and large schools in Class AA. Each class competed in twelve track events, alternating between A and AA. The 3200m was the third event; the 1600m was the tenth. Len would have a little over an hour to recover between races. But that was not his priority. He wasn't thinking of the 1600m. Focus on the moment and the task at hand. He wanted the 3200m first.

The first four events, the Class A & AA 4x800m relays and 4x200m relays, were competed under darkening skies. The Class A 3200m race was next, to be followed by Len's race. He was warmed up and ready to go.

Unfortunately, the skies chose that moment to turn apocalyptic.

There was no Lightning Detection Security system in those days. We tracked storms using the flash-to-bang method. See the lightning and then count how long it takes to hear the thunder. If the number keeps getting larger, the storm is moving away. If the number is getting smaller, you're screwed.

During those first four events, the gods had simply grumbled. The rolling, towering thunderheads moving over us jockeyed for position, but there had been no rain and no actual lightning, just a few sparks as cumulonimbus bulbs scraped against each other. So, despite dropping temperatures and accelerating winds, the meet went on. Until, in an instant, it didn't.

As the Class A runners lined up for their 3200m race, a bolt ripped across the sky and struck a tree in a field just south of the stadium, fewer than a hundred yards away. There was no flash-to-bang, just a FLASHBANG, a simultaneous jolt, blinding and deafening. I ducked, as did those around me, throwing my hands up to my ears in awed futility. Then silence. The entire stadium waited. A coach next to me lifted his arm to marvel at the hairs standing on end.

Another series of bolts fingered across the sky, cracking and popping, and then the clouds loosed the torrent. A waterfall of rain drenched the western bleachers and began advancing eastward. Security cleared the track and the stands, herding everyone into a large indoor fieldhouse next to the stadium.

We waited.

Downstate Illinois is more great plains than big city. Unobstructed storms blow through like a 100m dash. Potent, explosive, dynamic, and over. Seventy-five minutes after the apocalypse, the meet resumed under clear skies. A now vengeful sun seared away any remnant of the storm. The surface of the rubberized Mondo track steamed. The temperature, which had dropped into the 60s, stretched to beyond 80 degrees and the humidity pushed past 90%.

I looked at Len, and he grinned. No problem, that smile said. Easy-peasy. Just roll with it.

Len and I had talked the night before about race strategy for the 3200m. There were runners who might be able to run a *time* as fast as Len's, but no one in the field could run as fast as Len. He had more raw speed. That meant that regardless of how fast the race was run, Len should be able to out-kick his competitors at the finish. So, as he had done in the IHSA State Cross Country meet, he needed to sit back and let the other runners lead until the final 800 meters. Then, he would make his move and begin a gradual acceleration to break his competition.

The Class AA 3200m runners gathered for the start, 32 competitors stacked in a sweeping arch across eight lanes of track. With the fastest qualifying time, Len had the first position. As the runners steadied for the gun, I watched him expand his chest with a deep breath, then roll his shoulders forward, letting his arms hang limply in front. He closed his eyes, took another deep breath, and slowly exhaled, emptying every potential distraction. Fast and loose.

The official called the runners to set position, hesitated, and fired his starter's pistol. The runners burst forward. The penultimate race of Len's high school career had begun.

By the end of the first lap, the top four runners had already pulled away from the rest of the pack. Len sat fourth, a stride from the lead, but letting the others take control.

The group passed the 1600m mark, the halfway point, at 4:35, an ideal pace to set-up the other runners, not one of whom had broken 9:10. (Len's best was 9:04.) He was in perfect position. He needed to hold this speed for two more laps, and then, stride by stride, pick up the pace over the last 800 meters. This was cruising speed for Len, and I had no doubt he could close the race with sub-60 second final lap. No one here could do that. Patience. That was the key.

But there is also pride. Not vanity. The good pride, the determination and delight that push us to excel.

In sports, certain numbers have almost transcendent significance. Nine minutes is a magical mark for a 3200m runner. Only a dozen or so runners had broken that barrier in IHSA history. To run *exactly* 9:00.0 is nice, but pushing that limit, breaking through to 8:59.9 and beyond, is significantly better.

Len wanted that mark as part of his legacy, especially since, halfway through the race, he felt great. He looked up at the 4:35 on the scoreboard and thought, "We're jogging." Instead of waiting as planned, he took off.

The group of four had run the first 4 laps at 68, 69, 70, and 68 seconds. Then Len shifted gears. He ran the fifth lap in 64 seconds. The pack let him go. For all intents and purposes, they were now racing for second place. He cruised through the sixth lap in 66 seconds and slid into the zone.

The zone. Get your mind out of the way. Step outside and just admire what your body can do. No distractions. Len had gotten good at this his senior year. Once he decided to take the lead, he ignored everyone else and just went. In every other race, this worked, and he had finished alone, unchallenged.

With 800m to go, Len opened a near-insurmountable ten-second lead on the field. He ran the second-to-last lap in another 66. Unbeknownst to him, however, one runner had broken from the field in an attempt to secure second place. The pack let him go as well, and he surged forward on a wave of confidence. He had nothing to lose.

Into the bell lap, the final lap, Len picked up the pace a little more. He ran that final lap in 65, but he also completely zoned out the other runners. This is what I had taught him to do, what had worked for him all year. Run your race and everything else will take care of itself. But I had screwed up. I should have known Len better, and I should have known his opponents better. I should've known he wanted to break nine minutes, and I should've known that "upset" didn't only apply to stomachs.[22]

When Len entered the final 200 meters, the final stretch, the crowd was going wild. He ignored them, thinking they were cheering his attempt to break nine minutes. He picked up the pace, getting stronger, as he was coached, but never really shifting gears. He had no idea someone was closing on him.

With five yards left, a little under two strides, less than a second, the other runner caught Len and inched past. Other than shock, Len had no time to react.

8:56.05 to 8:56.21.

Len had broken nine minutes and finished second.

---

[22] In sports, "upset" refers to any competition where a significant underdog defeats a favorite. The term was popularized after the 1919 Sanford Stakes at Saratoga when a horse named Upset defeated the mighty Man o' War, the only loss of the latter horse's legendary career.

A week later, I was given a picture of Len at the instant he crossed the finish line. He is peeking to his right at the runner just in from of him. An epiphany of pain is awakening in his eyes. He had plenty of speed left, but no time to use it. I threw that picture out.

In the few seconds after the race was over, Len and the other runner looked the same, both overcome with disbelief, both drained. As he had done after every race that year, Len reached out instinctively to shake his opponent's hand. They exchanged a smile, and then Len turned away.

The other runner had spent every ounce of energy to capture his state title. He took a few wobbly steps, overwhelmed, and collapsed into a loosed marionette sitting sprawl on the edge of the track. The race attendants rushed to help him back up. He spent the next hour taking fluids in the medical tent to keep from collapsing again.

Len had had every ounce of energy sucked from him by the defeat. He took a few steps, lost and disoriented. Then, while I watched from the stands[23], he gathered his sweats and running flats in a crumpled heap and headed, alone, out of the stadium. He left through a gated maintenance exit at the south end of the track. I worked my way down to the track and followed him out. I found him in the open, empty field behind the stadium, sitting slumped, his back against a giant, solitary tree.

He had another race to run in sixty minutes.

---

23   I had volunteered to work as an official at the meet and could have been trackside, but I thought this gave me an unfair advantage over coaches who couldn't volunteer. So, I watched from the stands.

(3)

FOUR YEARS EARLIER, MY mother died. She died too young, barely 60, but her death, though tragic, was not unexpected. She had lived a hard life.

At her wake, I stood next to my aunt, my mother's younger sister, in the receiving line. After half an hour of politely greeting guests and mourners—neither of us knew well many of the people there—she turned to me and muttered, "Only idiots ask questions at a wake."

She was in her late thirties, and I was in my early twenties. I don't know what set her off, but she chose, over the next few minutes, in short bursts when the line momentarily stopped, to lecture me as if I had done something wrong, as if this were a decade or so earlier and she was babysitting my ten-year-old self who had dared to disappear on his bike for almost three hours without telling her where he was going. She gave me some advice then—along with a few bruises on my shoulder; she was a pinch-and-twister—and she offered more now, whether I wanted it or not.

At the next pause, still sotto voce, but with a whiny, condescending flair, she mocked the affronting phrases: "How are you doing? Are you feeling okay? Is there anything I can do to help?

"What morons." When the line moved, she greeted those she did and didn't know with bobbing nods and eyeless smiles. To those struggling to console her, she offered an occasional hand-pat that instantly morphed into artful guidance—a gentle push—to move them along. My aunt was not one to allow even well-meaning individuals to hold up the line.

"I know what you must be going through," she whimpered, followed by a pseudo-retch that drew a strange look from the closest mourner. She smiled as he passed, then murmured to me, emphatic, her face locked in a ventriloquist's pained countenance, "No . . . You . . . Don't!"

Soon, culminating the lesson, she stole another instant and grabbed my right biceps in a two-handed stranglehold. She squeezed, digging her nails through my suit coat and shirt and into the gap between bone and muscle.

"Just be there. Give a handshake, maybe a . . ." she searched a second for the appropriate descriptor, "*sober*, maybe a sober hug."

"And," she finished, jostling me to emphasize each word, "Shut! Up!"

I was a man, not a ten-year-old, and much more powerful than this firecracker of a woman. I had not asked for a lecture. This was my mother's wake. My aunt kept holding on, and I was tempted to jerk my arm away—Get off me!—but I didn't. In my heart, I knew she meant well, and that she was hurting.

Instead, I flexed my biceps, and patted her hands with two sober taps, and said nothing.

(4)

DYING, WHETHER LITERAL OR metaphoric, never comes easy.

Something important had died after the storm had abated on the track at Eastern Illinois University. Not a dream. More. Worse. A realistic, attainable responsibility

Len had inched closer to every day since his senior year began back in August. To be undefeated. To be the best. Len saw it, trained it, and lived it through the entire cross country season, the entire pre-State track season, and for 3195 meters of this 3200 meter race.

I know this is not the same as "real" death or loss. It's just a game; or, in this case, one race.

But it isn't *just* a race. Anything I do with passion, anything I pursue with resolve, anything I commit to over time, matters. And losing it, hurts. How Len handled this loss mattered, and it was important that I, his coach, guide him through well.

I handed him the Gatorade I brought. He was still wearing his uniform and racing spikes, the bundle of sweats and his training flats tossed down on the roots of the tree. I plopped down on the grass next to him. We didn't talk. I watched him vacillating between utter denial and unconditional acceptance of his vulnerability. He should never have lost, not this year, but he did lose, and therefore he could and would lose again.

We sat for ten minutes. Neither of us said anything. He drank nothing. The sun flickered through the leaves of the massive white oak that shaded us. I looked up through the branches and wondered if this had been what had drawn, and clearly withstood, that earlier lightning strike.

Len sat in the upright fetal position of a wounded child, legs pulled up to the chest, arms wrapped around them in defense, chin resting aslant on the knees. His eyes had no singular focus, and he had not stopped sweating, or, at least, the sweat on him had not bothered to dry.

Forty-five minutes to the 1600m race. I had to get him moving.

"Drink the Gatorade," I said. "Put your sweats on. Switch shoes." He did as I asked, sitting all the while.

"Stupidest race I've ever run." He was not a crier. There would be no tears.

I thought about his statement. I could've questioned his assertion. In cross country his sophomore year, Len had taken a wrong turn on a course that wove through a forest preserve. Turning right instead of left, he headed down a path into the woods. Luckily, it dead-ended at a river or he might still be following it. He spun around to see his opponents striding past the opening he had entered. He raced back out and managed to catch only a few of those who passed him. He went into the woods in first and wound up fourteenth. That was pretty stupid.

I could've also taken the blame. As his coach I should have known him better; I hadn't realized how important that nine-minute mark was to him. I hadn't coached him up enough on his opponents, either. I didn't find out until later that the kid who beat him had also been the anchor of his team's 4 x 800-meter relay for most of the season. He was used to running from behind, used to catching those with a significant head start. I should've known this. I should have also known that both the spacing out strategy and the "one race at a time" maxim had their limitations.

We could go back and forth, each taking blame rather than giving it, but a pity party over who was most responsible for the loss would benefit neither of us. Any attempt to understand what had happened, at this moment, was futile. Plus, talking too much, especially nervous rambling, only fucks things up.

"I saw you shake his hand, Len. That was classy." He couldn't look me in the eye.

"Habit," he said, and picked a few blades of grass that he tossed aimlessly onto the ground in front of him.

I stood up and turned to him. I reached out my hand and he took it, not looking up, but letting me help pull him to his feet. I squeezed his shoulder and gave him a gentle push. "Get running," I said. "Jog around this field a few times."

Keep it simple.

Len didn't need a big speech or a "snap-out-of-it" slap in the face. He needed a nudge. He needed activity, for his body—his muscles had to be locking up after running that fast in this heat—and for his mind. Fight grief by beginning with a simple task. Keep moving. He started jogging. One lap. Two laps. Three laps.

"Stop and stretch," I told him. "Drink some more."

Len is one of the toughest competitors I have ever met. I didn't ask him if he wanted to run the 1600. That would be as stupid as asking, "How do you feel?" at a wake. I knew he felt like shit, and I knew he was going to run the 1600m. He had no choice, not because I demanded it, which I did, but because he demanded it. He might lose, but he was not a quitter. We walked back into the stadium.

A little over an hour after running the fastest 3200m race of his high school career and suffering the harshest defeat of his life, Len stepped to the starting line with 12 other runners to begin the final race of his senior season.

(5)

AGAIN, THE OFFICIAL CALLED the runners to set position, hesitated, and fired his starter's pistol. Again, the runners burst forward. The ultimate race of Len's high school career had begun.

A pack of five runners, Len included, took the lead with a 62 second first lap and gained separation from the rest of the field. Instead of pushing the pace, however, the pack slowed, running the second lap in 66. This allowed four other runners to catch up. At the 800-meter mark, halfway through the race, a gangly group of nine jostled for position, Len caught in the middle.

With 600 meters to go, one of the runners surged ahead and over the next 200 meters the pack of nine spread out into a single file line.

The bell lap, the final lap. 400 meters. The nine remained stacked one behind the other. Len was fifth, two seconds behind first.

I watched him along the backstretch. He was laboring and chasing, two things he had not done all year.

The runners entered the final curve, fewer than 200 meters to go. And I saw it, from the crowded stands ten rows up, I felt it. Something clicked. Coming into the final straightaway, Len lifted his eyes from the heels of the runner in fourth and locked in on the finish line. The other competitors continued their valiant efforts bound by Newton's law of universal gravitation, but Len was now sprinting downhill.

After the race he told a reporter, "All of a sudden during that race I just fired up. I realized that the last

110 yards of my high school career were going down the drain. I had to do something about it."

He did.

He put on a finishing kick over the last 100 meters, accelerating past each of the four runners in front of him and nipping the final one at the tape, 4:12.61 to 4:12.81. He ran that final 100 meters—or, 110 yards, as he put it—in slightly over 12 seconds, an absurd speed to finish a 1600-meter race.

I have two favorite pictures from that day.

The first shows Len hugging two runners from Glenbrook North immediately after the 1600m. One of those individuals was the one Len just beat by two-tenths of a second, the one who had finished runner-up in the 1600m. The other was one of the few who, like Len, had run the double on this ridiculously hot day. He had finished eighth in the 1600m and third in the 3200m. All three individuals are smiling. Glenbrook North had been in our regional and sectional for cross country and our sectional for track. These three had seen a lot of each other. The picture demonstrates the respect they shared for each other and for the sport.

The second picture shows me with Len on the track a few moments after the first picture was taken. Ignoring a security guard, I had leapt from the stands as soon as the race was over. I ran to the finish line but stood back and waited for Len to congratulate and be congratulated by his competitors.

He saw me, shook one more hand, took two powerful stomps toward me and jumped into my bear hug. I squeezed hard enough to pop a few of his vertebrae.

The picture shows us hugging, his face to the camera, revitalized by what he had just accomplished, not victory in a race, but an affirmation of will, of resolve, not to be defeated.

(6)

An unfortunate reality of sports is that we remember the wins but relive the losses.

In fall of 2018, I went out to dinner with Len and a few of his teammates. Just a casual get-together to acknowledge my retirement from teaching. When the subject of the 1987 State Track meet came up, before any story was retold, Len cringed and groaned like someone had stabbed him in the gut.

He looked at me, smiled as if obligated to apologize, and shook his head. I shuddered and teared up. I had to dab my eyes with my napkin. Why is the loss his initial reaction? And why is that reaction so visceral? Because that is the nature of serious athletes, of sports fanatics. Wins are great and worth celebrating. But the losses hurt.

A few seconds later, Len shook off the agony, like snapping out of a trance. He brightened, and play-punched me on the shoulder.

"After the 1600, Coach almost broke my back!" he barked out, and we had a good laugh. Ours had been no sober hug of consolation, and I'm glad that he chose to embrace that memory as well.

CHAPTER 9

ESCALATION

It's not the mountain ahead that wears you down, it's the grain of sand in your shoe. Be master of your petty annoyances and conserve your energy for worthwhile things. —Unknown

(1)

"THE IRONY HERE IS that the bombing of Dresden, Germany, an atrocity overlooked in most U.S. history books, is perhaps the first significant act of Global terrorism—meant to scare both the Germans and the Russians—and," he pauses to clear his throat, "it was committed by the Allied forces."

When our teacher Mr. Antón is on a roll, delivering some poignant historical lesson he thinks foundational to the class and essential to our understanding of the United States of America, you better at least pretend to be listening. In this regard, Angus "Gus" Williams should have known better. You can kid around with Mr. Antón, he is cool, but when you see that vein start to rise in the middle of his forehead, when he clears his throat as if gagging on a little bile, you better back off.

Gus doesn't. He keeps farting around[24], ignorant of the lesson and distracting the students around him. On and off throughout the period, he's been quoting lines—under his breath—from *Young Frankenstein*, each time eliciting giggles from the students close enough to hear. Why this film and what got them started is unknown. Silliness.

"What knockers!" Giggles.

"SED-A-GIVE???" Giggles.

"Frau Blücher!" followed by a muffled neigh. Giggles.

Too many lines, too many giggles. Bad timing.

So enamored is Gus with his performance that he doesn't realize Mr. Antón, who likes to walk around the class while teaching, has circled behind him. He also doesn't realize that, for obvious reasons, he has pushed Mr. Antón into the red.

Gus hunches to his desktop and cups both hands over his mouth. He flutters his right hand to yield a jazzy, 1920's style vibrato and sings, "I-I-I ain't got no baaahhaha..."

His whimsical intonation is broken by a teacher's fist whiffling through the air and striking Gus in the back of the skull. He immediately burrows forehead first into his U.S. History text, folding both arms over his head in defense. The second fist smashes into Gus's forearm. The third only grazes the surface.

Mr. Antón—a *history* teacher—knows never to attack a walled city. So, he alters strategy. He assesses his quarry, and a crooked smirk creeps across his lips. He digs through the defenses, grabs Gus by the lobe of his

---

24 Mr. Antón's favorite admonishment: Quit farting around!

ear, and drags him out of his desk and up to the front of the classroom.

We are not children; we are juniors in high school. Gus, my classmate, is a long, angular kid, who always seems a little skewed to the left, as if leaning into a wind. He is six inches taller and twenty pounds heavier than Mr. Antón. But Mr. Antón is an adult and a teacher at an all-boy Catholic school, and our indoctrinated instinct is to obey.

They move to the front of the class.

We are silent.

I am neither shocked nor surprised. Corporal punishment and Catholicism go hand-in-hand. This is, however, original. I have never seen a teacher repeatedly punch a student with a closed fist. And, though I have heard tell of the disciplinary ploy I think Mr. Antón is about to enact, I have never actually seen it performed. I admit, I'm interested to see how this plays out.

Mr. Antón holds Gus's twisted lobe in his right hand. He stands Gus tall, studies him toe to head, and measures this man child. Then, with the dexterity of an artist, Mr. Antón takes a piece of chalk in his left hand and puts a dot on the board 49 1/2 inches off the ground. With Archimedean precision, he draws a circle two inches in diameter (with an area of π) around that dot.

He looks again at Gus, at the circle, and smiles. Mr. Antón approves.

Twisting first to inflict a little more pain and ensure compliance, he pulls Gus down to his knees and places the tip of the boy's nose square in the middle of that perfectly placed circle. Gus must kneel fully upright to keep everything in place.

"Stay there!" The words glottal from deep in Mr. Antón's throat.

With only a fraction of the class period left, it should have ended there. Gus should have stayed in place, and Mr. Antón should have finished the lesson. The after story might have been amusing. Not to be.

Gus left behind him, Mr. Antón turns to the class as if nothing has happened. The vein in his forehead has submerged, and his voice again has that slightly effeminate lilt, as if everything he teaches us is for our benefit, our pleasure. A gift.

I like Mr. Antón. He cares. About the curriculum and about us. He knows how important it is for us to learn the lessons of history. What he has done to Gus isn't personal, at least not toward Gus. It's about respect. It's about discipline and order, and now that order has been restored, to Mr. Antón's thinking, everything is over.

Gus, however, has been violated, degraded. Staring into the blackness of a chalkboard an inch in front of his face has given him opportunity to assess how fucked up this all is. Everything is not over. He cannot literally strike back at Mr. Antón, the canon of subordination to superiors is too deeply ingrained, but he must retaliate.

Mr. Antón is sitting on the front edge of his desk, facing us. His legs are loosely crossed; he holds an open history text in his left hand and gestures with his right, emphasizing this point and that. Gus is behind him out of his line-of-sight.

Gus, still on his knees, pivots from the blackboard to face Mr. Antón's back. He raises his open hands together, slowly, to just in front of his cheeks, and leans in as if preparing to dive out off a cliff. He grins, toothy, and pivots each hand inward, curling into fists all but his middle fingers which he leaves pointing up and in at 45-degree angles. He tilts his head, raises his eyebrows, and bites his bottom lip. He pauses, eyes wide, and then puffs out two breathless explosives: FUCK. YOU.

Mr. Antón doesn't need to see to know something is happening behind him; the collective shift of our eyes has given Gus away. But he won't spin around. He won't give Gus the satisfaction. Gus can't make him do that.

The vein swells and the bile gathers. Mr. Antón stands, but continues teaching, never impeding his lesson. He has no idea what exactly has happened behind him, but he knows from our grins and grimaces that it was bad. Still facing us, he glides to the side and then begins backing around his desk. He feigns tranquility, inching toward the blackboard where Gus—who after his defiance has spun around into position—kneels with his nose once again compliantly planted in the center of the circle.

We watch Mr. Antón. He stops. Gus is now next to him, just to the right, though they face in opposite directions.

Mr. Antón is still teaching, though none of us are listening. He has the history text balanced in his left hand. He raises his right hand to emphasize to us a significant point. He floats the hand back and forth as if orchestrating a lullaby. Then his pupils dilate, and his front teeth settle on his bottom lip. As we, his students, having realized what he is about to do, suck the air like drowning fish, he snaps the hand back, cracking against Gus's skull and driving the boy's face into the blackboard.

Gus's nose explodes; his blood sprays out in a downward fan, glistening wet but colorless against the dark background. Gus sinks back onto his heels. Blood spurts onto his shirt and spatters onto the tiled floor.

He will not stay on his knees. Fighting concussive dizziness, he stands, laboring, one leg, then the other. He turns toward us. Making no attempt to staunch the flow that continues gurgling out in spasms, he raises his palms and extends his arms to his classmates. The two-fold message is clear, at least to me: (1) look what *he* has done and (2) *we* are in this together.

Mr. Antón silences Gus's appeal by snatching some tissues from a Kleenex box on his desk. He stuffs them into Gus's hand and forces the wad up to Gus's nose.

He points to Simon, sitting in the front row, "Take him to the nurse. Now." Simon takes Gus by the elbow and leads him out.

The bell rings, and the rest of us file silently out.

I am the last to leave. I hesitate by the door, mentally snapshotting the scene before me. Mr. Antón stands by his desk, Gorgon struck, staring at the white circle on the board and the already sticky trail of evidence drizzled down the blackboard and puddled in penny-sized globs across the floor.

(2)

THERE ARE TWO GUIDING principles for corporal punishment in Catholic schools. The first I learned as a child, when I was often on the receiving end of such judgement. The second I learned from Fr. Heilmann my first year teaching when it was assumed that I would now be meting out this style of discipline. (He said it as a "joke.") These cardinal rules are best articulated through the following statements: "This is for your own good" and "Don't leave a mark."

Mr. Antón misfired on both accounts. Nothing he did was for Gus's benefit: no ethical motivation, no constructive lesson to learn. And he definitely left a mark.

This all happened on a Wednesday. Gus stayed out of school on Thursday, and Mr. Antón was "out sick" on Friday. Each of those days in class we watched an episode from the documentary series, *The World at War*. By Monday, both were back, and everything seemed to have passed. The only remnant was a shade of greenish yellow beneath both of Gus's eyes, and this too gradually faded. The rest of the year passed without incident.

Senior year, I took Mr. Antón's *History of the Iberian Peninsula* class. A group of us even went to Spain with him for seven days over winter break. As I said, I liked Mr. Antón. He had a subtle wit, a charismatic demeanor, and a toothy Cheshire grin that brightened a classroom. He was one of my favorite teachers.

Unfortunately, those adept at teaching aren't always as proficient at learning. Mr. Anton's actions toward Gus were neither isolated nor exceptional. He was good for one or two of these bouts of excessive force per year. One could argue that "only" one or two incidents a year constitutes more anomaly than pattern. "He's a really good guy," the hypothetical supervisor says, "except for this 'one thing,' and, God bless him, he's working on it!"

Or one could argue that since everyone knew his past and his potential and did nothing about it, Mr. Antón was not only enabled but also felt entitled to act on this potential from time to time. It was to be expected.

Either way, many years later I heard a rumor that the chickens finally came home to roost. Several individuals, apparently, jumped Mr. Antón outside his home. They roughed him up and closed the beating by "curbing" him, meaning, they forced his mouth open, wedged it against the concrete curb in front of his own house, and stomped on the back of his head. He lived, but that striking smile was shattered.

I'm not positive the rumor is true. I don't care. Its validity does not really matter to me. Its plausibility is enough.

(3)

I AM 23 YEARS old and in my first year teaching at Notre Dame High School. Second period, early in the day. I leave my classroom—my students are taking a quiz—and start into the hallway toward the bathroom to take a quick leak. I probably should not be leaving my class alone, unsupervised. I also shouldn't have had three cups of coffee that morning. Nature takes priority, though, so I hustle out, hoping to do my business and be back before anyone notices.

Okay, I need to clarify a few contextual considerations for this scenario.

First, I had graduated from NDHS just five years earlier, and I am self-conscious about now being a colleague of my former teachers and administrators. I want to be perceived as *professional*.

Second, I want and need to be respected by the students as their *teacher*. Age proximity makes this difficult; I am 23 and some of the seniors I teach are already 18. This is a typical struggle for all young educators. However, this is especially challenging for me because a few of the juniors and seniors are younger brothers of friends I had in high school. These students saw me as "Mike," their brother's friend who used to party at their house.[25] I must create separation from that persona. I am now "Mr. Burke."

Unfortunately, leaving my class unsupervised because I can't control my bladder will not enhance my status in either regard. That's why this pit stop needs to be quick and unobserved.

I turn into what should be an empty hallway to go tinkle in what should be an empty bathroom (no teacher wants to pee next to a student). Instead, hustling toward me from the far end of the hallway is a junior, a kid I do not know. He has a backpack slung over one shoulder, his shirt is partially untucked, and he keeps his head down.

---

25   I sat down with one of these younger brothers immediately after I was hired, over the summer, before school started. He was going to be a senior and had been scheduled into one of my classes. So, we cut a deal. He'd work hard and keep his mouth shut (he had a lot of dirt on me), and I'd cut him some slack when it came to grades. Not an easy "A," but an easier "A."

Oh, and he is wearing a fucking Cubs hat, the classic red "C" bright against the classic blue background.[26]

I should let this go. I should keep *my* head down, and we should pass unacknowledged like the proverbial ships in the night. I am, after all, on a clandestine mission. But the "C" glares at me, and I can't help myself. Part of what's ingrained in me as a teacher (and formerly as a student) is "No Hats in the Building!" Everyone knows this. Notre Dame High School is the *Home of the Dons*. A "Don" is a Gentleman of Our Lady. And a Gentleman takes his hat off indoors.

We are five yards apart and closing. He still has not looked up, might not even know I'm there.

"Take the hat off," I growl at him, my voice a low, rumbling snowball. There is a slight delay before the command reaches him. When it does, he snaps his eyes toward my presence, teetering sideways, tacking away from a collision, slowing, having heard but unable to listen.

Three yards.

I veer toward his trajectory, and he tilts his head at me like a puzzled dog and slides farther away, almost into the wall of lockers. The hat remains. A feral emptiness begins to ebb from his face as he struggles to shift paradigms, to leave wherever he has been and transport fully into "I'm in school" mode. He just needs a

---

26 I grew up a White Sox fan in a household of Cubs fans. I took a lot of shit despite the fact that the White Sox, over time, had been the better team, which isn't saying much. Neither team had won a World Series since the early 1900s. The summer before this incident, the Cubs had come out of a 39-year playoff drought to win their division, only to choke in the playoffs against the Padres. Still, everyone seemed to have jumped on the bandwagon.

little more time. I don't give it. I cut him off, and he stops, just out of my reach.

"Gimme the hat," I snarl. He knows now where he's at. I reach my hand out, not palm up as if to accept an offering, but palm toward him, my fingers curled into a kung fu claw, ready to snatch the hat if this kid doesn't comply immediately.

He does. He takes the hat off and hands it to me. I poke him in the chest with it and, stretching my chin forward, mutter, "No hats in the building."

Without any thought at all, I frisbee the hat toward a trash can at the end of the hallway. We both watch it flutter-spin through the air, on target, but falling short and clanging off the metal lip. It tumbles onto the carpet, coming to rest bill up, and having landed square at the feet of, quite likely, the most respected teacher in the school's history. "Sir" has somehow materialized next to the trash can at this most opportune time.

Mr. Maniere is in his seventies and in his umpteenth year of teaching. He is a thin, wiry man with speckled gray hair and glasses. He always dresses in sharp-creased, navy-blue pants; a long sleeve white shirt; and a micro-patterned tie with some geometric shape repeated ad infinitum. No one calls him by his name. Everyone refers to him as "Sir."

Sir had been my math teacher twice: Algebra when I was a freshman, and Advanced Trigonometry when I was a senior, a little over four years before this rather awkward moment.

In the movie version of my life, the camera follows the hat, center-screen, in slow motion, as it frisbees across the hall. The opening of Beethoven's *Moonlight*

Sonata rustles in the background but grows in intensity. We get three different angles of the shot: through the air, through the air, through the air, and then the climaxing super slow mo of it banking off the trash can, flipping, and landing bill up on the carpet.

Silence.

Close-up on the hat; the big red "C" is center screen. The black toe of a dress shoe peeks in from the corner. The camera slides in toward this shoe and then pans back and up and out to reveal the expanse of the hallway.

Tableau.

The three of us form a tall, thin, isosceles triangle. The student and I are close to each other in the middle of the hallway. Sir, hands on his hips, stands farther away by the garbage can. We are frozen, each staring, each locked on that hat at Sir's feet. Seconds pass.

In the movie version, the shot ends there. All of us stuck in time, bugs in amber. In real life, Sir ends the impasse with a sigh through his teeth, the sound escaping like air venting from an ancient radiator. He looks up to the two of us and folds his arms into an L. His right fist curls under his chin, his left hand cups his right elbow. He thinks.

He tilts his head, now resting his cheek, and assesses us—primarily me—through raised eyebrows. I can't meet his eyes, and instead, circle my focus to the background behind his head. I am painfully cognizant that I am far closer in age to this kid standing beside me than to Sir and that I am the one now being schooled. I agonize over his methodic deliberation.

Sir lets my humiliation linger just long enough for it to become indelible. Then he bends, exaggerating his fatigue and frustration at having to unnecessarily expend what is, at his age, a limited reserve of energy. He picks up the hat and motions with it to the student, who steps forward. I don't move.

"Can you put it in your locker, please? Thank you." His voice is the calming, tranquil susurration of a mountain stream.

The student nods, takes the hat, and escapes around the corner. Sir motions to me with a wag of his index finger, a beckon into the empty classroom he had vacated to investigate the voice in the hallway. I follow him.

He sits on the edge of his desk, and I stand, waiting, fully aware of how fucked up this all is, how I've fucked this all up. I *should* be in my classroom supervising students taking a quiz. I don't have to pee that bad. I don't even have to go anymore. I hug my arms across my chest and drop my eyes to the floor. I'm a naughty little kid. I can't help rocking from foot to foot.

I can't tell how much time has passed, how long I've abandoned my students, but I don't dare turn and look at the clock over my shoulder. I can't and will not further disrespect Sir. He breaks the silence. (I realized later he had been orchestrating this lesson, including the timing, since the moment he stepped into the hallway.)

"Michael," he says. Mercifully concise, he repeats the following, like a mystic chant, gently clapping his hands on the beats of Please, Thank, Ask, and Tell:

"Please and Thank You. Ask, Don't Tell."

"Please and Thank You. Ask, Don't Tell."
"Please and Thank You. Ask, Don't Tell."

That's one idiosyncrasy of his teaching style: to stress in patient, rhythmic repetitions of three, the crux of any lesson. I get it.

"Yes, Sir," I say. His eyes fix on mine to verify, then he motions with a nod of his head for me to go back to my class.

Fewer than four minutes have passed when I return to my classroom. None of my students look up; they haven't even noticed that I was gone. Their attention has been solely devoted to twenty-five multiple choice questions on the first half of *The Scarlet Letter*.

In one sense, nothing really happened.

(4)

JUMP AHEAD A FEW decades. I am now retired and trying to write. My primary focus is on significant memories, moments in my life that, for one reason or another, stuck.

I have the wife of a friend of mine read a rough draft of the two anecdotes that open this essay. She is a teacher at an elementary school, third grade through fifth grade, but not an English teacher.

We meet to discuss her impressions on a sunny summer afternoon at Lizzie McNeill's Irish Pub in downtown Chicago. We take a table outside, overlooking the main branch of the Chicago River. A nice breeze drifts in from Lake Michigan. I order a Guinness, and she orders a Pinot Noir.

After exchanging pleasantries, we sit in silence for a short while and watch a group of kayakers get organized and begin their ascent up the river. This is a moment to be savored; two teachers enjoying adult beverages in the early afternoon of a weekday. Something only summer can allow.

Despite the genial atmosphere, Winnie (short for Winifred) is agitated. She sits with her hands folded over a manilla folder that I assume holds a printed copy of the draft. She is waiting, however, for some signal from me to start. This does not bode well for my essay. I smile. Go ahead.

"I have some written notes," she begins, tapping the folder, "but I want you to answer two questions first." She leans toward me, peeking to both sides, checking the tables around us.

"I confess," she continues, "I didn't enjoy reading either of the anecdotes. That was very unpleasant." She shifts in her seat, takes a sip of her wine.

"Mr. Antón . . ." she fumbles, "that was . . . abuse. Criminal. What he did. And getting 'curbed'? I had never heard of that. Didn't need to either.

"And the thing with the Cubs hat; you were just an asshole. I did not like that," she stresses, one syllable at a time, like Sam-I-Am. She taps the folder with her index finger. "I don't think I benefitted from reading this at all. I mean, I would never hit anyone, and I already know basic manners. That's child's stuff."

She takes a longer drink from her wine glass and swishes the alcohol around a little to rinse away the bitterness of her criticism. "So, first, who is your audience? I mean," she shrugs, calmer now after having gotten through the worst of it, but still willing to be blunt, "who's going to benefit from this?"

She leans in again, "And second—not as important as number one, but still a mystery to me—why the opening quote? What did that have to do with anything?"

She settles back in her chair, arms folded across her chest. Her questions are not rhetorical. She'd appreciate answers. Had she been one of my students, I would have said what teacher-me always said in these situations: *Figure It Out.* I would have probed for her thoughts before sharing my own.

But she is a friend, and an adult, and she has done me a huge favor by offering to provide some feedback, to give me some non-male, non-high school, non-English-teacher, teacher perspective.

Winnie also seems to me to be a very kind person. That compliment can sound condescending, but I don't mean it that way. One should never assume that kindness suggests weakness. I don't. I assume that Winnie can be tough and strong. But she is kind. So, it took effort for her to be critical. I appreciate that.

She wants to understand why I wrote about those two moments. I think about it, and I try to explain.

(5)

WHO IS GOING TO benefit from telling this story? Who is the primary audience?

I am.

These two anecdotes taught me about discipline and escalation. What Mr. Antón did was criminal, and I did behave like an asshole. However, learning by negation is as important as learning by affirmation. I need to reflect on failures as much as I celebrate successes. I don't want to wallow in failure, and I don't need to gloat over success. But I need to remember and retell the stories of each so that the lessons of each stay fresh.

In matters of discipline, I know I have the potential to, let's say, get excited. "Be sand, not gasoline" is not one of my catchphrases by chance. I remember these two anecdotes because they taught me about escalation.

For Mr. Antón, his escalation—and the blind-eye of those who enabled and encouraged it—led to his being curbed. The violence that returned to him was not some sort of possibility, it was an inevitability. Cause and effect. Blood will have blood[27].

Fortunately for me, Sir put the fire out before I could have made things far worse. Who knows what would have happened in that hallway if he had not interceded. Moving forward, I needed to remind myself not to let the escalation even start. Sir would not always be there to intervene.

Unlike Winnie, "Please and Thank You. Ask, Don't Tell" are not common sense to me. I don't intuitively link manners and discipline. I have to work at being sand. I had to practice de-escalation. Remembering both Sir's advice and the entire story behind it helped me.

There's also the whole legacy thing. I care about how I'll be remembered. Mr. Antón's impulsion toward escalation turned his legacy from esteemed educator into cautionary tale. Sir, on the other hand, when he finally did retire, was a beloved legend, a man respected for

---

27 "It will have blood; they say, blood will have blood." (*Macbeth* III iv 150). My favorite Shakespeare play.

his gentle strength and sage advice, and a teacher who had positively influenced thousands of individuals.

I don't want to be remembered as a criminal or an asshole, so I work on it. And that's what I told Winnie. I am the audience. I need to remind myself of these stories and the lessons I've learned because I'm still working on it.

(6)

WHY THE QUOTE?

To explain, I'm going to share a long quote from *The Brothers Karamazov* by Dostoyevsky.

Father Zossima, an elder priest and philosopher, says this, but he is quoting a doctor he knew:

"I heard exactly the same thing, a long time ago to be sure, from a doctor," the elder remarked. "He was then an old man, and unquestionably intelligent. He spoke just as frankly as you, humorously, but with a sorrowful humor. 'I love humanity,' he said, 'but I am amazed at myself: the more I love humanity in general, the less I love people in particular, that is, individually, as separate persons. In my dreams,' he said, 'I often went so far as to think passionately of serving humanity, and, it may be, would really have gone to the cross for people if it were somehow suddenly necessary, and yet I am incapable of living in the same room with anyone even for two days, this I know from experience. As soon as someone is there, close to me, his personality oppresses my self-esteem and restricts my freedom. In twenty-four hours, I can begin to hate even the best of people: one because he takes too long eating his dinner, another because he has a cold and keeps blowing his nose. I become the enemy of people the moment they touch me,' he said. 'On the other hand, it has always happened that the more I hate people individually, the more ardent becomes my love for humanity as a whole.'"

There's so much to unpack here. The speaker is a doctor and unquestionably intelligent. He speaks with a sorrowful humor. He is passionate about serving humanity—willing to go "to the cross"—but incapable of living in close quarters with any individual because, that individual inevitably "oppresses my self-esteem and restricts my freedom." The petty annoyances the doctor should be able to ignore, but can't, do him in.

I often felt as the doctor does, and like I think Mr. Antón did. I wanted to help humanity, to teach great lessons that would change the lives of my students, to do worthwhile things. I got those opportunities, and they fed my ego, and I wanted to do even more, to have more of an impact.

So, when shit happened that I couldn't ignore and was compelled to address, I got pissed off. Why are you impeding me? And then I got mad at myself. I shouldn't be letting this bother me. And then I got madder at the individual for making me mad at myself for getting mad at this stupid shit. And so on.

Sooner or later, if I didn't de-escalate, if I didn't practice de-escalation, I'd snap. And it wasn't the big things that would get me. It was the little ones. In my role as educator, the simple, minor misbehaviors—the stupid shit—tested my character more than any crisis ever could.

For Mr. Antón, it was farting around while he was teaching. *He* could joke and make the students laugh, but God forbid that a student starts farting around, especially if it distracts other students from the very important lesson being taught. He took that personally.[28]

For me, it was redundant stuff like littering in the hallways, students packing up their stuff five minutes before the bell rings, or hats.

"Can you take your hat off, please? Thanks."

I am not exaggerating when I estimate that I made this request at least a thousand times over the course of my career. I could have just blown it off, ignored it—let the kid wear the fuckin' hat, who cares? —but I couldn't. I did not enjoy disciplining. I didn't get into education because I was on some power trip; but I knew, as a teacher, I had a moral obligation to enforce rules. I saw this as part of my service to humanity. I need adherence to established rules, not just because rules need to be followed, but because individuals need to learn to follow rules. Holding individuals accountable shows I care: I care about the school and I care about the individual. I believe that.

So, all the way to the end of my career, I tried to hold students accountable, even for those petty annoyances,

---

[28] Another essential for de-escalation: don't take anything the "public" does personally. This is easier said than done, but in so many ways crucial, whether one is a teacher or a nurse, a police officer or a Starbuck's barista. Many, many times over the years I've reminded myself, "This individual doesn't *know* you; don't take it personally."

those grains of sand that wear you down. And I thank Sir for getting me started on some simple, practical, de-escalation strategies to help me manage.

(7)

ON THE SECOND-TO-LAST DAY of my final semester, the day before I retired, I stepped out into what should have been an empty hallway at Wheeling High School and witnessed a student I didn't recognize spit his wad of gum onto the carpeted floor, toward, but a few feet short of, the nearest garbage can.

Our eyes met, and he paused, and I nodded toward the gum.

"Please," I said, assertive, but still a request.

And he went and picked it up and put it in the can, and I added, "Thanks."

And he said, "Sorry, Mr. Burke."

And as he escaped around the corner, I damn near wept.

CHAPTER 10

RIGHTEOUS INDIGNATION

(1)

WHEN I WAS IN fifth grade, I fell in love with Miss Portier and Chiquita banana football helmets.

Miss Portier wasn't sexy, this coming from a ten-year-old just discerning what sexy was. She didn't wear hip-hugging skirts or flout her cleavage by securing one-too-few buttons on her blouse.

That was Miss Micki-Johnson, our other fifth grade teacher. Even now, I am unsure whether her first name was, in fact, Micki, or if her last name was the hyphenated Micki-Johnson. She introduced herself day one as Miss Micki-Johnson, colliding the two names in nervous excitement, and was forever—or at least for the one-year she taught at St. Peter's Catholic Grade School—fused.

Rumor had it she occasionally walked to school and so, must live very nearby. The other fifth grade boys ogled her and made playground promises to follow her home some afternoon and sneak peeks through the windows of her apartment, but I was uninterested. She wasn't my type.

Miss Portier had long brown hair and warm brown eyes. She was handsome, petite, and athletic. She had an angular face with distinct cheekbones and a nose like the base and hypotenuse of a tiny right triangle[29].

Miss Portier had no cleavage. She wore loose, long-sleeve blouses buttoned to the top and calf length A-line skirts. She was a serious teacher, a good teacher, who tried hard not to smile until Christmas.

Often enough, though, one of my classmates—sometimes me—would say or do something harmlessly amusing and she would curl up the right corner of her mouth and her eyes would brighten, and she would tilt her head just a smidge in acknowledgement. All very deliberate.

I lived for those moments.

Miss Portier never smacked a single student. She disciplined with a modus operandi completely antithetical to my common experience in Catholic education: silence, a stern look, and patience.

My young heart stirred well before my genitals, and Miss Portier was the first object of this passion. She crushed me.

(2)

IN 1970, THE 16 teams of the National Football League merged with the 10 teams of the American Football League to form one, united body. The new NFL had 26 teams divided between the American Football Conference and the National Football Conference. A

---

29 With the proportionality of a Pythagorean triple where the base is 3, the height 4, and the hypotenuse 5. I didn't know the math then, but I knew her nose was perfect.

decade of animosity and derision between the former rival leagues had ended.

Chiquita bananas celebrated that merger by running an NFL promotion featuring helmet stickers, about the size of a quarter, emblazoned with the emblems of each of the 26 teams in the new NFL. Each bunch of bananas had one sticker.

The first sticker I collected I discovered by chance. I happened to be the first one home from school that afternoon and so snatched the top banana from the bunch. As I peeled the banana—pinching the fingertip on the bottom as a gorilla does rather than ripping back the neck—I realized the label was different. The typical Chiquita girl with her Latin fiesta dress and fruit-basket hat had been replaced by a Minnesota Vikings football helmet, purple with a white horn drawn from front to back. Hmmm. Interesting. I picked the label free, studied it more closely from the tip of my index finger, then stuck the helmet to the inside cover of my school notebook.

The next day at recess, I became aware of other boys commenting on the helmets they had collected. I had one; another had two; a third had three.

I lay awake that night in my top bunk imagining football helmets butting together like bumper cars on my bedroom ceiling. I resolved to start my own collection: a motivated pursuit rather than a random gathering, and to stick with the task until completion. My older siblings had collections of baseball cards and stuffed animals (tigers) and Hot Wheels and rocks (shiny ones). I had nothing.

My mom shopped every Wednesday. At the beginning of my quest, I waited patiently for her weekly trip to the grocery store. She always bought bananas. I'd retrieve the sticker from the bunch, then wolf down (gorilla down?) as many bananas as I could so she would be sure to buy more on her next shopping trip.

I celebrated the new stickers—the second was my beloved Chicago Bears—by mounting them, with purpose now, in my school notebook, the NFC teams on the right, the AFC on the left. I mourned any repeats, the waste of a week. My mother had no idea what I was doing, and I had no interest in her assisting with my pursuit—I wanted to do this on my own—so there was no guarantee that she would target a bunch of bananas stuck with a helmet I did not have.

I ate a shit-ton of bananas.

After six weeks of patience and alternating bouts of constipation and diarrhea[30], I had collected three unique helmets: Bears, Vikings, and Dolphins, and traded one of my repeats for a fourth: Jets.

At lunch, my friends and I would compare. We all had about the same number; there were, after all, only so many bananas one could consume in a week. We also had the same basic teams, though there were anomalies. Seems Chiquita was releasing some helmets in bulk and some in limited quantity. I had collected four helmets in six weeks. Amassing all 26 teams appeared an interminable endeavor. My resolve waned, and I considered quitting.

---

30 Fun fact: unripe bananas cause constipation; ripe bananas relieve constipation.

Then, one kid jumped way ahead. We pestered him until he confessed. He'd gone shopping with his mother one day after school, and while she was distracted gathering other items, he plundered the banana display for any stickers he didn't have. He snatched three new teams in one visit!

I had an epiphany: a vision of clandestine missions executed under the cover of night. Picturing the *Spy vs Spy* cartoon character from *Mad Magazine*, I saw myself as a secret agent, racing on my banana seat bicycle through darkened streets illuminated only by the occasional spotlight of a streetlamp. My trench coat capes out behind me; my wide-brimmed witch's fedora hat flops down to mask my features. I ghost into a grocery store; I slip through the aisles like a shadow; at the banana stand, one wave of my cape and the helmets are mine. I see my collection completed.

At that moment, a plan formed, and my resolve firmed.

We had four supermarkets within a few miles of where I lived. A Jewel and a Dominick's were north of my house. A Happy Foods and a mom-and-pop grocery called Bushman's Market were south. I figured I could case and pilfer from two stores a week. The helmets didn't get released and the bananas didn't get restocked to demand any more visits than that. Plus, I didn't want to go to any one store too often. I didn't want to be noticed. I didn't want anyone to suspect what I was up to.

First up, the Jewel and the Dominick's. Both lay, roughly, along the route my school bus took to St Peter's Elementary School.

Fortunately for me, in fifth grade, when the weather was tolerable, I rode my bike to school rather than take the bus. In fact, I didn't just ride, I *raced*. I'd wait at our stop until the bus arrived and then take off, the accordion opening of the bus's doors serving as our starting pistol. The bus could obviously go faster than I could, but it had to stop for students every block or so, and it had to obey traffic signals. The traffic signals usually determined the winner because, unlike the sensible bus driver, I would gladly put my life at risk by weaving through an intersection against the light to gain what advantage I could.

I liked racing the bus, and I imagined a rival's strategic kinship between the driver and me. On the mornings I rode, I arrived at school damp with sweat, but rested and calm and more receptive to learning.

In the afternoon, I took my time getting back. My mom knew that, riding more leisurely, I should arrive home each day about ten minutes after the school bus dropped off my older brothers and younger sister. This was my window of opportunity.

I passed the Jewel on my normal route home, and I could easily stop and peruse their produce section without adding much time to my travel.

The Dominick's, however, fell about half-a-mile off my direct route. This trip would necessitate some deceit. So be it. Once every two weeks, I could stretch my normal time to as much as thirty minutes by lying to my mom, by telling her, if she even asked, that I had stayed after school to clean erasers or stopped at a park for a quick swing.

I decided that on alternating Mondays and Wednesdays, only once a week, I would hit these two stores. Monday of week one to Jewel; Wednesday of week two to Dominick's; Wednesday of week three to Jewel; Monday of week four to Dominick's. And so on.

Pickings tended to be better on Wednesdays when the produce was freshly stocked, but I didn't want to become predictable, so I kept Mondays in play as well. All quite ingenious.

The Happy Foods and the mom-and-pop store were south of my home, the opposite direction of St. Pete's. I'd have to go past my house by over a mile to get to either of these stores, so I could never make it there and back under the guise of my ride home from school. I needed a different strategy.

I was a fidgety, ants-in-my-pants kinda kid, so I determined to use this apparent deficiency to my advantage.

On a Tuesday or a Thursday at dinner, I would allow my knees to bounce a little more vigorously and the thumb and pinky of my left hand to drum the dinner table a little more percussively. Inevitably, my father would point to our home's back door and direct me to, "Get the hell out of here! Go run around the damn block!"

I *could* run around the block, *or,* I could hop on my Schwinn Stingray and seek my favorite fruit. I glared at my father and feigned frustration each time I left the table, letting the screen door slam on my way out, masterfully hiding my true intentions. This week Tuesday to Bushman's Market, next week Thursday to Happy Foods.

That was the plan, and it went fairly well.

Massive chains, the Jewel and Dominick's paid me little mind. These were busy places, so, with minimal pretense, I could take my time checking out their bunches. I'd scan the display and pick off the stickers I didn't have—or repeats I thought worth trading—and add them right to my notebook. I then walked out, no one noticing me. Easy money.

At Happy Foods, I had to be more discreet. The produce was in the front of the store, next to the entrance/exit, right by the checkout lines. The cashiers and baggers had less to do. I couldn't go straight in and out. I had to pretend I was shopping, occasionally investing my allowance in groceries a boy's mom might errand him to acquire. I'd scout the helmets as I passed on my way in, then go to the aisles and grab a can of gravy or a jar of Maraschino cherries. On my way back, I'd work my way across the produce line, squeezing an avocado, checking the price on a bag of oranges, and, when I thought no one was watching, snatching the stickers I wanted before heading to the checkout line. Though it demanded a little more finesse, Happy Foods was manageable.

Unfortunately, the pop owner at the mom-and-pop caught me casing the bananas during my second visit and chased me out before I could nab the Houston Oilers sticker I coveted. I waited outside, watching through the window until he disappeared in back. Then, I went in and bought the bunch (after separating it down to just three bananas) that had the Oilers sticker.

I was afraid of the pop of Bushman's Market—he was a hulking, hairy man—but part of me on that day wanted him to step in and accost me at the register so I could claim, "Sir, I am *buying* these bananas!"

The fall breezed by, and though I didn't stay exactly on schedule, I held to my commitment. Just after Halloween, before the true chills of winter made it unseasonable for me to continue riding my bike to school or the stores, I completed my collection. Done. Finished. All 26 Teams. This coincided with the end of the Chiquita banana football helmet promotion as well. Which made sense. Because the promotion was ending, all the helmets were in circulation, and my frequenting four different stores had greatly improved my chances of getting them all. None of my classmates had reached that status; not one completed his collection.

My school notebook became my most prized possession.

It never left my sight, rarely left my grip. I carried it on the playground and to the cafeteria. If I had to tinkle or just escape to the bathroom for a spell, the notebook went as well. I continually peeked inside the cover, possessive of the helmets, pleased and titillated, seeing in their completion a victory I had won both physically—with my bike as my trusty steed—and, more important, strategically. I had outworked and outwitted the other students, my parents, and the various storeowners and employees.

I had done this completely on my own, and the fact that only I knew about it, added value.

Love might not have been too strong a description of my sentiment for this notebook, this physical manifestation of my accomplishment. Self-worth. I had done something I could be proud of.

But pride goeth before destruction, and a haughty spirit before a fall,[31] and who better to be the architect of my personal destruction and reconstruction than Miss Portier.

(3)

ONE MORNING, SHE MET me at the classroom door.

"You're distracted," she said and pointed to the notebook under my arm. I tucked it tight to my right side and tilted and dipped my left shoulder to ward off her attack.

She curled her index finger once, twice, and after thrice added, "Hand it over."

Donating a kidney could not have been more painful. I reached across with my left hand and struggled the notebook loose. I stretched it to her, but before releasing it, met her eyes. The eyes are the windows to the soul, glimpses into empathy and understanding. I was crushed. Miss Portier didn't fathom the gravity of her request or the depth of my acquiescence. Her eyes told me she viewed this exchange as being between a teacher and an unruly child over some silly trifle.

"You can have it back at the end of the day. Take it home then and *leave* it there."

She took the notebook and placed it on the bookshelf behind her in the far front corner of the classroom. For the first time in weeks, the notebook had left my side.

---

31   Proverbs 16:18 KJV

At lunch and recess, it left my sight—and Miss Portier's—as well.

At the end of the day, as we all exited the classroom, I went to get the notebook. I waited in front of her desk for her nod before retrieving it. The notebook was still on the bookshelf, but not where Miss Portier had originally placed it. It was in a different spot, askew. I shivered. No longer waiting for her permission, I darted to the bookshelf. I took the notebook into my hands and felt the defilement, bends and twists in the cover where it all should be smooth.

I opened it. A third of my stickers—the most rare and most valuable to me—were missing. In their spaces were scaled flakes of thin, white tears, the nasty remnants of theft.

I was furious.

"What happened?" I said this first to the book, then turned to Miss Portier.

"What HAPPENED?"

I had raised my voice to a teacher.

The straggling students who were still leaving for the day slowed and turned to look. Miss Portier had flinched at my outburst, but now regained her composure, shooting them a keep-moving stare. I got it too. I held my tongue, held still. She waited for them to leave and then turned to me, not pleased. We were alone, but not in any scenario I had ever imagined. Her hand trembling, she pointed to the nearest front row desk.

"Sit down," she hissed through clenched-teeth. She wanted to reestablish order, to put me in my place.

"No." My voice cracked and the tears welled. I lifted the open notebook to her, feeling oddly like an altar boy raising the Roman Missal for the priest to read at mass.

"This isn't fair. I listened to you. I gave you my notebook." I stood rigid, my arms still outstretched.

For the first time she took in the vandalized page. For the first time, she saw more. Her body softened. She drew a demonstrative breath in and looked upward, holding and slowly exhaling. Her eyes returned to me.

I closed and lowered the notebook, hugging it into my folded arms.

"Michael," she said, pausing after my name before continuing, enunciating each word, "you cannot raise your voice to me." Her tone was tender and assertive, reprimanding me, yet allowing me an out. Looking up to her, I couldn't stop feeling how beautiful she was. And I couldn't take it. How did she not know?

"That's not the POINT!" I let the injustice rage again inside me.

"Michael Francis!"

"NO!"

She folded her arms and pursed her lips and stated, as if reaching an unavoidable conclusion, "We need to go see Sister Geraldine."

"Fine!" I barked, staring her down, and with that I was off to the principal's office. I didn't care.

I left Miss Portier behind and stomped into the corridor. Though the school day had barely ended, the other students—having dashed to the exits—were gone. My footsteps (I wore hand-me-down hard-sole black dress shoes) clattered off the dulled tile floor and polished cinderblock walls and echoed down the long, empty hallway.

Our classroom was on the third floor, the principal's office on the first. I took a few steps toward the stairwell at the far end of the hallway, then stopped and waited, facing away from her. When I heard her closing the door behind me, I started walking, leading, not looking back. I marched down the hall and through the open double doors at the top of the steps. I paused before descending and, again, waited, still not looking back at her. I let Miss Portier get almost to my shoulder before starting down.

Four flights of stairs, two flights to each floor, zigzagged to the bottom. At the end of normal school days, I enjoyed skittering down these steps—surrounded by a chattery flock of fellow students—and out into the afternoon sun. Though I didn't dislike school, leaving at the end of each day felt liberating. Today was over; tomorrow could wait.

As I started down, I didn't quite skitter, but I did allow myself a slight rat-a-tat. I could feel the positive energy of these stairs gathering. The gentle taps through each flight softened me, and I couldn't hold my anger. They were stickers, not people. And as my mom often advised in similar situations, "No one died." Let it go.

At the bottom of the stairwell were two sets of double doors facing each other across the vestibule. Both sets were closed. The doors on the right led out into that afternoon sun. The doors on the left led to the administrative hallway, at the end of which waited the principal's office. I stopped.

Miss Portier had fallen more than a flight of stairs behind me. When she turned the last corner, I opened the door on the left and stood there, not smiling but not glaring either, waiting for her to descend the final flight and pass through. Ladies first. She saw me standing there like the doorman at a five-star hotel and almost tripped on the top step. Re-establishing her balance, she stopped, stood straight, crossed her arms, and stared at me. She began tapping her foot in frustration.

A mix of emotions welled through her eyes. She was angry at me for raising my voice, yet she knew I had been wronged, and it was partially her fault. She felt insulted that I had marched ahead of her to the principal's office, yet here was this little shit holding the door for her. I had challenged her judgment, not threatened her authority. I still respected both her person and her position.

The tapping stopped and her arms unfolded. She rested her hands low on her hips. The right side of her mouth didn't quite curl, but her eyes brightened—just a little—and she tilted her head a smidge before shaking it in mock disbelief.

"Go home," she said, a concession, not a command, and I melted.

The Chiquita banana football helmets were pretty cool, but Miss Portier was someone special.

(4)

A Positive Role Model

MISS PORTIER WAS A good person and worth emulating. She had the courage and compassion to accept her part in inciting (whether intended or not) my behavior. She reinforced my fledging appreciation for the power of manners. She taught me about passion, about what and why I love what I do. (I didn't love those football helmets; I loved collecting those helmets. The stickers themselves shouldn't matter.)

Most important, Miss Portier made me feel like her favorite Michael Francis in the class. She had a way of seeing her students as individuals, as real people. That's (unfortunately) rare for a teacher, and dangerous: part of my crush on her is that I imagined that she actually *liked* me. But she knew how to maintain distance.

Of course, the fifth grade me wasn't consciously learning any of these things. That's what's funny about positive role models; the best ones aren't trying to do anything more than set a good example. Their influence is subtle, like a time-release capsule, benefitting slowly over time. I had no idea that Miss Portier would help sculpt my future classroom persona.

At the time, I was just a kid who was bananas about his teacher.

CHAPTER 11

THE OLIVE TREE

Foolishness is bound in the heart of a child; but the rod of correction shall drive it far from him.
—Proverbs 22:15 (KJV)

To yield bounteous fruit, a child, like an olive tree, is best beaten. —Anonymous[32]

(1)

SISTER MARY JOSEPH LOVED history, especially ancient history, and she loved God. She was an Old Testament nun, well-meaning, but wrathful. She believed in corporal justice and devised creative ways to help us link certain crimes with certain punishments so that we might become like little Pavlov's dogs and avoid these transgressions in the future by sheer association with the physical torment each transgression engendered.

Sister Mary Joseph loved *Jeopardy!* She ate her lunch each day in the convent adjacent to the school—rather

---

32 I first heard this credo from a Dominican priest I taught with at Fenwick High School. He was a good man, a very old man at the time, and he said it as caution, not as advice. "This is what I was taught to believe," he told me, "by some in my community." He shook his head gently, with great solemnity, before adding, "It is not true."

than with the other teachers in the faculty cafeteria—so she could enjoy the show in peace.

Each afternoon, Sister Mary Joseph taught our sixth-grade class *The History of the Ancient World*. She conducted her lessons with a yardstick, gripping it in her right hand and tapping it methodically against her left palm as she glided up and down the aisles questioning us *Jeopardy!* style about last night's reading on the ancient civilizations of Mesopotamia. We sat with our backs straight, heads up, eyes forward, and hands steepled neatly over our closed history texts.

"These two rivers and their tributaries form an aquatic ecosystem essential to life in Mesopotamia."

We did not raise our hands to answer. Raising hands was for questions, not answers, Sister Mary Joseph had taught us. Since we all should know the answers, there was no need to raise hands. Instead, Sister Mary Joseph called on whomever she pleased.

"Mary Louise?"

"The Euphrates and the Tigris, Sister," Mary Louise would answer. (Despite her *Jeopardy!* style questions as answers, we were not to respond with *Jeopardy!* style answers as questions. That would be silly.)

Answer correctly, and Sister Mary Joseph nodded approvingly and continued her course, never breaking stride, up and down the aisles. The long tunic and scapular of her habit swished from side to side. With each step, one black patent leather toe—then the alternate—winked into the light before disappearing back beneath her robes. She was a big woman, but her hard soles left no footfall.

Sister Mary Joseph often called on students she knew could answer her questions. She rewarded and reinforced their work ethic. She also targeted those who needed her love and inspiration. Like the olive tree, they just needed a little extra thump to release their fruit.

"Credited with inventing writing, the wheel, and organized government, this Mesopotamian civilization is regarded as the first advanced civilization." Swish. Tap. Swish. Tap. We waited for her to choose.

"Jacob Dane?"

Sister Mary Joseph was big on using first and middle names, especially with the boys. This led to some interesting origin stories. "Dane" for example, didn't reference Jacob's Danish ancestry—he was in fact Irish—but his family's pet Great Dane, named "Dane," who was hit by a car and killed a few weeks before Jacob was born. Though I have my doubts about spiritual transference, Jacob Dane did resemble his namesake: a gentle giant. He was the biggest kid in our class, literally and metaphorically. He watched out for everybody. If a playground dispute threatened to turn aggressive, he simply wandered into the vicinity and cooler heads prevailed. He was everyone's best friend.

He wasn't dumb, but he wasn't in any hurry to be smart either.

"Jacob Dane?" Sister Mary Joseph repeated.

Fumble a response that at least demonstrated you had read—though clearly not closely enough—and Sister Mary Joseph might pause and poke you in the side with that yardstick, prodding you to reveal the few useless details you could remember. Freeze, and she'd stop, slide the yardstick under your chin, raise your head until your eyes met hers, and, knowing all the time that you didn't, ask:

"Jacob Dane, did you do your reading last night?"

Busted.

"No, Sister."

"Tsk. Tsk. Tsk." Sister Mary Joseph shook her head, and the righteous among her students waggled theirs in confirmation. "Take the extra textbook from the shelf and bear the weight of your transgression."

Jacob Dane knew the drill. This was not his first trip to what we called "skid row." He took his own textbook and the extra one from the shelf and headed to the back of the room where he would stand like Christ on the cross, both arms outstretched, a 5-pound tome of history weighted in each palm. He would, since this was our final class, stay that way for the remainder of the day.

Sometimes Sister Mary Joseph called on him late in the period, and he need only bear this for a few long minutes. Today, she had gotten him early. He would suffer, but he would not show weakness.

Jacob Dane had an unrequited infatuation with a Greek girl named Artemis "Artie" Theodosakis. She sat in the back of class, near skid row. Artie, an only child, had been taught incessantly by her single mother to never associate with *his* kind. Thus, she had no interest in Jacob Dane, and he was left to romance her only in his imagination. Despite this rejection, as he had in the past and would in the future, he resolved to be strong in front of her. The result—five pounds is a lot of weight to hold at arm's length—would be aching deltoids and, for the rest of the day, the tendency of his arms to float spontaneously upward like an angel's wings prepping for that initial thrust heavenward.

Jacob Dane was, without rival, the most frequent visitor to skid row. Still, he made the best of it and turned the immediate costs into long-term benefits. His aversion to homework and his misguided amorousness forged the iron will, the brawny shoulders, and the vice-like grip that eventually helped make him an All-State wrestler when he got to high school.

In Sister Mary Joseph's class, holding textbooks for Jesus was light punishment, relatively speaking.

Dig a booger in class and Sister Mary Joseph demanded (after she made you deposit your prize in a tissue) that you stand and hold the offending hand extended out in front of you like a one-armed zombie. She'd tap her left palm three times for emphasis and then *whack* the yardstick across the tips of your fingers.

First offense, she used the flat side of the yardstick and hit mostly finger. Second offense, she used the thin edge and deftly clipped only the nails. Either way, the result was painful and embarrassing, since, for the rest of the week, your purpled fingertips—the sixth grade Mark of Cain—screamed to any witness: "Nosepicker!"

Forgetting to do your homework or doing a little boogie were not the worst crimes in sixth grade. These were bad, but they were not personal. Only one affront could both belittle Sister Mary Joseph and trivialize history in general.

Maybe it was the noise of 1972, maybe it was puberty, but I had a lot of trouble sleeping at night that year.

While Sister Mary Joseph questioned on about Mesopotamian history, I fought to stay awake. I actually hoped she would call on me—I had done the reading (a benefit of insomnia) and knew all the answers—but she didn't.

"Around 5000BC, this metal was the first to be extracted from its ore and cast into molds to be used ... wah wah woh wah woh wah."

I looked at the clock: an unlucky thirteen minutes left in class. I peeked back to skid row. Poor Jacob Dane! I stared forward, darting my eyes around, trying to find anything interesting to focus on at the front of the classroom. Portrait of the Virgin Mary holding Baby Jesus. Analog clock. Podium with crucifix affixed. Pulldown map (retracted). Larger, graphic crucifix centered above the blackboard. Glossy of *Jeopardy!* host Art Fleming[33] taped to the blackboard upper right. White erasure smears across the black board. Blackboard. Black board. White noise.

I felt the periphery of my vision blurring. I shook my head hoping to rattle my brain. I zeroed in on the auburn hair on the back of the head of the girl who sat in front of me. She had a blue butterfly hair clip just above her neckline and her ponytail fanned out between her shoulders and her long hair stretched almost to my desktop, the gentle tips almost touching ...

My head slid forward.

Shit!

I snapped it back, jarring me into full consciousness. No one had noticed.

Up and down the aisles Sister Mary Joseph progressed, her black and white habited face shadowing over us, her long tunic gently sweeping the floor, her

---

[33] Alex Trebeck didn't take over *Jeopardy!* until 1984.

voice a monotoning hum, the synchronized tapping of the yardstick. It was too much. All my energy concentrated on keeping my head up and staying awake. Stay awake. Stay awake. Stay awake.

I managed to keep my eyes tooth-picked open a little longer. I could win this battle. I could do this. Seven more minutes. I placed my respective index and middle fingers beneath my eyebrows and pushed up. Still my consciousness waned. God, please end this!

And God answered.

I took in a long, deep breath, held it, and exhaled. My chin, of its own accord, conceded defeat and bobbled to my chest. I quit fighting and embraced the heavenly drift up and away from my corporeal form. I found near orgasmic pleasure in this utter release of tension, the total relaxation, the feeling of being an empty body falling forward and gently plunging into a welcoming abyss.

Ahhhhhhhh.

This was the '70s. I had done no drugs, but my older siblings had, and I had heard their tales of out-of-body experiences, which is what I was having now. I floated above myself, momentarily at peace. A quiet thump. I saw myself blissfully snoozing face down on my desk. But not to last. My respite ended, and my essence was sucked like water down a toilet, swirling back into my physical being.

I opened my eyes to silence and an unconscious awareness of something missing, of Sister Mary Joseph's absence. My arms had slipped limply to my sides, and both the bridge of my nose and my forehead were plastered to my history textbook. A little drool had leaked out and pooled on the cover. Without moving my head, I peeked to the right and left. I couldn't see her. The students on either side sat straight-backed, eyes forward, as they should. Nothing except their near imperceptible tremors and lock-jawed silence seemed amiss.

Then, I could feel her gathering. Behind me. Still for the moment. The air pregnant with potential energy. I whiplashed upright, my head snapping back, my mouth opened in a voiceless "oh." At the same time, in harmonic convergence, the yardstick came whiffling forward. The story was delivered in sound.

BAWP. CRACK. Ooh! Aah! Crackle. Clatter.

Sister Mary Joseph's yardstick, swung with great vengeance and furious anger, met the base of my skull at the crest of its rise, the two forces intersecting at the peak velocity of each. Unable to bear the strain, the yardstick snapped. The dismembered half rocketed forward—much to the amazement of my classmates who reacted like kids at a fireworks display—until it shattered against the blackboard at the front of the room and splattered to the floor.

Once again there was silence, my fellow students wonderstruck by this awesome display of physics.

Open your mouth, round your lips as if to whistle, and knock your knuckles a few times, firmly, on the back of your skull. That hollow sound, jacked up a hundred decibels, was the initial "BAWP."

I was awake now.

I didn't cry or cringe. It didn't hurt. Thankfully, the countless smacks-upside-the-head I had received at home had sufficiently hardened and/or numbed my skull. I dared to glance back over my shoulder.

Sister Mary Joseph stood ping-ponging her eyes between the broken shaft of the yardstick in her hand and the jagged head on the floor at the front of her classroom, some fifteen feet away. She seemed a bit naked, something lost, and we were all a little ashamed to look at her. Thankfully, the bell rang, and we were all excused.

Somehow, I had won, and for a brief time, I was a playground legend. A few girls, including Melissa Astraea, asked to rub the back of my skull, to feel the hard, swollen spot. For an eleven-year-old boy, that was golden.

(2)

I used to tell this story to my students, usually after I had introduced some minor disciplinary consequence that they thought extreme. "You think that's extreme? You never met Sister Mary Joseph …" and on I'd go. When I finished, a few always asked, "Didn't you go home and tell your parents?"

A furrowed brow and a tilt of the head was my sufficient response. Really? Go home and tell my parents that I fell asleep in class? That I *forced* Sister Mary Joseph to discipline me? No, I didn't tell anyone.

(3)

Affirmation and Negation

Sister Mary Joseph is one of my role models, by both affirmation and negation. There are things she did as a teacher that I found well worth emulating. There are other things she did that I never want to forget. She had a profound influence on me. She taught me that if the disciplinary consequence for a given transgression is clearly delineated, then students will abide by that consequence. My job was to be sure that consequence was both reasonable and proportional.

Through my final year of teaching, I had my own "skid row" for my AP Language and Composition (APLAC) class. If a student didn't do his homework, he[34] wasn't allowed to participate in class discussion that day. My philosophy was simple: you're not allowed to *get* if you have nothing to *give*.

I didn't yell at these students; I didn't demean or condemn them. I gave them a choice. They could go to the library for the period, or they could sit silently on the cold, hard floor in the back of the classroom. These were juniors in high school, 16- and 17-year-olds. AP students. Sitting on the floor at the back of the classroom—forbidden from participating—seems demeaning, so going to the library might be the preferable option.

I taught three periods of APLAC: 70+ students a day. Almost every day, a few students failed to do the previous night's homework. I had my "skid row" policy in place for over a decade. During all that time, through all those class periods, I can't recall one student opting for the library. Students chose to sit on the cold, hard floor and at least listen in on the class discussion rather than be banished to the library.

34 I'm using the masculine pronoun here because, to be completely honest, boys *were* much more likely to "forget" to do their homework than girls.

At the end of each school year, I asked my APLAC students to complete an anonymous survey and give me feedback on the class. One of the prompts was: *Mr. Burke should continue his Machiavellian practice of checking homework[35] and relegating students to "skid row."*

Over all those years, 80% of students checked "Strongly Agree"; 13.3% of students checked "Somewhat Agree"; 6.7% checked "Somewhat Disagree"; and 0% checked "Strongly Disagree."

Students need and want discipline. They know when they are engaging in "foolishness," and they too want to "yield bounteous fruit."[36] They need and want parents and teachers—anyone acting *in loco parentis*—to hold them accountable. Fairly. Justly. Reasonably. Have expectations for me, and I will rise to meet them. Have no expectation, and I will sink to unfathomable depths.

Sister Mary Joseph was right in principle. It was my job to improve on her practice.

---

35 I "checked" by simply asking students to "Give me a Thumbs Up if you completed last night's homework." Students either gave me a thumbs up or knew to head to skid row. If a student lied, if I asked a question and he didn't have a reasonable answer ready (the answer needn't be correct), he would lose 10% of his score on the next unit exam, the equivalent of one letter grade. The "Thumbs Up" policy gave students an opportunity to work on their integrity.

36 I've seen olive trees, but I've never tried to pick olives. I've read, though, that using a long pole and beating the interior branches of the tree is an ancient and effective way to harvest the fruit.

CHAPTER 12

OUGHT VERSUS ACTUAL: CLARISSA

Sticks and stones will break my bones, but words will never hurt me.
—Childhood Adage

I SIT ALONE IN my classroom collecting my thoughts and gathering a few ungraded essays I need to look at over lunch. I enjoy the quiet and solitude for only a moment before my teaching radar tunes up. I can hear it, a distinct deadening of the normal hallway bustle. The wave of humanity flowing through the corridors has stopped, and instead of footsteps and chatter, I hear a brief collective groan of disgust, followed by a mass inhalation, a dull *thud thud thud*, and another groan.

Emotion often preceding intellect, my body reacts before my mind finishes processing. Cue the dilated pupils, the goosebumps sprouting, the accelerating heart rate. Something is wrong.

I start to rise from my chair as Adriana pokes her head in the door. Her eyes are a saucered mix of sorrow and revulsion.

"Mr. Burke," the words shiver, "you better get out there."

I speed up, brushing past her on my way out.

In that tableau vivant of my memory—the super slow mo instant when I pass her—I am hunched like a sprinter, my shoulders forward and my arms pumping, a long aggressive stride. Adriana does not turn to follow me with her eyes or her feet. Instead, she shudders into the empty classroom, her head down, her arms clutching high across her chest. As I pass, I hear and feel the first spastic puffs of her weeping. I leave her alone.

Normally, the hallways during passing periods are evidence of hope and great humanity. Hundreds of teenagers pour from their various classes into twelve-foot-wide corridors lined with metal lockers set in cinderblock walls. They scoot to their next destinations, flowing in both directions, and covering considerable distances in those close quarters in under five minutes. This minor rite of passage occurs ten times each school day in thousands of high schools across the country, all with minimal disruption. Literally millions of high school students do what they ought to do. These teenagers, often oblivious and always mercurial, behave well.[37]

Until one doesn't.

---

[37] When I first started teaching at Notre Dame High School, one of my colleagues (Sir) taught me to anticipate the actual but acknowledge the ought. He meant that, as a teacher, I should prepare for students behaving as they actually would; in other words, they would make mistakes and do some foolish things. However, I should also look forward to and appreciate students behaving as they ought to. Don't let the one student late for class negate the twenty-five who got there on time. I should know that some students will be late, and have a consequence ready, but I should celebrate, instead of taking for granted, the twenty-five who did as they ought to.

The crowd has circled, but unlike typical fights where instigators lean in and egg on passive combatants, these onlookers cringe, heads skewed to one side, hands raised, hesitant to witness this through more than a shuttered eye.

I wedge my way through and there, in the middle, is one of my former students, Clarissa. She is facing toward me, genuflecting, as in supplication, her right knee down, her left knee up, her shoulders bent, her head bowed. Her right fist is planted on the ground for balance. In her left arm she cuddles something. She is still. An arch of spattered blood fans out on the floor in front of her.

I step closer, circling slightly to the side, not sure of what I am seeing, not wanting to be a threat. I whisper her name, "Clarissa?" Again, gently, inching closer, "Clarissa?"

She straightens a little, lifts her head and her shoulders, and turns to my voice. I stop, aware now of what she is cuddling, not sure how close I can get. Her face is slack, vacant, her eyes distant.

A limp body, a girl's body, extends out behind her. The girl is on her back; her arms are stretched at her sides, palms up. They twitch and are still.

Balanced on Clarissa's left thigh, in her forearm, she holds the girl's head, face up, the chin tucked into her left armpit like a football. The fingers of Clarissa's left hand are woven into the girl's hair. In Clarissa's right hand, the one knuckled on the floor, she holds a Master lock, silver with a blue dial. Her face and her shirt are splattered with blood.

The girl's face is a smear. There are vicious gashes across her forehead, five or six fleshy, oozing one-inch slits. The girl is conscious; her eyes are open; her right pupil is grossly dilated, a black disk. Again, her arms twitch, shiver for an instant.

I look to Clarissa, brushing my hand through the air, hoping the movement catches her attention.

"Clarissa?" She sees me and puzzles; I am not a part of this. Go away. She shakes me off. I slip from Clarissa's focus, and she turns back to the girl. Methodically, she again raises her right hand. The fist and lock arch high, gathering. The crowd sucks in the air around me.

"Clarissa!" I slide forward, close enough to block the blow, but not touching her. My hands brace the air in front of me. I plead. "Stop. Clarissa. Please. Stop. Let her go."

Clarissa.

Clarissa is a good kid, a nice kid; I know that. I had her in class for an entire year. I saw her every day at her best. But niceness doesn't mean weakness.

She pauses and for the first time we see face to face. She doesn't just recognize me; she knows me.

"Mr. Burke." Clarissa mutters, pants, her right hand still poised like a viper set to strike. Her eyes turn down to the target, "She dissed my little sister!" The hand and her lips tremble, her voice rasps with indignation. "Mr. Burke . . . my LITTLE SISTER!" Her right arm flexes.

"Clarissa, NO!" I am inches from her face, and I am no longer asking. She starts. The pitch and severity of my voice slap her out of a trance. And it's over. Her right hand collapses to her side, the metal lock clangs off the floor. She sighs and slumps, as if exorcised from some demon. This violence, however, was not an unconscious act driven by some outside force. Clarissa knows who she is and exactly what she has done. This is not her, but it is. She looks up to me for direction.

"Clarissa, you need to let her go."

"Yes, Mr. Burke."

Always respectful, Clarissa. Such a sweet kid. She had been a favorite of mine last year in Sophomore English. A work ethic "B." She had a chance to break through the stigma of her "low socio-economic background" and go to junior college and beyond.

"Please, Clarissa."

She works her fingers from the girl's hair and lays the head on the floor. The girl turns away to her side, curls into a fetal position. Clarissa stands.

"Go in there and wait for me." I nod to a classroom across the hall.

"Yes, Mr. Burke." Clarissa, slouched, shuffles toward the open door. The Master lock, plucked from the scene, dangles from her index finger. The students in front of her part.

I slide forward to check on the girl. She is still curled, her back to me. As I kneel beside her, I unbutton and remove my dress shirt. I gently touch her shoulder, "Young lady?" She tries to lift her head and I gently, slowly, turn her on her back and cradle her elevated head in my lap. I press my balled-up shirt softly, but firmly against the violence, staunching the bubbling gouges crowned across her forehead. She is concussed. But her face, at least, is unharmed.

"What's your name?" I ask.

"My name," she echoes. She thinks a second, then murmurs, "Julene."

"Okay, Julene. We're going to wait right here until the paramedics arrive. Okay?"

"Okay." She closes her eyes. A damp stickiness bleeds up through my dress shirt, reddening my fingertips.

I notice now that other teachers and a security guard have begun dispersing the crowd. They have taken Clarissa away without incident. Eventually the paramedics arrive and take over. I get my shirt back and go into my empty classroom—I have lunch this period—and wonder what I should do. The assistant principal comes in, and we debrief about what happened. He tells me I should go home and take the rest of the day off.

"I can't," I say. "I have cross country practice after school."

Instead, I drive home (I live only fifteen minutes away) to change my shirt. There were no cell phones then, so my wife is nonplussed when I show up mid-day and walk in from the driveway wearing just a T-shirt. I hold up the crumpled, crimson mass in my hand.

"Is that blood?"

"Not mine," I offer. I explain what I can while I change, and head back to school.

This happened in September. The following June, I left Proviso East to go teach at Glenbard South. During those nine months, I neither saw Clarissa nor heard anything about what happened to her or Julene. I admit, I didn't ask either. No one who witnessed it talked about it, at least not to me. And I preferred it that way.

CHAPTER 13

THE DOUBLE BIRD

(1)

"THIS ISN'T FAIR!" SHE cries out.

Sitting at her desk, dumbfounded, Therese waves the print blue scantron I have just handed her as if I should take it back. There has been some mistake. She didn't fail. She *doesn't* fail. Take it back.

The rest of the class ignores her outcry, each too engrossed in their own joy, contentment, misery, or despair, all contingent on a test score and percentage stamped in red at the bottom of each scantron.

124/185 67.0% Not good. Despair.

155/185 83.7% Not bad. Contentment.

Therese, in fact, did not fail; she got a "C," 141/185 76.2%. But to her, rightfully so, a "C" is failure. Of herself, she expects "A"s.

I notice but ignore her gesticulations. Therese rises from her desk. She stands in the aisle. I am one aisle over handing back the last of the results. She thrusts the scantron at me, again, and again, stomping her foot like a fencer lunging for a hit. Her bottom lip is pinched between her teeth; a bulging vein throbs from her hairline to the middle of her eyebrows. Her constricted throat emits a low, feral growl. She's pissed.

She's not alone. I hear mutters under breaths as I head back to the front: "We're not in college!" "This is freaking ridiculous." "I need to see my counselor."

I have seven years' experience, but this is my first year at Glenbard South. I am a new teacher here. I have little ethos, no earned credibility. We are four weeks into the semester. These students are juniors; the course is American Lit & Comp. For Therese's class, this exam, the first of the semester, has blown their minds. I could see it shocked into their faces as they worked their way through the Quote Test[38] on Tuesday and then the True-False & Multiple-Choice section on Wednesday. The universal reaction was, "SHIT! He actually expects us to *know all* the crap we talked about!"

Therese remains standing, now still, in the center of the room. Her arms are fisted at her sides; she hunches, cored out with her torso flexed, as if ready to receive or deliver a blow. She demands an answer. This isn't fair.

I work my way back to the front of the room, turn, and sit-lean against the front of my desk, facing the

---

38 I've found that the best way to assess if a student has not just read, but worked to understand and reflect on both the language and the meaning of a text is to give a Quote Test. I select several key quotes from the various readings we've done that unit, list them in random order, and then require students to match the quote—ones we've discussed in class as being seminal—to the author and the work. A typical unit might cover ten different works: a mix of poetry, short stories, and nonfiction. The quote portion of the test has maybe 25 quotes from these ten works. If the student takes a holistic approach to reading—read, annotate, answer the study guide questions, and ask about their annotations in class—they'll be fine. Anything less is a crapshoot. If they read the way some have in the past: skim the work and then wait for the teacher to tell them what is important, they'll crash and burn on the Quote Test portion of the unit exam.

students, so there is no barrier, no bulwark[39] between us. I cross my legs, at ease, loafing. My hands are folded across my lap, and I am tapping my thumbs together, killing time. Mocking by contrast—yes, I admit it—the consternation of my students.

Therese waits. She has no interest in sitting or backing down. I give in and give her an answer.

"What isn't fair? That you didn't read? That you didn't study? That you didn't ask enough questions in class about what you didn't understand? Which one of those is unfair?"

Therese again stomps her foot. "I *did* read. I *did* study." She has clenched her hands into fists. Her upper body trembles.

"Good! I'm glad you read and I'm glad you studied, but that still leaves one out, doesn't it?" I pause and give her a tilted-head, raised-eyebrow, tight-lipped, I-Gotcha smile. (I was kinda being an ass.)

I stand and address the whole class. "The class average was 73%. That's a 'C'. That's average. If you're not happy with that, figure out why." I tell them what is so obvious, yet so difficult for most students, most individuals to do: they need to advocate for themselves if they want more than average. "This is the first test. You'll have plenty of time to raise your grades. However," I lean into them, "you *all* need to ask more questions!"

I point an admonishing finger at Therese—she cringes, frustrated to tears—so I sweep the finger around the

---

39   Too many teachers build bulwarks to protect them from their students: desk in the middle, podium on the right, bookshelf and filing cabinet on the left.

rest of the class, singling out random students, taking the focus off her and giving her, if she wants it, an out.

"What we read and the way I want you to read it is not easy. I get that. I'll help, but I'm not *going* to help unless you *ask* for that help. Raise your hand and ask questions. Read, annotate, complete the study guide, then ask questions. Ask about what you didn't understand and verify what you think you did understand."

Though the feeling is not mutual, I could almost hug Therese because she's helped me set up beautifully one of my favorite life-lessons. I knew and I know that one of the most important skills I can help students develop is self-advocacy. Ask questions!

I'm finished. Therese remains standing in the center of the room, fuming, but she is no longer acknowledged. Her classmates have acquiesced, and her angst is being drowned out by the shuffling of their putting away scantrons and taking out pens and notebooks. I avoid eye contact with her, pick up some notes from my desk, a piece of chalk, and turn toward the blackboard to begin outlining key concepts for the next unit: *Rationalism in America*.

I begin writing on the board, my back to the class, notes to kick off the next unit. I start explaining what I am writing, then I stop, mid-word, and turn to make sure all the students have transitioned. As I pivot, I realize the white noise has silenced and a tense stillness tinged with giggling anticipation has overtaken the room.

And then I see her.

Therese stands boldly in the middle of the room flipping me a magnificent double bird. She has a beautifully athletic stance: feet planted, knees flexed, ribs arched.

Her chest is high. Each arm is fully extended, each middle finger points up and in at a 45-degree angle. Her tilted-head, raised-eyebrow, bite-the-bottom-lip, FU sneer perfectly parodies my earlier smirk at her. I was not meant to see this. This is pure venting, but she's busted. We hang together for a moment.

Emotional content.

I have never been a status quo teacher. I try to push individuals outside their comfort zones, to engage them both intellectually and emotionally. I want a reaction. The key for me is to not push too hard, to play the fine line, and, most of all, to realize when I do go too far and some student reacts, that *I* caused it, that I, not the student, am responsible for this. I have taught long enough now to recognize this dynamic as it unfolds. Therese did it, but I started it.

So, I smile and snort-laugh. I waggle my head and look to the ceiling, and turn back around, allowing Therese a moment to slip into her desk. I put chalk back to blackboard and write and explain and move on.

After class, Therese waits at my desk, flanked by two of her friends, until the other students have left. I sit at my desk, shuffling through some papers and pretending not to notice her, not ignoring her, just not wanting to be awkward. When she starts to speak, I look up and give her my full attention. She is 100% sincere.

"I'm sorry, Mr. Burke . . ."

I raise my hands to cut her off, then I tap my chest and dip my head in a humble mea culpa. "Don't worry about it." I hope my nonverbal cues are clear: no hard feelings, no grudges, no problem. She takes a deep breath, in through the nose out through the mouth. Her rigid shoulders relax.

"I'll see you tomorrow," I say. I look to the other two, "See you tomorrow, ladies."

Therese nods and they leave.

(2)

SIGNING YEARBOOKS IS A common ritual among high school students, especially seniors on the cusp of graduation. Most seek only fellow students, but some ask a teacher or two as well.

I am now finishing my second year at Glenbard South. A few seniors stop by my classroom after school during those final days of May to say goodbye before casting off to adulthood. Therese is one of these. Jackie, another of my former students, is with her. We talk about college—Therese is headed to Ball State; Jackie to Bradley—and their future plans.

Therese asks me to sign her yearbook. I keep it simple, "Therese: Good luck in college and in life. Remember to always *Seek Thyself!* Take care, Mr. Burke."[40]

Under my name I draw two little m-shaped birds, a reminder of a meaningful moment we had together.

---

40   *Seek Thyself!* was one of the catchphrases of my junior American Lit class.

CHAPTER 14

WRESTLING WITH AN EXISTENTIAL CRISIS

(1)

IN GRADE SCHOOL, I had the distinction of being the first of my peers to sweat profusely.

Each morning I'd steal into the medicine cabinet and spritz my armpits with my brother's Right Guard deodorant spray: "One shot and I'm good for the whole day!" The slogan was catchy, and the commercials were clever[41], but the product never worked for me.

I was damned if I didn't and damned if I did.

Locked in a desk all morning had me squiggling out of my skin, drumming fingers and bouncing knees to vent my pent-up vitality. I broke a sweat struggling to

---

41 These 1970s commercials featured two neighbors whose modern apartments share a medicine cabinet. The first man greets the rather shocked second man with a boisterous, "Hi Guy!" After a brief exchange about the benefits of using Right Guard Deodorant, the nonplussed second calls to his wife for relief, "Mona!" I remember this being the first serial commercial I found entertaining, one where the characters were more worth following than the product. I didn't know at that age what "absurdity" was, but I know I empathized with the character who opens his medicine cabinet and finds a totally different person staring back at him.

sit still. Before the school day's first hour had ended, moist beads were popping through Right Guard's protective barrier and tickling their way down my sides.

Recess, as with most of my classmates, was not a time to rest, but a time to run around. I had to move, wanted to be active, liked my energy, so I conceded and let my body go.

There is a euphemism that states, "Horses sweat, men perspire, but women merely glow." By the end of each mid-day romp, I achieved a sort of equine-androgynous[42] effect: My body sweat, my forehead perspired, and my face merely glowed.

I tried to dry off as best I could before heading inside, but the cobalt cotton polo shirt I wore as my school uniform betrayed me. The light blue of the shirt turned a deep, dark blue when wetted accenting the rings of dampness draped under each armpit and the Rorschach blots on my sternum and in the center of my back.

In addition, even without lifting my arm for a manly whiff, I could smell my own stink. I stank, like red onions sautéing in butter, a pungent, but not altogether unpleasant stench, at least not to me.

But so be it. Like Popeye says, I am what I am and that's all I am.

That year, one of my classmates, an exceptional caricature artist for a twelve-year-old, started a cartoon strip based on students in our seventh-grade class. He'd draw a new strip every few days, the storylines loosely parodying stuff that happened during the school day.

---

42   I know I'm blending Latin and Greek roots, but hippo-androgynous sounds too, well, round.

One of the characters was named "Mike B.O.", an obvious reference to yours truly. I was a loner, and I did not appreciate this attention.

I was smaller than the cartoonist, smaller than almost all my classmates, but I knew I could take him. I had been whacked around enough at home to know how to deliver a blow. He was soft, and I could make him stop. I saw myself driving a fist into his stomach. But I would lose. I knew that even then. I couldn't win that fight. I'd look like a jerk and be a bully, something I detested. Besides, I *was* sweaty and stinky. He drew what he saw and smelled. Hard to argue.

So, I avoided the comic strip, hoping it would all go away, but it grew in popularity, and so did I.

For some reason, the kid doing the cartoons decided to turn Mike B.O. into a superhero who would rescue fellow students from eighth grade bullies by using his armpit blasters to douse the villains in noxious gas. Suddenly my sweat was cool.

One day a girl I liked but would never dare speak to (she was the first to sport a woman's fuller figure) snuck up behind me while I sat at my desk reading and poked her finger into my sweaty armpit. I spun and caught her sniffing and then waving the digit at her girlfriends who shrank back in giggling horror.

I wasn't sure whether to be flattered or repulsed by their behavior. These girls were interested in me. But I had no response. I turned back to my book and kept quiet, but this only added to the allure. I was suddenly the shy, quiet, Clark Kentish alter ego of Mike B.O., the most popular character in the comic strip.

Somehow, I got invited to an actual party at the house of another girl I liked. I decided to go.

I ironed my best jeans, spray-layered on the deodorant, and perfectly parted my hair (I had soft, sandy-blonde hair that one of my aunts loved to tussle). I stole a dark blue, long-sleeve, button-down dress shirt from my brother. I rolled the cuff of each sleeve back two times, not because the sleeve was too long, but because I thought the mid-forearm look was radical.

The doofus was a dude.

I hopped on my bike and slowly (so as not to exert myself) rode the three miles to this girl's house. She had not asked me directly, her friend had, but she had nodded her assent. I was about to join the ranks of the invited.

I parked my bike by the side of the house and gathered myself at the front door. I heard the noise of a party already started and drifted over to glance through a window well that opened into a basement rec room crowded with my classmates. I watched them talking, laughing, jostling each other.

Despite the cool night air, I felt nervous sweat beading under my arms and dappling my sternum. I looked up to the sky and thought about what I was doing. I took another look through the glass, and then drew in a deep breath, held it, rounded my lips, and whistled a tranquil sigh. As I let the air out, a tremor slid down my spine, through my thighs, and out my toes. I shivered, and then flexed and stretched, as if now awakening. One more deep breath.

I was not Mike B.O.

I returned to my bike and began a circuitous five-mile ride home. I didn't run away. I took some time to think. I didn't fit there. I needed to figure out where.

(2)

I DIDN'T LIKE WHO I was in grade school. I wanted to be different from who I thought I was perceived as being. Or, if not different, at least in some control, to believe that I was who I was by choice and not the assumptions of my peers or the default history of my siblings. I wanted some control of others' perceptions, or at least more control of my own self-perception.

I also felt on the fringe of everything. Present, but not really in any specific group. Part of that was fine. I didn't mind being on my own. I didn't need anyone else. But I also didn't want to be left alone. I wanted somewhere to belong without needing to belong there. It was all so confusing, and, typical of adolescence.

So, I started looking forward to high school's fresh start. Like most kids that age, I couldn't wait to get out and move on. But I struggled. What if I screwed up? I feel like I didn't sleep through the night or take a solid shit over the last few months of grade school. I maintained as best I could a stoic veneer, but inside I was a nervous, hyper-introspective kid. What if I screwed up?

(3)

EIGHTH GRADE ENDED, AND one hot summer day I took a first step toward becoming someone different.

My parents owned a second house on Lake Marie in Antioch, Illinois. That is where I spent my summers, away from the kids I knew at school and my friends in the neighborhood. I imagine most people would consider having a summer home on a beautiful lake a great privilege, and it was, but it also put me on an island. Most of the time, it was only an older brother and my younger sister to hang around with. Sometimes, close quarters bred conflict.

One afternoon, my brother and I got into an argument. He was two years older and about to enter his junior year of high school. This brother and I were out on the end of our pier—it stretched about thirty feet into the lake—arguing about whatever. I don't remember. We were both dressed in regular clothes, not swimming trunks, I know that. I also know the conflict got heated and threatened to turn physical.

I had four older brothers. I was also a little shit. I got picked on and beat up (nothing too serious and often deserved) a lot. When I was younger, my defense had always been to bust out the tears. When I got a bit too old for that, I was forced to simply acquiesce without defending myself. Take it. Back down. Walk away. Like a coward. Fighting back was futile. Fighting back would only get me beat up more.

On this day on the pier—I didn't do this consciously; it just happened—I changed. I stood up to my brother, and something in my eyes must have caught him by surprise because his reaction to my not backing down was to cheat.

When he stepped toward me, I didn't cower. I also stepped forward, my chest as high as I could raise it. I challenged him. In response, he gave me a sudden push, and I stumbled back off the end of the pier and splashed sideways into the lake. Instead of standing there gloating and laughing at me—like he normally would have done—he retreated off the pier and into the house. I stood in the water and watched him turn his back to me. He hadn't fought fair (whatever that would have been). I was not finished. Soaking wet in my street clothes, I plowed through the water to the shore and strode across the front lawn up the concrete steps into our front porch.

The porch was screened in on three sides. Suspended from the ceiling on one side was a bench swing. My brother stood in front it, not knowing how to react since my behavior was so out of character. He stood waiting. I never hesitated, never broke stride. I stepped forward and drove both palms into his ribcage; this was easy to do because he was several inches taller than I was. I drove him backwards, into the porch swing, which cocked sideways; the bottom corner jumped up and ripped through the screen behind it. I held him pinned, trapped between me and the swing, an edge of which had dug through his shirt and into his back.

"If you ever touch me again, I'll fucking kill you!" I had never sworn before at anyone in my family, never even raised my voice.

"Michael!"

My mother stood in the doorway between the porch and the house itself. I had had enough of her too, her having spent too many useless days smoking cigarettes and playing solitaire at the kitchen table, killing time, waiting for what? I couldn't even look at her.

But I relented, giving my brother another shove and driving the edge of the bench a little deeper into his back ribs, before letting go. I went right past my mother, through the house, and out the door on the other side. I went across the lawn and out behind the garage. A baseball mitt and a few rubber balls lay scattered in the grass. I picked them up, paced off fifteen strides from wall to mound, and spent the next half hour whipping fast balls at the chalked-white batter's box scored onto the back of the garage.

That evening, when my father got home from work, I expected to get in trouble, to be yelled at—or worse—for fighting, and then to be grounded for ripping the porch screen. But nothing happened. And at dinner, it was as if nothing had happened. Whatever my mother did or didn't say, totally defused the situation.

I couldn't let it go, though, and that night I lie awake thinking. I didn't like that part of myself, that anger, or, that rage. It had never felt so consuming. But another part of me was glad it was there. That I was capable of fighting back. Now, I needed to channel it. But first, I had to make up with my brother. I did, and the next day we spent the morning fishing off the pier, catching and releasing tiny bluegill and perch.

(4)

IN MID-AUGUST, TWO WEEKS before the academic portion of my freshman year of high school began, I joined the football team. Two of my older brothers played football, and my father had been an exceptional football player[43], so this seemed a natural starting point to becoming someone I respected.

43 My father had played for Vince Lombardi at Fordham University. Years later, as Lombardi coached the Green Bay Packers to their

I quit, however, after three days.

Each of the three practices I attended concluded with the same "separate the men from the boys" drill: the nutcracker. For this drill, a coach would place four orange cones in a two-yard by two-yard square. The forty or so members of our freshmen football team broke into two long lines extending back from opposite sides of the square. The lead players in each stack would drop into three-point stances—balanced on their right fists with their back feet trenching at the dirt—and face off across this six-foot gap. (Note that a normal "line of scrimmage" in football is only 11 inches, the length of an actual football; for this drill, the coaches had us farther back so we could get some momentum going and really pop each other.)

The coaches stood on either side of the square, our own tiny gladiatorial stadium, to initiate the drill and observe this ultimate test of toughness. We freshmen—clad in shoulder pads, thigh pads, knee pads, hand-me-down single bar plastic helmets, and jock straps with snap-in plastic cups to protect our fledgling cojones—wanted to impress.

The two teammates waited, their eyes glaring across the void, growls rumbling in their throats until the coach's whistle released them. They exploded forward, colliding with titanic force, the crowns of their helmets cracking together (no targeting rules in those days), their legs driving forward, their arms pushing and

---

third straight NFL Championship (including winning Super Bowls I and II), my sister wrote him a letter to verify my dad's claim. Lombardi wrote back, a handwritten letter on Green Bay Packer stationary. He said that, yes, he remembered my father, especially for his grit and tenacity. Lombardi wished our family and my father well.

twisting to try and throw their opponent to the dirt. A second whistle ended this struggle, and two new combatants sprang to the front, and so on, and so on.

The first two practices had ended with one round of this obligatory brutality, each player getting one crack at a teammate. I was 4'11", slower than a dripping faucet, and not yet 100 pounds. Those first two practices, I had matched up with someone equally inept, in ability if not in size. Each round had been noticeably nondescript, the coaches' indifference signaling to me that I had displayed nothing that might contribute to the team's success.

On the third day, as I moved toward the front of the line, I did some counting. I wanted to make some impression, and I hoped for a favorable match-up. I was fifteenth in line, and I counted down the other side: . . . 13, 14, 15. Butterflies awoke in my stomach and a slither of nausea snaked up my throat. You've got to be kidding me. God, please.

I counted again, slowly. The butterflies in my stomach morphed into baby dragons. By dumb luck I lined up with Ziggy Lewis, the heaviest kid on the team. He was only a few inches taller than I was, but he weighed over 250 pounds. He was a wrecking ball with two shoes and a head: immobile, but immovable as well.

Shit.

I looked around for help. The whistle blew again and an ecstatic "Hit somebody!" sounded from the front as I took another step forward.

The first day of practice, two days ago, as we lined up for our first go at the nutcracker drill, Coach Francis looked us over and saw the outright fear on most of our faces. "Ah, Shit Piss, Boys," he chided us. "If you don't feel it, FAKE it!"

Now I understood. I rolled my shoulders and clenched my fists. I scowled and started bobbing my head from side to side as I had seen hooded boxers do on their way to the ring. I bounced up and down on my toes to get amped. I stomped each foot into the ground like a raging bull.

My cockish display of bravado proved impotent; I couldn't fake it to myself. I was terrified, and all this movement did was leak some tinkle out of my peepee. Good thing I had a cup on to catch the discharge.

Our turn arrived.

I loaded myself into that three-point stance and resolved to let whatever happens, happen. On the whistle, I shot out like a bullet at a brick wall, with a similar result. I bounced off my opponent and spiraled onto my backside, ass planted in the dirt. I may have shaken a few drops of sweat from his facemask, but Ziggy remained unmoved. I popped up, the tears of frustration that welled in my eyes thankfully hidden by my oversized helmet.

Shoulders fighting to stay square, I moved off to where the other players waited. Blessedly, no one laughed. We were the Notre Dame *Dons*, after all, and a Don is, above all, a gentleman. At least it was over, and I had done a good job *trying* to fake it.

After the last pair finished, we gathered around the coaches, ready for final inspiration. "Boys," Coach Francis complimented us, "that was the best round of nut-cracking yet! Wasn't a turd-bird in the bunch." He looked from face to face, sincere, and we looked back, petrified.

"So what the hell! Let's do it again!"

An audible groan emitted from somewhere within our ranks, morphing quickly into a sort of sea lion barking followed by hands clapping and shoulder pad slapping as our huddled band dispersed again into two lines.

I filtered into the back quarter of the line heading south and began my waddling procession to the front. At first, I ignored the concussive crack, crack, crack of plastic on plastic as my teammates engaged each other. Eventually though, I had to acknowledge that my turn would again come. So, I decided to do the math. I counted to my spot in line. Tenth. I counted the other side. Full sized fire-breathing dragons. You've got to be fucking kidding me! God help me, please. I counted again.

No help.

I said three Hail Mary's and one Lord's Prayer. I crossed myself, begged for a reprieve, and counted a third time. Denied again. I was cursed; each count yielded the same result. I would get another shot at Ziggy. My cup runneth over.

No one had laughed at my initial failure, so I resolved to hold that respect. I moved to the front of the line, dug into my stance, and damned the misty eyes betraying me. I looked up at Ziggy and saw . . . boredom.

He was bored.

Asshole. He didn't even see me. I was nothing to him. As it had with my brother earlier that summer, something in me clicked. Fuck him. Now, I didn't need to fake it. I snorted like a bull and dug my left foot, then my right, into the turf. When the whistle blew, I took one low, slow step forward, then a second, and on the third coiled all my weight and drove my forehead up into his facemask while punching both my fists into his chubby tits. He "oofed" and took one step, then another, backwards to regain his balance. Before he could recoil and roll over me like the bowling ball he was, mercifully, the second whistle blew.

I stood as tall as my nearly five-foot frame allowed. The coach nodded at me, and one of my teammates, Ed-Joe, smacked me on the back of the helmet.

That day I chose to walk home after practice rather than take the bus. The five-mile trek took me for three of those miles down a forest preserve path through the Miami Woods, alongside the North Branch of the Chicago River. The August sun was hot, but other than a few twinkling beams, it couldn't penetrate the thick cover of the trees. The path I walked was cool, quiet, and calm.

Ambling along underneath oak, hickory, and ash, listening to the water ripple beside me, I could collect my thoughts and scatter my anxieties. I didn't fit. I could survive; I knew that now. But though I loved and still love the game itself, football was not my sport. This wasn't me. I resolved to quit. In the woods, walking alone, I embraced my decision. I took control. I felt good.

"I bought you those spikes for nothing!" my mother screamed at me when I broke my decision to her as I entered our home. "I can't bring them back!"

I looked down at the football spikes, tied together by their laces and draped across my shoulder. They were used, by one or more of my brothers. I didn't know what she meant or what I should do, so I waited, as I often did with my mother. Stupefied, she stood glaring at me with her arms folded and her jaw wired. (My mother had already had her first Manhattan, though it wasn't yet five o'clock.) "Quitter," escaped under her breath. She *fffft*ted at me—a curse without cursing—and turned to go water her plant, her favorite coping strategy.

Years earlier, my mother hung a hand-carved bamboo birdcage, round and domed, inside the garden window above and behind our kitchen sink. The birdcage had belonged to my mother's maternal grandmother. My mother, who hated birds, kept a fern locked inside. When she was like this, she would turn to the fern and sprinkle it from a watering can kept ready on the window ledge. Then she'd gaze past its leaves and through the window glass and out across the tops of the trees in our backyard and into the somewhere in the distance.

That's how I left her, standing there, staring. As I went up to my bedroom, I began feeling the weight of a terrible gravity with each step up the staircase. For all her nonsense, she had a point. My mother was right. I had not merely made a decision; I had set a precedent. I had quit.

(5)

IN GRADE SCHOOL, ACADEMICS had been my strength. I had been smart on my terms. I didn't need to study or do anything beyond the required homework. I aced the exams by paying attention in class; if you waited long enough, the teacher always explained everything. I listened and I learned.

Eventually, since my grade school didn't have any "gifted" classes, I got moved—along with several of my classmates—to *Independent Study: Accelerated Enhancement Activities*. One period each day, our group would move to an empty classroom and be left, unsupervised, to do our individual work. I got to progress at my own pace and study content I selected. I loved it. I blew through each day's suggested schedule of self-guided activities and spent most of my time on independent reading and daydreaming. I cruised.

Freshman year of high school, I tested into honors classes that, for the first time in my life, put pressure on me academically. I couldn't just pay attention in class; I had to study and do homework. I made mistakes. I struggled to keep up. I worried that I didn't belong in those classes. That worry manifested itself at night.

I'd fall asleep easy enough, then snap awake at 2 a.m., my mind racing over some triviality: an organ I marked incorrectly in biology lab (God love the sacrifice of fetal pigs) or a stupid subtraction mistake on an Algebra quiz. This anxiety would morph from academics into some crazy scenario extrapolating from a meaningless confrontation. Did the kid who bumped me while I had my back turned at my locker do it on purpose? Was he looking for trouble? Was he the one who left chewed gum on the seat of my desk? Did he piss in my gym locker? Stupid shit that I knew was stupid shit and yet I couldn't get my imagination to stop spinning absurdity.

I'd lie in bed agonizing, counterproductively chastising myself that I have to be up in seven, six, five, four hours. I refused to get up and do something productive like going for a walk around the block or moving onto a couch in the living room where I could turn on a light and do some reading, either of which would help bring me down and put me out. Instead, I just waited.

I paid for this the next school day.

If the teachers were dynamic and engaging, I was fine. But if they weren't, I sank. In classes where the anesthetic content and the teacher's white noise voice sirened me to oblivion, my cheek would rest on my folded arms, and I would slip into a semi-conscious zombie state. More than once I fell sound asleep, not just nodding off, but the-entire-class-walks-out-during-a-fire-drill-and-leaves-me-there asleep.

I slipped from easy A's in grade school to barely B's in high school. And sleeping in school only made sleeping at night more difficult.

Worst of all, I didn't care.

September and October drifted by. I lay awake many nights, staring at the tree outside my bedroom window, watching for any wind that might gently bend the boughs. Soon I could glimpse indifferent stars through the barren branches of fall.

I wanted high school to be different, *I* wanted to be different, but different so far had only meant worse. I was a quitter and a shitty student.

I was fucking it up.

(6)

THE WINTER SPORT SEASON began. I had now sprouted to 5'1" tall and broadened to 104 pounds. I stayed after school that chilly November day to try-out for the freshmen basketball team. I had never played organized basketball, but I had spent many an afternoon dribbling around my driveway and shooting at the backboard and hoop fastened to the front of our garage. I thought I could play.

I survived warm-ups without consequence. I could stretch, and do jumping jacks, and follow directions well enough to execute—after a few tries—the stance and footwork drills we were taught.

After warm-ups, we broke into two groups and ran three "suicides," one group resting while the other took their turn. A suicide is a conditioning drill run on a basketball court. The players start on one baseline and sprint back and forth between various lines on the court—free throw, half court, opposite free throw, opposite baseline—and the original baseline. Because of all the stopping to change directions, suicides demand effort and will, not skill or even speed. I did fine.

Three kids couldn't finish the suicides without walking and were told by the coaches to go sit in the bleachers and rest for a second. "It's okay," they were told. "Get your energy back." They were never acknowledged again.

For me, so far so good. I felt like I belonged, that the coaches could see my hustle.

This was, however, a *basketball* tryout, and the coaches had to determine which fifteen athletes would make the freshman team. To expedite the winnowing process, the coaches broke the remaining thirty of us into six groups of five so that we could scrimmage, a good way to identify who already had basketball acumen. We would play actual games with two coaches as referees and a third coach on the sidelines observing and taking notes.

Two teams played on one half court; two played on the other; and two teams sat out. (Our gym only had room for one full court and a half dozen side baskets.) My team, the "E" team, sat out the first round, so I had a chance to watch my competition, the other twenty kids playing, and see where I stood. I watched and evaluated. I'm not stupid. I realized that all the kids on the "A" and "B" teams would most likely survive tryouts. Fine. I just wanted to make the team. I could work my way up to the starting five once we began actual practices.

The kids on the "C" and "D" teams seemed closer to my level. There was nothing they weren't doing that I couldn't do.[44] Still, there was a reason the coaches had assigned me to the "E" team. I knew I had to impress them with my hustle and determination if I was going to make it through.

Team "E" finally got a chance to play, but instead of matching us with team "F", the coaches pitted us against team "C" and had team "F" play team "D". Teams "A" and "B" practiced free throws and lay-ups on the side baskets. They didn't bother watching us.

---

44   Yes, my logic was somewhat muddled, arguing that I was their equal because there many things we both couldn't do.

I was positioned at guard, and though I knew I couldn't shoot well *yet*, I thought I could definitely play defense. "C" team started with the ball. The kid I was defending dribbled toward me, his head up, his eyes looking past me for an open teammate. I got in a low crouch, as the coaches had instructed, and timed his dribble: one... two... three... On his fourth dribble, I dove forward and knocked the ball away before crashing into his legs and staggering him backward. The whistle blew.

"That's a foul," the coach informed me.

"But I hit the ball first?" I asked.

"Doesn't matter."

The coach gave the ball back to the kid I was guarding who started dribbling again, looking beyond me for an open teammate. He turned a hip to me and started backing his way up court, dribbling with his right hand. I put both my hands on his left butt cheek and stopped his progress. I didn't really push him; I just sort of used my body weight and position to keep him from going anywhere. The whistle blew.

"That's a foul!" In lieu of any explanation, the coach sent me to guard a much bigger kid under the basket. I jostled around with this kid as best I could, refusing to give ground as he tried to bump me out of the way. A shot went up and clanged off the rim in our direction. The kid leaned into me to box me out, but instead of resisting, I slid to the side and with both arms, gently swept him by as a matador dodges a bull. His momentum met no obstruction, and he tumbled to the floor. I didn't trip him, I swear. He fell on his own. The whistle blew.

"That's a foul," the coach stated. I started to plead, but he shushed me with a wave of his hand.

He leaned back and sized me up from the double-tied shoelaces of my Chuck Taylor hand-me-downs to the tip of my blonde cowlick. In fewer than two minutes, I already had three fouls. No one had even scored a basket yet. Hell, my team hadn't even had possession of the ball.

The coach waved to one of the "B" players on the sideline to come take my place, and I waited for him to relegate me to irrelevance on the bleachers. Instead, he looked at me and laughed, not maliciously, and directed me toward the third coach who stood on the baseline taking notes. That coach, Coach Hinger, was a big man, maybe six-four, and he squatted down to my height and kindly fathered a hand on my shoulder. He also laughed—a low, quick chortle—and then squeezed my shoulder. With his other hand, he pointed to a hallway off the back corner of the gym.

"Son," he advised, "down that hallway, through the door on the end, that's the *wrestling* room." He met my eyes and nodded to affirm that I understood. I did, so I listened. I left the court and opened that door and fell in love.

That night I told my mom I was joining the wrestling team. "I am not buying any shoes!" She told me.

But she did, eventually. A new pair.

Wrestling practices were grueling. The other kids on my team were literally trying to beat me up, and if I didn't fight back, I'd be crushed.[45] After each workout,

---

45   One of the mottos of wrestling is, *Create Legal Pain*. This dictum is not hyperbole.

I found myself refreshingly exhausted. The impact was immediate. I could sit still at night and finish my homework. I slept better. I paid better attention in school (this was also attained by my conviction, in boring classes, to write down notes on everything the teacher said, whether it mattered or not, and to do so in random patterns across my notebook). By the end of the semester, my grades climbed back to A's. I became the student I wanted to be.

Wrestling taught me that if I could level the playing field, I could compete with anyone. Given my flyweight frame, I couldn't defeat the 250-pound Ziggy in the nutcracker drill. In wrestling, however, there were weight classes, so I always competed against someone my own size. Though I got my ass whipped on occasion, I won more than I lost and eventually got moved up from the freshmen to the sophomore squad.

Best of all, wrestlers didn't just tolerate sweat, they worshipped it. Sweating profusely meant I could cut weight easily, which meant I could eat more because I could quickly dump a pound or two of water weight if necessary.

Wrestling also fed my introverted nature. In competition, I didn't have to rely on teammates. The matches were all one-on-one. Yes, we were a team, but once I stepped on that mat, I was on my own. I could also do much of my training on my own. I weight lifted alone in my bedroom, interspersing blocks of studying with sets of curls, bench press, and cleans. Late at night, after finishing my homework, I threw on a few layers of sweat clothes and went out for a solitary four- or five-mile run—no ear buds or Audible then—just me and my thoughts.

We all face existential crises in our lives, transitional moments when we must redefine who we are and why we exist. Moving from grade school to high school was a crucial one for me. I found answers at the end of a hallway. Wrestling gave me a high school identity I liked and a sense of purpose and belonging.

(7)

Co-Curricular Activities

YOU CAN STOP HERE, if you want, but I feel obliged to rant for a moment.

This essay was inspired by a philosophy podcast I sometimes listen to while I work out.[46] The hosts, on this particular segment, were talking about our search for identity and the two existential questions all human beings ask themselves at transitional phases of their lives: Who am I? and Why do I exist?

Their discussion triggered me back to my transition from grade school to high school, and my struggles. For me, finding some answers to those existential questions started in that wrestling room. I can look back now and see how obvious it is, how much of my character, my work ethic, my ability to manage and route energy, and my personality in general were shaped at the end of that hallway.

I won't play the "what if" game: What if Coach Hinger hadn't pulled me aside and pointed down that hallway? What if he had, instead, condemned me to

---

46   *The Partially Examined Life* by Mark Linsenmayer

the bleachers? The questions are irrelevant. The fact is he *did* pull me aside, and that's all that matters. I am by no means a perfect person, but I know that that wrestling room helped me toward a better version of myself. I learned more about *life* in the wrestling room than I did in any other classroom in my educational career. That's not to say the other classes weren't important. They were. But if there was a "most important" to me, wrestling was it.

I also know I am not unique. Co-curricular activities (including athletics) are as fundamental to an individual's education as any academic class. This is especially true for grades 6 through 12.

Want to see the difference between a good school district—one that is effectively preparing students for life in a democratic society (not just how to get a job)—and a struggling one? Look at how much is invested in facilities, equipment, and staff to support Co-curricular activities. If the students want to start a debate team, will the district support it? What about robotics or jazz band or women's wrestling? Does each school in the district have a student government and service programs? Is there a spring musical? A math team? An anime club?

I am fortunate that the high school I went to prioritized and invested in Co-curricular activities. Many other school districts do as well. But too many don't; and, big surprise, the places where these programs are lacking are often the places where they are most needed. This needs to change.

CHAPTER 15

Survival

(1)

Safe Zones

IN MY FIRST YEAR teaching at Proviso East High School, several students were murdered, all in separate shootings, during an explosion of retaliatory gang violence that played out on the streets of Maywood and the surrounding communities over a brief stretch of time from the end of summer into early fall.

The teenagers killed were students in name only. They were either habitual truants or dropouts. The difference depended on age. At 17, a child could legally dropout; 16 and under and that child was still obligated to attend school. The distinction didn't matter; none of them showed up. All should have been working alongside their classmates toward a rite of passage: graduating with the Class of 198—. Instead, each was dead.

I didn't hear about any of the murders until a month after the senselessness had finally stopped. And then, I only found out because I overheard several of the runners I coached joking about how, "Maywood (is)

Maywood again, no more Tombstone."⁴⁷ I perked up when I heard the Tombstone reference. What were they talking about? I knew not to question the runners; they didn't mind my hearing their banter, but it was not my place to join the conversation. So, the next day, I asked the Dean of Students what they were alluding to, and I learned what had been happening.

I found this odd: had I missed something? Why didn't I know about this? Despite their attendance issues, these murdered individuals had to have friends and acquaintances who attended school, friends and acquaintances who carried daily the emotional burden of previous and possible subsequent violence. Why had there not been some sort of general announcement, or, at least, a memo sent out to staff, an advisory to watch for students who might be in distress?

I had never taught at a school like Proviso East. Poverty. Crime. Homelessness. Gangs. My students faced these challenges daily. I was from the white, middle-class suburbs. I had no experience in this sort of environment, and for the first time in my life, I felt incredibly sheltered and naïve. I realized that serious shit happens here every day.

As far as these murders, I didn't know about them because I didn't need to know and because I lacked the social intelligence to pick up on what was happening all around me (at least until I heard the Tombstone reference). The Dean helped me understand this. At the school, there would be no general announcements or staff memos. No publicity.

---

47 Tombstone, Arizona is where the Gunfight at the O.K. Corral, and subsequent retaliatory violence, occurred in 1881.

The Dean explained why the administration had chosen, not ignorance, but a sort of strategic stoicism. They weren't going to let themselves or the school get worked up about what was beyond their control. No sense pouring gas on a fire. The surrounding community had its struggles; that was not about to change. The school, however, was trying its best to be a safe zone.

The administration wasn't in denial; they cared about their students and the community. But running the school and keeping it a safe zone for students, not just today, but tomorrow and tomorrow, demanded making choices, especially during crises that were, again, beyond their control. In a sense, they had built a wall around the Proviso East campus and then broadcast the unwritten rule that what you do out there is up to you, but don't bring it in here. If you come in here, leave it out there.

For example, during the years I was at Proviso East, the administration had no tolerance for gang activity on the school campus. No one wore hats, there was no graffiti on the walls, certain color combinations were banned, tattoos were covered by Band-Aids or clothing. Violators were dealt with harshly. Suspensions and expulsions were common. If you don't want to be here, fine. We won't force you. It's your choice. The benefit all students got from this "no tolerance" policy was that, during school hours and on the school campus, for the most part, they didn't have to worry about gangs. Fear and despair could be kept at bay.

The administration hadn't turned a blind eye to those murders that fall. They all knew what was happening. The Dean told me that the security team—the civilian para-pros who walked the halls—knew which students to keep an eye on, which students might be involved or impacted. However, the administration operated on a strict need-to-know basis. I didn't need to know, so no one had told me. I understood. To keep Proviso East safe, it was essential to keep that wall in place, and to not let what happened in the community seep into the school.

I have no doubt that literally thousands of students over the years found solace in the safe zone the Proviso East administration established. These students benefitted because, at least in the building, they were able to pursue the education they desired without constantly being on guard or on edge.

Later in my career, when I taught at Wheeling High School, I became one of the English teachers whom the counselors sent troubled seniors to. "Put him (or her) in Burke's class. That'll give 'em the best chance to graduate." I took this as a great compliment. I liked being known as a teacher who could help struggling students get across the finish line. I did it, I realize now, not by enabling kids, but by making my Senior English class a safe zone, in principle.

Okay. I need to pause here to clarify that there was no sudden epiphany, no lightbulb moment back at WHS when I realized, "Gee, I need to make my classroom a safe zone, just like they had at Proviso East." It is only now as I critique my career that I see the parallels. The essential features I'm about to describe were put together—to show off some Latin—*a posteriori* rather than *a priori*.

Here goes. In principle, a safe zone has five essential features: a boundary, a targeted behavior, a benefit, strict but fair rules and consequences, and a choice. At Proviso East, the boundary was the school grounds, the targeted behavior was gang activity, the benefit was a safe environment in which to learn, the consequence was suspension or expulsion, the choice was whether or not to show up at school and engage in gang activity.

In the "Struggling Students in Senior English" case, the boundary was my classroom. The targeted behavior was five required essays and subsequent revisions. The benefit was that everyone who does all five essays, making an honest effort on both the essay and the revision, will earn at least a "C" and thereby meet the graduation requirements for English.[48] The consequence was that anyone not meeting this targeted behavior would fail and not graduate. The choice was to do or not do the essays, or, to drop my class and try and move to a different teacher.

In this class especially, I had a very broad standard for a "C." These students—the ones just fighting to pass—were not going on to be English majors in college. Most would never write another essay in their lives. My goal was to get them to argue some issue in their essay, to begin with a personal anecdote that introduces their voice and their thesis, to provide a few paragraphs of contentions and evidence to support that thesis, to at least attempt a counterargument, then to loop back to their opening anecdote to complete the circle and close their argument. I didn't judge them (harshly) on the quality of their argument, and I sure as hell didn't dink them to death for grammar errors. I noted these things

---

48   Part of that "honest effort" meant getting the essay done on time. Deadlines matter. I deducted 10% per day late. After five days, an essay could earn no more than half credit.

for the revision, but for a "C," students just needed to make an honest effort to argue a point and correct the blatant grammar errors I had pointed out. (I graded and marked up the "final" draft; the students then completed one more revision based on my comments. This revision, if done conscientiously, raised the final grade anywhere from 5% to 15%. Any student who didn't do the revision lost 10%.)

Along with receiving a passing grade, there was an additional benefit for following this process: the students learned how to construct an argument and improved the quality of their writing. This is not, however, a benefit that would have appealed, at the time, to most of these seniors. They wanted the grade. They wanted to graduate and get the hockey puck out of there.

I had a reputation for being a strict, but fair teacher. As each essay came due, I reminded the class, without judgment, "If you do not do this essay, you will fail. That's okay, I'll still love you, but because I love you, you will fail. It's your choice." I was being completely honest, and I was not kidding. I tried to continually reinforce the concept that I'm holding you accountable because I care; if I didn't care, I'd let you do whatever the fuck you wanted.

All the seniors who were struggling had some sort of chaos in their lives. I couldn't help with that. However, I could give them one stable environment where they knew the rules and the expectations *and* could meet those rules and expectations, and where they had a choice. Some invariably failed, but the vast majority passed and graduated.

Four times in my career I had the strictness of my safe zone philosophy affirmed by former students. That may not be a lot for almost forty years of teaching, but it's enough for me. In each case, years later at some random location, I ran into a student (or a student almost ran into me[49]) whom I had failed as a senior and thus prevented from graduating on time.

All four students either hugged me or shook my hand, and each thanked me for kicking their ass. All were doing well. One had become a high school counselor. They taught me that in a safe zone environment, even those who fail can sometimes benefit.

(2)

The Parable of the Starfish

I FIRST HEARD "THE Parable of the Starfish" in a very simplified form in an Educational Psychology class I took in college.

This is the parable as it was told then:

> *One day, an old man was strolling along a beach that was littered with thousands of starfish that*

---

[49] This happened while I was teaching at Notre Dame High School. My wife and I lived on Oak Park Avenue in Chicago, a rather busy street. I was mowing my front lawn on a Saturday morning when I heard tires screech. I turned to see a car swerving in my direction. Before stopping, the right front tire jumped the curb and came to rest on the edge of my lawn. Jeff threw open his driver's side door and came charging toward me. I didn't recognize him at first, and my initial thought was how to defend myself against this lunatic. Then I realized he was beaming, calling my name, "Mr. Burke!!!" and reaching out to me with both arms. We hugged, and he told me a little about his being a sophomore at the University of Illinois, and how failing my class was the best thing that had happened to him.

had been washed ashore by the high tide. Soon, he came upon a young boy who was eagerly throwing the starfish back into the ocean, one by one.

Puzzled, the man looked at the boy and asked what he was doing. Without looking up from his task, the boy simply replied, "I'm saving these starfish, Sir."

The old man chuckled aloud, "Son, there are thousands of starfish and only one of you. What difference can you make?"

The boy picked up a starfish, gently tossed it into the water, and turning to the man, said, "I made a difference to that one!"

I loved Ed Psyche because the teacher was a healthy skeptic who encouraged our class to way-over-analyze seemingly innocuous stories meant to inspire future educators like us. We tore this parable apart.

The overall intended meaning is clear: a teacher saves the world one student at a time. That's great. However, imbedded into that simplistic message like fleas and ticks feasting on a puppy are images that suggest a more fatalistic reality. Here are some of the contradictions we extracted from this version:

Poverty, failure, and despair—the factors that leave thousands of kids behind every day—are as inevitable as the tides.

Save a few, but realize the vast majority is beyond you.

Young people are naïve; they believe they can make a difference all by themselves.

Old people know no one can make a difference. What is, is.

The young boy will become the old man soon enough.

We had fun, our class, playing devil's advocate, pretending to be cold-hearted and cynical by shunning the optimism of saving the world one student at a time and instead embracing the underlying pessimism of this parable. Our teacher, Professor Wool, had the audacity to tell us (regarding teaching as a career): "It's just a freaking job!" The implied reality? Few teachers make any difference at all.

None of us believed that, but it felt rebelliously blasphemous to hear it out loud, to challenge the fates by articulating a dark reality: teaching could become "just a freaking job," and if it did, why was that the career we were pursuing when we all knew we could make a hell of a lot more money in business or law.[50]

Professor Wool, psyche teacher extraordinaire, did a great service by providing me a continual reminder of what I could not allow to happen. Over the years, every time I heard this parable repeated at an institute day or saw it posted in a colleague's classroom, I flinched. I knew that too many of the teachers and administrators

---

50 I wrestled with this "dark reality" most of my career as I saw men and women I graduated with banking three or four times what I was making. I got shit from my father after I told him my intentions when he asked me, rhetorically but not, "Why did you go to Notre Dame to be a *teacher*? You could have done that anywhere." Sidenote in a footnote: The University of Notre Dame does not have an education program; I had to take my education classes at St. Mary's College, an all-female school across the street. My Ed Psyche class could have had fun with the underlying implications of that reality.

I worked with had resigned themselves to doing their job until they eventually retired, that they had lost all hope of making a difference. Too many young boys and girls had become old men and women.

I'm retired now, and I crossed the finish line still trying to make a difference. I'd like to think there was still enough of the "young boy" in me right up to my last day.

I like the simple, intended optimism of "The Parable of the Starfish." I just didn't like all those underlying contradictions.

So, with deference to Professor Wool, I've written my own version. Here it is.

> The night after a brutal storm, an old man woke and went for his normal morning walk along the beach. The man was disheartened to see thousands of starfish washed onto the sand, stretching as far as he could see in either direction. He shook his head at the waste; he knew the day sun would dry out and kill those not returned to the water. "I guess this is as nature intended," he conceded.
>
> As the sun rose and the light spread, he saw a young girl in the distance. She would walk a little, then bend down, pick up a starfish, and throw it back into the ocean. After watching for a while, the old man approached her. "Save your energy," he counseled. He swept his hand across the expanse. "All these are gonna die as the sun rises. You can't possibly make a difference." The young girl smiled and picked up another starfish, "I can for this one." She tossed it back in the ocean. The old man shook his

head from side to side and smiled. Then he bent to pick up a starfish himself. What the hell, he thought.

Okay, I know that sounds even mushier than the original. But I like it because it suits me. There are those who will make a big difference in the world, but for me, if I leave the world just a little better than how I found it, progress will be made. I don't have the temperament for macrocosmic efforts. I have no ambition to do great things. I'd much rather be George Bailey than George Washington.

I am not being disingenuous. I don't want the pressure or the scrutiny. I liked writing my own curriculum and being in control of my own classroom. I liked being a head coach. I like what I'm doing right now: writing this essay. I value my independence. Trying to have a major social presence doesn't fit my personality.

That being said, I am enticed by the notion of tipping the scale. The Butterfly Effect in chaos theory posits that the flap of a butterfly's wings in Brazil eventually becomes a tornado in Texas. In short, little things now can have a huge impact later.

In the classroom, this is the Teachable Moment Effect. One philosophic discussion in my classroom about the absurdity of man's inhumanity to man alters the trajectory of one of my student's lives just enough to, ten years down the line, have her hug her child instead of spank him. The 6:00 a.m. five-mile loop I make my cross country runners do every Wednesday (in addition to their regular after school workout) teaches just enough about work ethic to help one of them get the promotion that will benefit both him and his fledgling family.

Trusting that if I do simple things well, some good will come of it, gives me hope. This becomes especially important when shit happens—in my life or in the world—that just blows my mind, and I think, questioning myself and my God, "Why?"

The Parable of the Starfish, my version, is meant for average women and men working to survive an apparently desperate situation with their hope still intact. What then are the primary lessons of this version?

Frequently, the shit hits the fan. Storms strike. Crises inevitably arrive. The situation appears desperate.

In those moments, shift from the macrocosm you can't control to the microcosm you can. Don't see the beach. See the starfish in front of you.

Act. Do Something. Don't just accept things "as nature intended."

Start small and grow by setting a positive example. Don't try to lead. Just do what you think is right. If it is right, others will join you, in action by doing what they think is right, or in principle by learning something from your example.

Don't be afraid to build on someone else's example.

Applying these lessons over the course of my career helped me continue to see teaching as more than "just a freaking job."

(3)

The Lesson of the Lake

I ORIGINALLY LEARNED THE Lesson of the Lake when I was a seven-year-old in pool safety class at

Oakton Pool in Skokie, Illinois. Oakton was a beautiful, spacious facility with two pools. The first was shaped like a large L. The foot of the L was only three feet deep and designated for wading and little kids. The stem or length of the L was 25 yards long and wide enough for six lanes. At the base, it too was three feet deep, but it gradually deepened to five feet at the top.

The second pool was a square, forty-by-forty-foot perimeter, twelve-foot-deep diving well. There were three diving boards along the west edge. The outside two were 1-meter springboards. The inside one was the high dive, an impressive 3-meter springboard that didn't look that high from the ground but would definitely squeeze your sphincter from up top.

Children under seven were not allowed in either the diving well or the deep end of the main pool. They were relegated to the "baby section" and had to be supervised by an adult family member. Children seven and over who had passed pool safety class had free rein of both pools (including the right-of-passage privilege of jumping off the high dive).

To gain that independence, one summer morning, three young boys and four young girls stood shoulder to shoulder like soldiers at parade rest, our hands clasped behind our backs, our feet toeing the line made by an expansion joint splitting the concrete deck.

Pool safety class was taught by two high school-aged lifeguards, Ted and Jenny. They both had the rounded shoulders and chiseled core of accomplished swimmers. They towered over the seven of us and spent the first few moments circling our little line in a slow, deliberate stroll. We stood silent, staring straight ahead, squinting at the morning sun glinting off the pool water. Ted took the lead while Jenny served as both enforcer and, paradoxically, comic relief. While he talked, she glared at us like a drill sergeant, standing with her arms folded and her muscles flexed, her body cut like a superhero's beneath her skintight, Red Cross, one-piece swimsuit.

Ted started with a rudimentary review of basic pool hygiene and etiquette. "Always take a shower before coming on deck," he reminded us. "Clean yourself! Use soap! Don't just dash through the water. And . . ." He hesitated before lowering his voice and snarling in a hushed tone that forced us to strain to hear him, "wash between your toes!" He froze, and we held our breath.

"SPREAD 'EM!" Jenny barked, and we all jumped.

I looked at the kid next to me, both of us wondering if she meant for us to do so now or if she was just being rhetorical. At Oakton Pool, the staff made a big deal about cleaning between your toes. A guard sat immediately outside the locker rooms. Every time a kid like me came on deck, the guard made sure I was wet and told me to bend down and spread my toes to make sure I wasn't carrying any toe jam, slime, or fungus onto the deck.[51]

I looked up at Jenny for a clue as to whether she was being literal—I was ready to do whatever she commanded—but she was looking at Ted, her face a stern mask, so I stopped my slow squat toward my toes and stood straight up.

---

51 I eventually learned to spread my toes without using my fingers (this meant I didn't have to bow down before the guard), a dexterity I developed at Oakton Pool over the next several summers and still possess today.

Ted continued his tutelage. "No running on deck! No splashing! No HORSEPLAY!"

At this Jenny whinnied aggressively and then flapped her lips, her eyes bulging, and her head shuddering side to side. She never cracked a smile, her feet stayed planted, her arms firmly crossed. Only her head moved as she perfectly parodied a wild stallion. Ted acknowledged her aside with only a slight pause in his delivery and continued unruffled.

They were good, very good, and I was impressed. I was terrified, amused, and befuddled. They had my undivided attention.

After he had finished the basics, Ted presented us with a scenario. "Pretend all the lifeguards happened to be on break at the same time. That would never happen, but just pretend. Picture it in your mind."

"Okay, I'll play along," I thought. I liked these two. I closed my eyes and tried to imagine a guard-less pool. I tilted my chin up to the sun to help me concentrate. It worked. I slipped into day-dream mode which is probably why Ted picked me out of that small audience of 2nd and 3rd graders. He slid in front of me.

"Well?" he asked. I had missed some question he had posited and was, therefore, dumb. Jenny glared, and I waited for her to kick my ass.

"Okay," Ted conceded, demonstrating a very mature patience for a seven-year-old's attention span. "Now, I repeat." He leaned into my bubble. "What would you (demonstrative pause and point at me) do, if you saw her (demonstrative pause and point at the redheaded 3rd grader standing next to me—her name was Eileen) drowning in that (demonstrative pause and point at the diving well) pool?"

I froze. I looked at Eileen, over at Jenny, back at Ted. Was this a trick question?

"I'd," I stumbled, "I'd jump in to get her?" I framed this as a question, not because I doubted its accuracy, but because it seemed to me such an obvious answer. Of course I'd jump in to get her.

"No!" he snapped into my face. "Never!" He took a step back so he could address the whole group. "Never jump in the water to save a drowning person. In their panic, they'll drown you too."

I smiled at Eileen and she at me. Her freckles blushed, and she shrugged as if to say, "Sorry, but that's probably true. I'd drown you." I thought so as well.

"First," Ted continued, "call for help—get an adult, or if another kid is there, send them to get help."

Jenny chimed in, pointing out various safety items on the deck as she spoke, "In the meantime, throw a life preserver, reach with a pole, or toss a rope." She paused. "And don't forget to hold on to one end of the rope!" She wasn't joking; we were just kids, after all.

She went on, pointing to things we took for granted that could be useful in an emergency: "Use a towel, or a shirt, or a few shirts quickly tied together, but NEVER, EVER, jump in the water to save someone!"

Jenny moved in front of me and squatted to my height, locking my eyes with hers. "Jumping in to save her," her eyes glanced to Eileen then back to me, "might seem like the right thing to do, but it's not. Get help. Don't try to be a hero."

In the movies, after she spoke, she would have tousled my hair or given me a playful punch on the chin, but she didn't. She stood up, and that lesson was over.[52]

Twenty-five years later, I lived what those two lifeguards had taught me, and that became the Lesson of the Lake, one of the anecdotes I told my high school English classes to get them thinking about how to save a life.

My wife has three siblings who all live relatively close to us in the suburbs of Chicago. Each summer, we'd dedicate at least one Sunday to getting together en masse with her family, including spouses, children (my own four, plus seven nieces and nephews), and a few friends who were family as well. My wife's parents had died a few years before—her mother of cancer, her father of heart disease—and these scheduled gatherings were meant to slow the inevitable drift that occurs in all families once the matriarch and the patriarch pass.

This particular summer, my wife's oldest brother organized for us to do a beach outing to Crystal Lake (the actual lake, just outside the town of the same name). Located northwest of Chicago in McHenry County, Crystal Lake is shaped like a russet potato, a little over a mile long and a little under a half-mile wide. The main beach is at the top of the tater and is an ideal spot for family gatherings.

My wife's oldest brother's family arrived first. They settled on the edge of the grassy picnic area, away from an umbrella of trees, but adjacent to the beach. A steady

---

52   Years later when I saw the movie *The Sandlot* I knew exactly what Michael "Squints" Palledorous felt for Wendy Peffercorn.

trickle of relatives and friends followed. My family arrived last, about a half hour late.

We, the adults working together, set up our grills and circled five picnic benches as close to the water as permitted; food and drink were not allowed on the beach itself. From our spot, we could supervise the young cousins—who immediately sought the water—and still interact with each other.

Over the next few hours, the adults talked, cooked, talked, and ate. The kids played in the sand and shallow water, splashing, screaming, sunning. They trudged away from the shore only when ordered to *Eat something*, then wolfed down a dog or burger and a hand full of chips before racing each other back to the beach.

After lunch and the requisite cleanup, my wife, a friend of the family named JT, and I decided to swim out to a floating platform where the three older cousins were playing king-of-the-raft. The raft was no more than sixty yards offshore, the first twenty or so of which were shallow enough to wade. The three of us started out, sploshing just past our waists, our arms lifted, hands tapping the surface, before beginning the relaxed swim into water well above our heads.

The cousins, seeing the old guard approaching, dove off the raft and headed in.

Forty yards is not far to swim, especially if I'm going slow. But open water is a terrifying environment. Once I go deep, once I'm over my head, I am committed. If I run out of energy, if I need to stop to rest, I sink. There are no time-outs; there is no opportunity to catch my breath. Even treading water takes effort.

And the biggest threat isn't even the water. It's the panic that sucks me under.

Though we started together, the three of us soon separated. I arrived first and climbed up onto the raft to watch the others approach. My wife was doing fine; she enjoyed swimming her slow, flat strokes, taking her time. I could tell, however, that JT was struggling. He was ten years older than my wife and me, and to be blunt, not very athletic. He started out swimming with decent form, but gradually degenerated into a doggy paddle and sidestroke hybrid. After each stroke or two he'd pop his head up, forward rather than to the side, and gulp for air. I stood up and waved him forward, "Go slow. Take your time." My wife arrived, climbed the ladder, and stood beside me.

Ten yards from the raft, JT stopped swimming and started treading water. He spun his head around, trying to gauge distances. He couldn't go back, and he convinced himself—I knew this when he bit into his bottom lip—that he couldn't make it forward. I could see his eyes ballooning, fear stripping away logic.

"Shit," I said aloud.

JT closed his eyes, stopped treading, and slipped under. He burst back through the surface, whirling his arms, spinning himself in a circle. I scanned the raft for a rope or a towel or anything, but there was nothing I could use to help. He was too far away anyhow.

"JT!" I called to him. "Keep swimming. C'mon. You got it."

He snapped in my direction, then turned his head up toward the open sky, mouth gaping, eyes bulging and vacant. His hands started slapping the surface of the water trying to push himself up and out. He was burning through any strength he had left, and I worried, despite the crystal clarity of the water, that if he went under, I'd lose him in the darkened depths. I dove off the raft.

I came up a few feet to the side of him. Water gurgled from his mouth, and again, he stopped fighting and slid down. His eyes, open, touched the surface of the water, and I reached out to grab his arm. That's when he saw me and lunged, latching on to my wrist and dragging me toward him. I stiff-armed him away, "Get Back!"

He clawed up my arm with both hands, scratching, breaking the skin, grabbing for my shoulders, pulling my hair, whatever he could grasp to lift himself out of the water.

"Goddammit, JT!"

He may have been older and wiser, but I was a lot stronger. I held him back with my left arm, coiled my right fist, and popped him on the jaw. I heard my wife gasp from behind me. I didn't knock him out or do serious damage, but I stunned him enough to freeze him. He let go, and instead of pushing him away, I now drew him in. I spun him on his back, wrapped my right arm around his neck, hooked my fingers into his left armpit, and sidestroked to the raft.

Just trying to survive, he would have drowned us both if he could have; he had no idea what he was doing.

In the few moments it took to get to the ladder, he recovered, his panic subsided, and, to my and my wife's amazement, when we arrived and I let him go, he climbed onto the raft as if nothing extraordinary had happened, as if he himself had swum the whole way alone. I looked down at the scratch marks on my forearm and wanted to pop him again, just as a reminder, but I didn't.

In English class, after I share this anecdote with my students, cautioning them to never—literally and metaphorically—jump in the water to save a drowning person, some kind-hearted skeptic always chimes in, "But you did dive in the water! You did save him!"

Not quite. I didn't blindly dive off that raft. I knew what I was doing when I went in; I knew the risk for me was minimal because I was bigger, stronger, and more than willing to pop him if I had to. If he hadn't settled enough for me to approach him, for me to help him, I would have let him drown. At least I think I would have, I don't know for sure.

I do know that if the situation had been reversed, if I had been the one panicking and drowning, he would have been a fool to dive in and try to rescue me. I would have killed both of us.

The nightmare I envision is if, instead of me, my ten-year-old son had been the one on that raft, and I had been trapped on the beach yelling advice. I would have screamed, "Talk to him Mike, encourage him, tell him it's not far, try to help, but DON'T YOU DARE JUMP IN THAT FUCKING WATER!"

(4)

Simplify

I TITLED THIS ESSAY "Survival" because I turned to the principles of safe zones, starfish, and the lesson of the lake throughout my career to help me survive.

When I felt I was losing control, when frustration or despair were trying to take hold, I took a step back and tried to simplify things: make sure my classroom is a safe zone; act, do something, while focusing on what is right in front of me; toss out plenty of life preservers, but don't jump in the water.[53]

Often, the bigger the problem, the more important it is to start small. That type of thinking kept me sane. I consistently reminded myself not to try and do too much. I wanted to do the simple things I could, to do them well enough, and to survive to the end of my entire career still caring and still trying to make a difference.

---

[53] One example. During my last year teaching, one of my student's apartment caught fire. She lived with her mother and most of their possessions were destroyed. The apartment was uninhabitable, and they were left homeless. I, along with many others, donated money to put them up at a motel until they could get organized and to buy clothes and other essentials to replace what they had lost. My wife and I were empty nesters at the time, and we had two open bedrooms. I thought about inviting my student and her mother to live with us until they found another apartment, but I didn't. That would have been jumping in the water. That wasn't my place. I was her *teacher*.

CHAPTER 16

A HEALTHY DOSE OF SKEPTICISM (x3)

(1)

A Fish Story

I TAUGHT FRESHMEN PREP English at Proviso East High School during the 1987-88 school year. At the time, Proviso East, located in Maywood, Illinois, was 95% Black and 76% at-risk. I mention these stats to give the following anecdote context.

One of the books we read in Freshmen Prep English class was *Treasure Island*, the classic Robert Louis Stevenson tale of pirates and adventure. Written in 1883, the novel is a staple of the "old dead white guys" literary canon. It is written by a Scotsman, takes place in England during the 1700s, and has no characters of color. Today, that might be noteworthy, and I would no doubt wonder why we were not teaching something more inclusive. At the time, however, there was no question. I taught *Treasure Island* because that was what the curriculum guide said to teach and because those were the books on the shelf in the book room. I focused on the content and taught this novel to these students to the best of my ability.

In fact, the novel was right in their wheelhouse. Most of my students' reading levels fell within the 3rd to 5th grade range, hence their designation as "prep."[54] *Treasure Island* has a 3rd grade reading level and a 6th to 9th grade interest level, and the story *is* interesting. Most of the mystique about pirates comes from this novel: buried treasure on remote tropical islands, maps marked with an X, the cursed Black Spot, and the one-legged pirate with a talking parrot perched on his shoulder.

The universal themes of Search for Identity, Loss of Innocence, and Man's Inhumanity to Man (in this case, as driven by greed) are relevant to any adolescent. The main character, young Jim Hawkins, is a pretty average and likeable lad both boys and girls can appreciate. He's thirteen or fourteen, on the cusp of adulthood. He has spent his life hearing of the *outside world*—his parents own an inn on the English coast frequented by sailors—but he has yet to experience this dangerously compelling world for himself.

The death of his father and some subsequent quirky occurrences present him the opportunity to gain that yearned-for experience. His adventure is a philosophic coming-of-age journey that teaches him, primarily, about the corrupting forces of greed. Our class focused on that aspect of Jim's education: what he learns about

---

[54] Still, what exactly they were prepping for I never found out because the prep level went through 12th grade—aptly called Senior Prep English—and too many of these students never left it. What could you be prepping for if you were still prepping when you graduated?

getting quick money and how the characters in pursuit and in possession of that quick money ultimately suffer.

I didn't present the text as a cautionary tale or as a metaphor for the quick money to be found in gangs and drugs, a common panacea for despair. I left that association unstated. My students couldn't read at grade level, but they were socially and emotionally acute. They got the point without me sticking it in their faces. By not moralizing, I made the book something they could identify with, not agonize over.

I gave the students a study guide to review before and to complete after each reading. The goal was not to test the students. It was to give them things to think about while they read. My assumption was that they would read, so I felt no need to grade their answers. Sometimes I had the students read at home and then complete the study guide—in small groups—together in class. Other times we read together in class, and they completed the study guide on their own at home, to be discussed the next day. If a student didn't read or complete the study guide, he or she was simply left out of the conversation.

The study guide questions were shaped by my 4 Level approach to analyzing literature.[55] I tried to give my students ways to conceptualize each question as being Literal, Metaphoric, Philosophic, or Aesthetic. Literal Level questions require simple recall; Metaphoric questions challenge students to "see beyond the obvious" and dig for symbolic meaning; Philosophic questions focus on aspects of human nature examined

---

55 See Burke's website for more on the 4 Level Analysis/Individual Art Assignment.

by the text; Aesthetic questions look for beauty: what stirs your (the reader's) emotions?

For example, in pursuit of treasure and guided by an X on a map, the pirates in the story dig a hole and find . . . nothing. The hole is empty. On a Literal level, the hole is a hole and empty means there's nothing in it.

Metaphorically, the hole represents the futility of their pursuit. Even if they find the treasure (which they don't), their lives will remain empty and meaningless. On a symbolic level, the hole in their lives can never be filled by what Greed[56] might bring.

The Philosophic message: Greed doesn't give life value. Greed can't fill the holes in our lives, at least not the ones that matter. We discuss this aspect of human nature as presented by the text, then I ask my students to *Be a Filter, Not a Funnel*: Do you agree? Can money or power make us happy? Does what Greed yields ever "fill" us? I want them to question what the novel implies. For most literature, this level, the Philosophic, is the most important. What does the novel say about human beings, and do I (the reader) agree? Through this work, what can I learn about myself and others?

Finally, on an Aesthetic level, does this scene (the pirates staring into an empty hole) stir your emotions? Does it make you feel anything? If so, what and why?

I helped my students through this process, but I never told them how to react on the Philosophic or Aesthetic levels. They were free to think and feel, honestly.

We had many teachable moments, and by the end of the unit most of the students had (1) read the entire

---

56   I explained to the students that I used a capital "G" in Greed to personify it; the Greed in the novel has a life all its own.

novel; (2) enjoyed their reading; (3) learned how to apply the 4 Level Analysis; and (4) extracted some good philosophic concepts to think about. Again, I didn't try to make the lessons "life-changing"; I just threw the concepts out there and let the students decide what each found useful.

On our last day of reading, as we closed the text, I saw in some of my students' eyes the slight, moistened glow that every teacher dreams of. My students had done and learned something valuable, and I was the reason for it. Their faith in me was spiking. I had made a difference. So, instead of soaking up their admiration, I chose to pull their legs a little. I couldn't help it.

Spoiler alert. At the end of the novel, one of the main characters, Long John Silver, the cook on the pirate ship and an individual with whom young Jim Hawkins has had a most complex relationship, escapes with a few bags of gold and is never seen again. He is the only pirate to avoid consequence. The audience accepts this as just because, despite his often despicable behavior, Silver has been kind to Jim.

Long John Silver's also happens to be the name of a Midwest fast-food chain known for inexpensive seafood and battered fish and chips. Long John Silver's has a very popular location nearby in the heart of Maywood. Such synchronicity shouldn't be ignored.

"The interesting follow-up to the novel," I tell my students with rich earnestness and sincerity, "is what happens to Long John Silver and the legacy that lives on to today." I pause to nod in affirmation on the cusp of my profound revelation.

"Long John Silver learned a valuable lesson about quick money. Instead of blowing his bag of coins, he traveled up the coast of England and, following the lead of Jim's family business, opened what became a very popular inn. His inn focused on the two foods pirates eat the most: fish and bread. However, instead of preparing these separately, as everyone else did, he blended them together and is credited with inventing breaded fish, fish sticks, and the fish sandwich."

This all makes perfect sense to the students. Long John Silver, though fallible, is one of the few heroic characters in the novel; they want to know he turned out okay. So, I add the pièce de resistance: "When he died, Silver passed the inn on to his daughter, who passed the inn on to her son, who moved to America and turned the idea into a restaurant and then built more restaurants that were passed on to his children and their children, all of which eventually became today's Long John Silver's restaurant chain!"

As I mentioned before, we have one right in the neighborhood, just a few blocks from our classroom. The students are ecstatic; they have a practical connection to this novel! I nod and smile, "Part of the recipe for that delicious, breaded fish you enjoy on All-You-Can-Eat Sundays traces back to the original Long John Silver." I pause to let this all settle in.

I have always been an effective bullshitter, and the students take the story hook, line, and sinker. And why not, the teacher they have newfound trust in has told them all this in most convincing detail.

While they smile and salivate imagining a tasty fish sandwich slathered in tartar sauce, I go to the board and write the word FICTION in capital letters. This was 1987. I was young, and new to Proviso East, and trying to show off, so I did what inexperienced teachers sometimes do. I tried to force another teachable moment on top of the perfectly fine one we were enjoying. I fucked this whole situation up by overdoing it. I had bonded with my class, and even the practical joke at the end would have been okay if I hadn't overplayed it, if I hadn't tried to force in some bullshit point about "fiction."[57]

What I *should have done* is write the equivalent of "JK LOL" on the board (unfortunately text-speak did not yet exist). Even writing this now, I realize I sounded like such a pedantic asshole. Not one of my better moments. What I *did* was point to the word in capital letters on the board and turn to my class.

"What is fiction?"

"Something made up." A young man answers.

"Something made up." I repeat. "Something not true. Never happened. It's just a *story*."

I pick up a copy of *Treasure Island* and hold the cover out for the class to see. "What is *Treasure Island*?"

There's a pregnant pause. "Fiction." The same young man answers.

"Which means?"

"It never happened." There is an audible suck of air from the room.

"So what about the story I just told you about the restaurant?"

---

57   The point about recognizing what is fiction is valid; the timing and tone of my delivery of this point is what was bullshit.

A young lady, her chin tucked to her collarbone, glares at me behind raised eyebrows. "Fiction," she grunts, and curls her lips into her teeth as if she just sucked a lemon.

"Fiction," I repeat (oblivious to the fact that she probably would have slapped my cheek if she were close enough to me) and point to the word on the board. "But I want to go deep for a second."

I know I'm going way over their heads, but that's okay. We have all year to think about this. "In this class," I continue, "I want you to think in principle about the value of stories because every story *is* part fiction and part truth. Behind all the fiction, every story has a philosophic message that is true to someone, and if we can figure out what that message is, we can decide whether or not that message is true, or even relevant, for us as well."

"As far as Long John Silver's," I smile and playfully admonish them, "if something sounds too amazing to be true, it probably is. *Be a Filter, Not a Funnel.* Maintain a healthy dose of skepticism. Don't be afraid to raise an eyebrow now and then."

A few of the students lean back in their desks and concede: You got us. They get it: Don't be a sucker.[58]

A few are pissed off: You lied to us. Teachers shouldn't do that.

The bell rings.

One of my students, a female, not the one who grunted "Fiction" earlier, waits for me after class. As everyone else leaves, she stands in front of my desk

---

[58] If you're thinking I should have bought a few dozen Long John Silver's fish sandwiches that I could now pass out to the students, yes, that would have helped.

staring at me with her arms defiantly bear-hugging her books. The room empties. I wait for her to speak. She can't; she seethes.

"Tamika?" I ask. I am standing behind my desk gathering some materials before heading to my next class.

She growls through her clenched teeth, reining in her anger and her pain, "You made us look stupid."

My first reaction is defensive and typical of my worst-case-scenario impulsiveness: I think about perception, about parent phone calls, about meetings with the division head and the principal. I see the headline that will end my career (this was my first year at Proviso and my first year teaching in a public high school; I had neither equity nor tenure): "Pretentious White Teacher from the University of Notre Dame[59] Flaunts his Academic Superiority over Young Black Students." I will be released at the end of the year which will essentially blackball me from any other public school job. I can't afford to teach at a private school—the pay just isn't enough to support my growing family—so that will be that.

Except, that isn't what I was doing. Though I fucked up the delivery, I wasn't flaunting, and I wasn't trying to make anyone look stupid. I was teaching about literature and about life, about the value of stories and the need for a little skepticism. It's okay for students to feel a little stupid if it eventually makes them smarter, right? Thankfully, I have enough commonsense to pause and collect myself before responding too defensively.

---

59   How do you know if a person you just met graduated from Notre Dame? Wait ten seconds; they'll tell you.

I admire Tamika. She is one of my best students. I sit down in my chair so as not to tower over her 4'11" frame. I do this by design to show my appreciation and my respect. I want us to see eye-to-eye.

"Tamika, I would never try to make anyone look stupid. But sometimes I have to, well, mess with people to help them learn. My main point is about stories. You heard what I said. I know you get that point."

She nods, barely perceptible.

"As far as the restaurant story, I'd say I was just kidding, but I wasn't. I want you guys to always be a little skeptical, to never trust anyone too much or too soon. A teacher. A coach. A friend."

Smiling, I add, "Especially a *boy*friend." She doesn't react, not the way I hoped. She sucks her bottom lip, biting into the flesh. My face flushes, and my commonsense screams at me: Stop trying to be fucking funny!

"Trust is built over time," I say, "but even then, like I said in class, you need to maintain that healthy dose of skepticism." I know I'm rambling, so I stop. I stand. I have another class to get to. But I wait on her honor.

She looks up at me, now pursing her lips and shaking her head, questioning what I've said, but her eyes have softened and she's no longer squeezing the life out of her books.

"Thanks." I tell her. "Thank you for having the courage to talk to me directly."

She concedes, still a little upset and still a little hurt, but willing to stay her conviction for the moment. She wants to peel one hand free and prod her index finger at me, like a schoolmarm rebuking a petulant child, but she doesn't. Instead, in her mind, she carefully edits out most of what she would like to say.

"Tomorrow, Mr. Burke," is all she advises. My second chance. She heads to the door and then pauses, composed, and, sneaking in one final glare, repeats, "Tomorrow."

"Tomorrow, Tamika," I say.

I may be a pit bull when I think I'm right, but I've learned that a mea culpa when I've screwed up works much better than doubling down on my own stupidity. I didn't have the brains or the balls to just apologize that day (or to be concise), but I made my best effort over the rest of that year to regain the trust of Tamika, and my Freshmen Prep English class. I didn't stop joking with them; that would have diminished my teaching ability and weakened our relationship. And that wasn't the problem. The problem was what Tamika so clearly articulated: she thought I was trying to make her look stupid. I needed to be sure that was never the case.

(2)

Fred Newton

This class made me feel so smart and so stupid, often at the same time, that I almost couldn't take it. —Student comment, 2016 APLAC End-of-Year Survey

Do you have APness? —Front slogan of student-designed APLAC shirt, 2014

OVER THE LAST DECADE or so of my career, I taught 11th Grade AP English Language and Composition (APLAC) at Wheeling High School. I wrote the curriculum for this class, and I designed it to accomplish a number of goals.

First, I needed to prepare students for the APLAC exam at the end of the school year. I am not one to teach to a test. However, I didn't mind doing so here since the analytical and rhetorical skills needed to pass this test are essential to being a critical thinker.[60] If I can't both present and deconstruct arguments, I can't fully participate in a democratic society.

Second, I wanted to teach students about American Literature. In most high schools, "average" students study American Literature during their junior years. However, in too many high schools, if students take APLAC, they miss out on American Literature because the course focuses solely on prepping for the AP Exam. I didn't want my students to miss out on American Lit. More important, I didn't want to miss out on teaching my students American Lit.

Third, I wanted to parallel the AP US History (APUSH) class most of my students also took. To accomplish this, I chose to organize the literary analysis units around philosophic periods linked to American history. I sat down with the APUSH teachers before each school year to be sure our syllabi aligned as often as possible.

Fourth, and most important, I wanted to blow my students' minds. I seriously wanted to mess with

---

60 By contrast, the "skills" needed to score well on the ACT or SAT tests are useless for much other than passing standardized tests.

their heads, in a good way. I had a big sign in the front of my class reading, "Seek Thyself!" That's the primary reason why I structured the class around philosophic periods. I wanted to use literature to introduce different philosophic outlooks, to help my students understand that there are many ways to approach or consider our reality.

I broke the year into eight units. We covered Classicism, Rationalism, Transcendentalism, Dark Romanticism, Realism, Naturalism, Existentialism, and general Absurdity. I kicked off each of these units with "board notes" to introduce the overarching philosophy of the period, the key historical events,[61] and the authors and works we would read over the next three to four weeks. However, instead of conveniently organizing everything, I scattered brief sets of tidbits and teasers, in no particular order, across the whiteboard at the front of the classroom. Picture a refrigerator door tacked with a few dozen different colored Post-it notes randomly smacked up here and there; each Post-it contains an important hint or clue, but nothing is complete, and there is no discernible pattern.

I learned early in my career that the easier I made it on my students, the less they would pay attention to what I was actually teaching, and the less they learned. Therefore, I started—at times, not always—purposefully

---

61 I need to note that though we followed the chronology of American history, I didn't limit the literature of each unit to that period. For example, the Rationalism Unit had the subtitle, "Violence versus Nonviolence: Managing Conflict in a Just Society." We began the Unit with Ben Franklin, Patrick Henry, and Thomas Paine; but then integrated Thoreau, Gandhi, and MLK; before comparing articles by Elie Wiesel and Arthur Miller; and closing with Spike Lee's film, *Do The Right Thing*.

being unclear or difficult to follow to force my students to advocate for themselves: to ask me to slow down or to clarify or repeat some point.

I'm going to be deliberately redundant here. I did not use a PowerPoint or well-organized handout to deliver my unit notes. I knew if I did, students wouldn't listen to my added and essential commentary and would simply work as fast as they could to jot down all the information listed in the PowerPoint, or, worse, assume the handout had all the answers and just space out.[62]

In my system, the students had to stay actively engaged: they had to listen to me, visually follow me, *and* take notes for 45 straight minutes. My tidbits and teasers style meant my students had little idea what each set meant until I added essential details. The randomness meant the students had no idea where I would start or finish, so they couldn't get out in front of me. I would jump from set to set and point out why these concepts or individuals were important to the works and philosophy we'd be discussing during the unit. Using a variety of colored markers, I jotted extra notes on the board, drew arrows linking ideas, circled key words or phrases.

It was an ADHD student's dream and an OCD/anal retentive's nightmare.

---

62 When the visual aid becomes more important to the presentation than the speaker, the speaker should be eliminated. Just send me the PowerPoint and save the redundancy of your reading it to me. How many institute days have I endured where an administrator reads a PowerPoint packed with data, written in a font no one can decipher from the auditorium seats, in a meeting lasting over an hour? I long for an administrator who can model excellent pedagogy on an institute day.

I always added a few puns and a little bit of bullshit to make sure students were thinking about the notes they were taking instead of just mimicking stenographers. For example, one of the sets I saved for the end of my lesson introducing our second unit on Rationalism and the American Revolution deals with key scientific revolutionaries of the period, including Sir Isaac Newton.

My "teasers and tidbits" list for Newton looks like this:

Isaac Newton
3 Laws
God Watches—Pun!
Illegitimate Brother Fred

PRIOR TO MY EXPLANATION, no student knows what each clue means. After, or eventually (some of this might not become clear until much later in the school year), everything should make sense.

For this set, I start with Newton's 3 Laws of Motion, focusing on the first law: *unless acted upon by another force, an object at rest tends to stay at rest and an object in motion tends to stay in motion;* and the third law: *for every action there is an equal and opposite reaction.* I tell my students that I've referenced the first law in every sport I've coached; it sounds cool to quote Newton while reminding badminton players to keep their feet moving between shots. The third law is referenced in Vonnegut's *Slaughterhouse-Five*, a novel we'll read at the end of the year. Both laws apply more to life than to physics, I tell them, especially when it comes to managing relationships, something we will discuss further later.

Many of our founding fathers were more Deist than Christian, including Thomas Jefferson, Ben Franklin, and Thomas Paine. Deists believe that God created the universe and then stepped back to let it run. God gives us everything we need to be successful; now it is up to us.

The "God Watches—Pun" alludes to the following extended metaphor for Deism attributed to Isaac Newton, himself a Deist: God is the master clock maker; the universe is the clock he made; once finished, he sat back to watch, though he does tinker from time to time. Why does he mostly watch and not get more involved? Because he's God, he built the universe to work, he gave us everything we need right here.

Most of the students I have are either Christian or Jewish or Muslim. They believe in a God actively engaged in the daily affairs of humankind. Deism challenges these students to contemplate a supreme being who leaves most of our fate up to us (a stark contrast from the predestination-focused Puritans we studied in our previous unit). The good news is: we're in control. The bad news is: we can neither blame God nor ask God for help. We're pretty much on our own. What God did give us is the clock itself; so, we can study its workings—in other words, scientific laws and principles—to help us along.

In my board notes, the pun I included brings a little humor: God is a clockmaker who "watches." I re-emphasize it before moving on. This helps ease some tension. (These puns worked better as I got older: I was not some young goof trying to be funny; I was a father-figure telling dad jokes.)

However, despite my levity, many of the students now have the bleary-eyed stare of minds on overload. The notes on Newton's laws and Deism are just a fraction of what I've introduced to them.[63] We've hit some pretty deep concepts and covered a lot of detail in a very short amount of time. The students are taking water through a firehose. They are writing down whatever I tell them, as fast as they can, just hoping to survive a few more minutes until the bell at the end of the period.

So, I choose this moment to shift from scientific and philosophic revolutionaries to one famous for culinary innovation. I point to the last item in this set (and the final notes of the day): Illegitimate Brother Fred.

Isaac Newton, I inform them, had an illegitimate brother named Fred. Fred wasn't much into physics, mathematics, or astronomy like his more famous half-sibling. However, like Ben Franklin, he was an inventor. In fact, he developed a process by which mashed dates were wrapped in pressed cookie dough. Later he switched from dates to figs—I write FIG on the board—because figs have a crunchier texture due to hundreds of tiny seeds (and a few wasp thoraxes) inside. This crunchier texture contrasts delectably with the smoother consistency of the cookie dough.

Isaac Newton's illegitimate brother Fred gifted us a rather tasty treat! Here I pause and wait, pointing to

---

63 All the concepts introduced will be revisited and fleshed out as the unit and the year progresses.

the word "Fig" and then the word "Newton" until some perceptive student shouts "Fig Newtons!"

Many of the students are ecstatic. We are nearing the end of class, and this is the first detail of my entire lecture they can understand and relate to. Finally, they've learned something that makes some sense. The bell rings. They smile as they pack up their notes, and they head off to their next classes thinking, "Hmmm. When was the last time I had a Fig Newton?"

I don't have the heart to tell them I had made it all up just to bust their balls; the few students who saw through my ruse don't have the heart to either. So, we let them believe, for now. I even include a question about Fred on the unit exam.

Later in the year, as my students learn to recognize when I am toying with their gullibility, I leak that poor Isaac did not have an illegitimate brother, who in turn did not invent the Fig Newton. A few students bow their heads at this revelation, saddened that their God has allowed such deception, but, perhaps, a little wiser for the wear.

I do share with them two facts about Fig Newtons (I swear):

First, Fig Newtons (now, just "Newtons") are named after the town of Newton, Massachusetts, not after Sir Isaac.

Second, due to the miracle of symbiotic reproduction there is a little wasp—providing essential fiber—in every fig. The female fig wasp burrows into a fig to lay her eggs. In doing so, she is stripped of her wings and antenna and rendered immobile. After laying the eggs, she dies. The eggs hatch and immediately mate in an incestuous orgy. Afterward, the wingless male wasps tunnel out of the fig and convene on a nearby leaf to talk politics and smoke cigars (actually, they tunnel out and die). The impregnated females escape through those tunnels and fly off to find new figs in which to lay their eggs, thus spreading fig pollen and perpetuating the life cycle of each species. Pretty good stuff.

(3)

Spills

MY WIFE AND I used to host a Burke-family get-together each New Year's Day. The families who could make it would meet at our house to celebrate the holidays. A few years ago, I started messing with my grand-nephew and my grand-niece. Gerard was four and Aella[64] was seven.

I am watching football in the family room with my wife, some siblings and their spouses, and a few older cousins. The younger kids are all havocking in the basement.

At some point, Gerard comes up to grab some snacks off the coffee table in front of me. After he snarfs down a Donkey Chip (the best tortilla chips) loaded with his grandmother's spicy taco dip, I point to his shirt, my forefinger touching a spot at the top of his sternum.

"You spilled," I tell him.

---

64 The name Aella (EYE-ell-uh) means tempest or whirlwind. In Greek mythology, she is an Amazon warrior. Her parents named my niece Aella because she was a terror in the womb; once she started moving, she rarely rested, continually punching, kicking, and twisting. She wanted into this world!

When he looks down, I flick my finger up across his face and say, "Gotcha." I smile. He is befuddled. He looks at his shirt again, straining his head backwards to try and see the non-spot. Finding nothing, he puzzles at me, then shrugs and goes back to the basement.

A few minutes later Aella comes in, grabs a chip and scoops not so much dip. I pull the same trick on her, pointing at her shirt, telling her she spilled, and then flicking my finger into her face when she looks down.

"Gotcha." I smile.

She doesn't look for the non-spot. Instead, she sneers at me, huffs, and turns away. My wife of thirty-two years shakes her head and semi-snorts, wondering why I always have to be *that* guy.

A half hour later Gerard returns for more chips and dip, and I get him again. "You spilled," I say, and point to a spot just under his chin and outside his vision. He reacts with the same befuddlement, this time pulling his shirt away from his chest to find the spots that aren't there. Another shrug and back to the basement.

I kinda feel bad. He just isn't old enough yet. "You're a jackass," my wife observes. I smile and wink at her.

Then Aella comes into the room. She plucks a celery stick with her left hand and dips it in some ranch dressing. She raises it to her lips, hesitates, then takes a luscious bite. She never looks at me, and I pretend to be engrossed in the football game.

She crunches the bite, mouth open enough to allow a spit of saliva to slip onto her lower lip. The remaining half-a-celery stick she holds out in front of her like a conductor's baton. She finishes chewing, bends, double dips the half-stick, and rises to take another bite. *Chomp.*

Never averting my eyes from the TV, I nonchalantly lift a finger to her shirt. "You spil..."

Before I can get the words out, she snatches my index finger with her right hand and snaps it backward to my wrist. I slide off the couch and down to the floor, limboing under to limit her leverage, then wrench my forefinger free. Were she stronger, she might have broken it.

The little stinker: she set me up!

She stands with her feet spread, arms folded, and chin high. I am sitting on the floor, flexing my finger, assuring myself that she has *not* broken it. She stares at me, a crooked smirk mocking my stupidity. Seven years old. I lift myself back up onto the couch. She milks her victory by shaking her pointed chin at me. I smile and wag the offended finger at her.

"Smart girl," I say.

I let her gloat, then call a truce. "Come here."

I open my arms, and, after a hesitation, she comes forward and barrels into my chest, knocking us backwards into the cushions. After a brief bear hug, she plops next to me on the couch, comfortable enough with us adults to watch a football game she has no interest in. She lasts a minute or two but soon leaves, the siren of childhood laughter luring her back to the basement. I grin at no one in particular.

"You're still an ass," my wife mumbles, again shaking her head, but this time, not unable to smile.

(4)

ALL THINGS IN MODERATION, and my practical jokes—my kidding around in general—were just one tool in my teacher's toolbox. I wasn't a comedian. All the same, I did enjoy being, at times, *that* guy. I didn't want to rob anyone of their innocence, but I thought it important, occasionally, to whisk away a bit of naïveté, and, hopefully, bring a smile.

Still, I needed to be sure that, regardless of my intention, the end result was never to degrade, never to make anyone look stupid. Tamika taught me that.

CHAPTER 17

THE MASK

(1)

IN THE EARLY 1990s, as an assistant wrestling coach at Glenbard South High School, I was fortunate to help coach one of the classiest individuals I have ever met. He also became a hell of a wrestler.

As a sophomore—his first year wrestling[65]—John was an unknown commodity. His background was in judo, not wrestling. No one knew him. He won most of his matches, but he lacked the requisite experience to beat the best. In short, he was good on his feet but lacked what in wrestling are called mat skills.

Judo is competed almost exclusively on the feet with points scored by foot sweeps, trips, and hip tosses. The combatants wear a three-part *Judogi*: a heavy, canvas, long sleeve jacket; lighter canvas pants; and a cotton belt. The clothes are loose, and much of the battle is contested at close quarters with opponents fighting to secure a grip on their opponent's clothes to tug him (or her) off balance before executing a throw. The perfect throw, an *Ippon*, elevates an opponent above the hips

---

65   Folkstyle wrestling, as competed in high schools across the USA.

and slams him with significant force into the mat. This perfect throw ends the match.

Judo matches are also won with submission holds that threaten to choke out an opponent or dislocate one of his limbs. In these instances, the opponent usually "taps out" before passing out or losing an elbow joint. Matches can also be won by immobilization: holding an opponent on his back for twenty seconds.

In contrast, wrestlers wear tight, one-piece singlets with no sleeves, no pant legs, no belts. Grabbing clothes and submission holds are illegal. So are slams. Much of wrestling is fought on the mat with one wrestler on top working to control and turn his opponent while the other battles to escape or reverse position. Wrestling matches are usually won on points, but sometimes won by fall, also called a pin, because the winning wrestler pins his opponent's shoulders to the mat for three seconds.

Judo and wrestling are similar—they are both, after all, controlled forms of hand-to-hand combat—but also very different. John's judo background made him exceptional in some wrestling situations, but vulnerable in most others. The better wrestlers, and their coaches, figured this out. By the end of his sophomore season, no one would tie up with John, no one would let him get close. They went right after his legs and forced him to wrestle, not just throw. He lost to these better wrestlers and was passed off as a one-trick pony: don't let him throw and away he'll go[66].

---

66   One-trick ponies are common in wrestling, especially kids whose only real move is a hip-toss (like John) or a headlock. Take that one move away—usually by getting into their legs—and they can be beaten.

In the off-season, to catch up, John put in hours and hours of work in the weight room and at various summer wrestling camps. He got significantly better. In 1991, as his junior year progressed, he won, he kept improving, but he stayed under the radar.

At that time, the Illinois High School Association (IHSA) Class AA state championship series was conducted over three weekends. The first weekend was the Regional meet. Every school was assigned to a Regional, and every varsity wrestler—one per weight class—was eligible to compete. The top three finishers in each Regional advanced to the next weekend's Sectional meet. The top three finishers in each Sectional advanced to the final weekend's State meet. There is only one state champion in each weight class. In 1991, over 250 schools competed in the Class AA state championship series.[67] The point is, every week, the pool of qualifying wrestlers shrinks, and the competition gets more intense.

That year, John won the Regional championship. In the Sectional semifinal, he wrestled a young man who was 34-0. This sophomore did not know John, did not know anything about him, and made the mistake of letting John get inside and tie him up. The former one-trick pony went back to the well and hip-tossed this undefeated opponent into the air and onto his back for a first period pin.

John won the Sectional Championship and qualified for the IHSA State Championships at 152 pounds.

---

67   Much of this has since changed. At the time, though, Class AA was the most competitive class with the largest schools and, generally, the best wrestlers.

Despite a 38-2 record, he was not considered a favorite. He was not ranked in the top ten.

As a Sectional champion, John had a bye[68] in the first round. In the second round, John won his first match of the day, 7-2. More important, five of the other seven Sectional champions in his weight—including the three highest-rated wrestlers—lost. The tournament was now wide open. With all the favorites gone, John had a realistic shot at winning it all, and he didn't waste his opportunity. He won 7-6 in the quarterfinal and 17-7 in the semis.

In the final, he faced the same sophomore wrestler he had pinned in the Sectional semifinal. The young man had learned his lesson and wouldn't let John get inside. The match was wrestled the full six minutes: a battle, a struggle, the entire time. John won 5-3. He was an IHSA State Champion.

(2)

IT MAY BE DIFFICULT to win a championship, but it is far more difficult to defend that championship.

As a junior, John wrestled without expectation. In a sense, his state championship was won on house money; he, personally, had nothing to lose. The only pressure he felt was to work his hardest and do his job. This was the mantra both the head coach and I preached: Do your job! And what was that job?

Respect yourself. Respect your opponent. Respect the sport.

---

68 As Sectional Champion, he automatically advanced to the second round of the tournament.

Respect yourself by working your hardest: do the extra rep, run the extra lap, push not *to* but *through* the end of each period. Respect your opponent by always giving your best effort and demanding that he give his as well. Respect the sport by following the rules, exhibiting sportsmanship, and being intense (i.e. give a shit, give a BIG shit).

If you did your job, everything else will take care of itself. John had no trouble with the above pillars.

(3)

JOHN HAD WON THE State Championship his junior year as an underdog, quietly and outside the radar of most opponents and the press. Senior year, however, the game changed. He was a defending State Champion. He was ranked #1 in his weight class to start the season. No one overlooked him. The noise was constant.

In his matches, unfortunately, that notoriety too often elicited fear from his competition rather than forging mettle. Most of his opponents conceded victory before they ever stepped on the mat. They wrestled without commitment. Some sought merely to keep the match close, to gain a moral victory by not getting pinned or only losing by a few points; they stalled and blocked and stalled and blocked. Others wrestled in wild desperation, trying crazy moves or feigning a hyper-intensity to prove to everyone that *they could win!* even when everyone knew they could not. Some coaches had their athletes forfeit to avoid injury or embarrassment.

Only a few opponents showed the requisite respect for themselves, for John, and for the sport. They still lost, but they did so with honor.

John went undefeated during the regular season, but too many of his matches fulfilled an obligation rather than affirmed those pillars of respect. He was winning, but he wasn't having fun, not like he had the year before when all this winning was new. Doing his job too often withered to doing a job. Wrestling became mundane.

The challenge of the State Series could change all that. Each round of competition meant better opponents: wrestlers John had not seen during the regular season, wrestlers who would concede nothing. John was excited. This was the challenge he trained for.

The Monday before the Regional meet, John and I were drilling double-leg takedowns. A double leg takedown is pretty much a football tackle: lower your level and drive your head and shoulder into the opponent's gut while hooking your hands outside both his legs and lifting. Done with quickness and force, the move drives the opponent back onto the mat and scores a 2-point takedown. It should be noted the points awarded for a takedown have since changed.

Every good takedown begins with a good set-up, a move that gets the opponent slightly out of position or off-balance and gains you the advantage on an attack. Given his judo background, John preferred inside setups at close range: an overhook, an underhook, a shoulder pop, a head tug, an arm drag. Most of his opponents knew this but could do little to stop him. Their effort to block his inside set-up served as the very set-up he needed.

The best wrestlers, however, knew to stay away. They would circle at a distance, never letting him get close enough to feel comfortable attacking. To prepare for these opponents, toward the end of our drilling, we worked on outside setups: feinting up and down, reaching out and tapping your opponent's forehead, cutting angles side to side. We were drilling at half-speed with John trying out different setups before shooting in on my legs and taking me to the mat. I was giving reasonable resistance: sprawling back on each shot to make sure he was getting enough penetration to finish his move.

On one repetition, John faked with a short jab step to his left before diving at my legs. The fake, unfortunately, was too good. I reacted to it, not to his actual shot, and sprawled back early. Instead of him slipping under me to my legs, we collided, butting like rams, my forehead to his face.

This is not an uncommon occurrence; wrestlers bang heads often, hence their scored brows and cauliflower ears. Most times, the damage is inconsequential. This time, however, I caught John square on the bridge of his nose. I have a hard head. On impact, John's nose erupted, a thick spray of blood fanning onto the mat.

Bloody noses happen. Take your fingers and wiggle the tip of your nose (or, if you're a witch, do it Samantha-style). That approximately two-inch mix of flesh and cartilage stretching from the tip of your honker to the nasal bone between your eyes is your septum. The septum serves as the divider between your two nasal passages. In most bloody noses, the blow rips aside a segment of that cartilage and shreds some of the lovely veins running through it; hence, the sudden profusion of loosed crimson. Messy as they are, most of these injuries are minor. The septum is merely displaced and eventually straightens back into position on its own.

Not this time. My forehead caught John with significant force at the exact midpoint where the septum meets the bridge bone of the nose. The damage was extensive. His septum was shattered; the x-ray looked like miniature vehicles slammed together at zig-zag angles after a multi-car crash on an icy expressway. He had both a severely deviated septum—completely torn free in places—and a nasal fracture: the bone between his eyes was cracked. This was serious.

John had surgery Tuesday morning to realign the septum and reset his nasal bone. He returned for classes that afternoon, his face swollen, his eyes sporting pretty purple and black half-moons of make-up. As his doctor advised, he agreed to skip the State Series and give up wrestling and all physical activity for the next six weeks to let everything heal properly. His high school career was over.

Ummm, no.

Despite the gravity of his injury, John had no intention of retiring.

As mentioned, dented faces are common in wrestling. Thus, there are specially designed masks that wrestlers can wear while recovering from the injuries that enhance their rugged good looks. Picture Jason's hockey mask in *Friday the 13th*: big eye holes to see through and tiny worm holes to breathe through. Take that mask and wrap both the inside and outside in half-inch thick foam padding. Affix the mask to your head with athletic tape. Go wrestle.

John was back at practice Tuesday afternoon, ready to work out and get used to the mask. He struggled. His was not a typical injury; his face was, to be blunt, fucked up.

John had an extremely high pain tolerance, especially regarding weightlifting and wrestling. Squeeze out that extra rep on the bench press when the body screams failure, no problem. Will yourself to explode to your feet to earn that escape in double-overtime, no problem. Embrace the hunger pangs that tear through your stomach as you cut your body fat to 2.5%, no problem.

Pain tolerance doesn't mean the individual feels no pain. It just means that, through repetition, the pain has been normalized, and the individual has learned to not only accept but also desire what could be called positive pain: pain that makes the body feel stronger, pain that feeds the psyche.

That being said, introduce new pain or pain not perceived as "positive" and the individual suffers. John could adjust and adapt faster than the average person, but that adjustment would still take time and exceptional will power.

As a wrestler, John had developed a level of unconscious competence—the ability to do without thinking—that helped him react to situations well before the average individual could. He could sense when an opponent was about to attack or when that opponent had left himself vulnerable. John's body acted before his mind was fully aware. Part of this unconscious competence was innate, a kinesthetic intelligence, but the majority was honed through hours upon hours of practice, repetition, and visualization. These habits of preparation are what slow time and distort reality for an elite athlete.[69]

Under normal circumstances, John possessed these superpowers, these elite abilities to slow time and distort reality. But not in this new world. Circumstances had changed.

It was Tuesday. The Regional meet was on Friday. John had three practices to adjust to new pain and a new paradigm. The wrestling world, as he knew it, had been scrambled. John spent that first practice drilling on his own, gliding through various moves against an imaginary opponent, trying to acclimate and adapt. The mask was a major distraction. The eyeholes may have been large, but they limited his peripheral vision and restricted the light. He looked out as if from inside a tunnel. He could see, but he couldn't.

The worm holes by his mouth and nose physically provided enough air, but the perception—because of all the padding and the fact that no air could get through his nose because of the swelling—was claustrophobic,

---

[69] For example, to a baseball player in this zone, the 100mph fastball seems to have been tossed underhand; the baseball itself looks like a beachball. As far as wrestling, I remember one good wrestler shooting a double on John. Before the kid could drop and close the 18 inches of distance between them, John swept his opponent aside like a bullfighter, pivoted his own hips and legs to the side and into the air with *Matrix* agility, and landed behind him. The kid finished on all fours looking up and wondering where the hell John had gone.

like trying to wrestle with a throw pillow over his face. He could breathe, but he couldn't.[70]

In addition, every minor jostle sent a migraine laser bolt up through John's sinuses, off the inside of his skull, and back out through his forehead. His eyes spontaneously welled. With the mask firmly affixed, however, he could only power-blink away the tears that blinded him.

And, he wasn't even facing an opponent, an opponent whose first move would be to pop him in the mask. One brutal reality of competition is knowing to attack an opponent's weakness, to aggravate a wound. If done within the rules, this is not only acceptable but expected. John understood this. No mercy. He persisted and endured, but he left practice that Tuesday dispirited. His final act was to fire the mask off the top of the concrete wall at the back of the wrestling room.

Thank goodness for dads and dentists.

John's father knew his son, knew that he could not compete with that mask. John needed to wear some protection for his nose, but not that. That mask had to go.

Adversity breeds genius. Through some incredible succession of ideas—this to that to this to that—John's dad thought to call his dentist, who was also a family friend. The two talked and determined that, yes, they could build a Lone Ranger type mask out of a combination of porcelain and the ceramic resin used in fillings.

---

70   Athletes breathe in through their noses and out through their mouths. This slows oxygen intake and prevents hyperventilation. One sign of an exhausted (and out-of-shape) athlete is that he becomes a mouth-breather: panting and gasping like a fish out of water. John didn't know how to regulate his intake during exercise when breathing solely through his mouth. He had to learn how to not take in too much air, how to purse his lips like a reverse whistle when inhaling.

The mask could be form-fitted to John's face and terminated just past the tip of his nose, giving him enhanced vision and no restrictions on his mouth-breathing. This mask could be ready in 24 hours.

John had another non-contact practice on Wednesday with the original mask. At practice on Thursday afternoon, he wore the new one.

Perception.

A good restaurant host always tells customers the wait will be fifteen minutes longer than the host thinks it will be. Tell me the wait is thirty minutes and call me in thirty-five, and I'm upset; tell me the wait is forty-five minutes and then call me in thirty-five, and I'm one happy camper.

For John, struggling with the original mask for two days made the adjustment to the new mask remarkably easy. He progressed from drilling on his own to drilling with a partner. The new mask was light and thin and strong. His face still hurt (though tempted, I did not make any jokes about this[71]) and his eyes still watered, but both inconveniences were becoming normalized. Both could be managed.

On Friday night, three days after surgery, John wrestled in the Regional tournament. He had one match that night and won easily, pinning his opponent in the first period. On Saturday, though clearly and increasingly uncomfortable, he dominated, wrestling with an urgency to get off the mat as soon as possible. He pinned his semi-final opponent in the first period

---

71   Speaker one: Does your face hurt? Speaker two: No. Speaker one: Well, it's killing me!

and his final opponent in the third. No one had provided much resistance. Sectionals would be different.

The novelty of the new mask wore off during Regionals, and John returned to practice on Monday clouded with doubt. The brackets for the upcoming Sectional meet had been published. In the quarterfinals on Friday night, the first round of wrestling, John was scheduled to wrestle a young man who was 34-2. This kid was very good. If John could win and advance into the semi-finals on Saturday, he was projected to face the same wrestler he had defeated in the Sectional semifinals and the State finals the previous year. That wrestler was 67-2 over the previous two seasons, his only losses having been to John.

In sum, to even make it to the Sectional finals, John would have to defeat the best two wrestlers he had faced that year all while wearing a mask and enduring a broken nose that limited both his training and, potentially, his ability. Oh, and he was sucking weight this entire time.

John wrestled at 160 pounds; his natural weight was closer to 185 pounds. Weight loss is simple math, and the fact that he couldn't burn as many calories at practice—because of his injury— meant he had to sacrifice more calories at the dinner table. At night, he'd throw on two layers of clothes and go jog a few miles just to burn a few more calories and get out of the house and away from the temptations of the refrigerator. Occasionally on those runs, he told me years later, he'd stop, make a snowball, and eat it like an apple, just to savor the illusion.

John was sluggish at practice on Monday, but he picked up the pace on Tuesday. On Wednesday morning, he went back in for a second surgery to realign his septum and try and clear some airway. He returned to school and to practice, though he reverted to drilling on his own.

Friday night arrived. From weigh-ins through warm-ups, John followed his normal routine and seemed his normal self. He smiled, chatted with other competitors, bopped around in what we called a soft-focus mode. He looked like his old self. I should have known better.

About forty-five minutes before his first match, John began shifting to a hard focus. The smiles and chatting slowed and stopped. He went to the warmup room with a partner to stretch and do more purposeful drilling. Over the next thirty minutes, internally, John should have been visualizing success, watching himself set-up and finish various moves in different scenarios against this specific opponent. A blend of physical and mental preparation.

Fifteen minutes before he was to wrestle, John should have stopped, emptied his head, zoned out all the preparation, and moved toward the realm of unconscious competence. Time to let my body do what I have trained it to do. Let my head help, but don't let it get in the way. That's what he should have been doing. Instead, he disappeared. When I went to check on him in the warmup room only minutes before his first match was called, he was gone.

I found him in a maintenance hallway, alone, just outside the main gym. He sat against a cinderblock wall, knees up, head down, twirling the mask over and over in his hands. He didn't look up.

"John, what's going on?" I squatted down in front of him. To say I had never seen him like this is an understatement. He spun that mask around and around, wondering, doubting, feeling the dream fade and part of his identity dissolve. Losing faith.

"I can't do this." He shook his head. Real tears welled in his eyes. "I can't do this."

"John . . ." I started. In the background, I heard his match get called to mat 3. There was no time. My emotion for John quaked. No time. No time to explain that I understood. No time to encourage. No time to convince. No time to inspire. He was due on mat 3. Now.

Or he could stay here and forfeit. Quit.

I lifted his chin with my left hand so that our eyes met. I didn't see a quitter. So, I slapped him across the face with my open right. This was no love tap; this was a "Snap out of it" *Moonstruck* Cher-smack, powerful enough to whip his head to the side. Still squatting, I leaned in and growled into his ear, "You could beat this guy with a FUCKING BUCKET on your head!"

He turned his face to me, so I stood up. "With a FUCKING BUCKET!" I repeated. I didn't reach out a hand to help him up; he could get up on his own. He rose to his feet. I pointed to the gym. "Get out there and do your FUCKING JOB!"

Rage.

First at me, then at all this fucking bullshit. Broken nose. Lost training. Lost faith. Bullshit. His shoulders rolled forward for an attack. He nudged by me to the gym, not a nice excuse-me nudge, a you-better-get-the-fuck-out-of-my-way nudge. Inside him was a gathering that would not be channeled until the referee's whistle started his first match.

John won that quarterfinal match 10-4. He won the semifinal 3-1, scoring a double-leg takedown in overtime to secure the victory. He dominated the final 17-2.

In that final, John's mask broke.

The next week, sans mask, John defended his State Title, winning 1-0 in the final against the same wrestler he had now beaten four straight times: twice in Sectional semifinals and twice for the State Championship. They hugged after their last match. The next year, with John now in college, that young man went undefeated and won the State Title at 171 pounds. Over three years, his record was 116-4.

(4)

ANY VIOLENT ACT EVENTUALLY demands some degree of retribution. Risk and cost. John had no petty need for retaliation. But he did get some retributive justice, and I welcomed the reminder that there is always a price to pay for expedience.

That summer, long after the high school wrestling season ended, John filled out to a more normal, healthy weight of 190 pounds. He asked me to come work out with him before he went to training camp for the Junior Nationals tournament. That was his work ethic; he wanted to squeeze in an extra workout just to get ready for the *training* camp.

John and his father met me in the now dormant wrestling room. We flicked on the lights and were greeted by a 45' by 90' rectangle of padded floor and padded walls. The smell was delicious. We began with some loose drilling and gradually picked up the pace. Not good.

I don't say this about many men, but John had tremendous hips. In all sports, but especially in wrestling, all strength begins in your core, with your hips. On one repetition, John jab-stepped to get me off balance, shot a double, scooped his hips into a full squat beneath me, and then popped me up into the air. After letting me float for a second, he caught me under my arms like a dad catching his toddler son and set me back on my feet. I just shook my head.

For the next fifteen minutes, he took me down at will. He worked at half speed, focusing on his set-ups and overall technique, while I did everything I could to provide at least some resistance. On a couple hip tosses he could have seriously injured me, but he had the control and the restraint to lower me to the mat with a less than assertive thud. This session had a definite "The Student has become the Master" tone.

I needed to quit—the workout had become parody—but I didn't want to sacrifice what little ego I had left. Thankfully, John's father, who had been sitting mat-side and passively enjoying this demonstration, intervened.

"John, that's good," he said. And then, smiling at me, he added, "Coach, you look a little . . . peaked[72]."

---

72 (pē'kĭd): having a pale or sickly appearance. John's father was soft-spoken and unpretentious, but on this occasion he picked the perfect adjective to describe my condition. I still wonder if his playful pun

I turned and glanced at my reflection in the glassless training mirror on one wall. Ouch. My face was whiter than my T-shirt, and, lacking the strength or energy to stand erect, I slouched like a humbled troll. I looked old and broken.

I felt good, though. This needed to happen.

(5)

JOHN WON THE JUNIOR National Championship that summer.

A few years later, as a junior at the University of Oklahoma, he won the 1996 NCAA Championship at 190 pounds.

The following year, he suffered tears to his ACL, MCL, and meniscus two days before the Big 12 Championships. He didn't sit out. He donned a full brace on his right leg and proceeded to win that tournament. Two weeks later, still wrestling on one leg, John won four consecutive matches to make the NCAA final at 190 pounds. He lost the championship by decision in double-overtime, but he also delivered one of the most courageous and inspirational performances in NCAA history.

(6)

Intentionality

RESPECT YOURSELF. RESPECT YOUR opponent. Respect the sport. John needed to be reminded to do

---

on "peaked"—as in hit my peak and began my inevitable descent—was deliberate.

his job and let everything else take care of itself. Everything he needed to do that job was already inside of him. He just needed it unfettered. A slap helped do that.

The crux of this story is about John's courage and tenacity as a wrestler. But the philosopher—and professional educator—in me can't help at least considering what could have gone wrong. My intentions were noble but *why* matters little when *what* goes awry. What if...?

I think a lot about intentionality. How the past seems to have occurred by design, especially when everything works out for the best. Everything did work out for the best, but was that by design? I don't know. The degree of retribution for my violent expedience could have been so much more severe. I'm fortunate that the resolution was constructive for both of us as individuals and for our relationship. I'm glad John made me pay in his own way. I deserved it, and it felt good to get my ass kicked.

CHAPTER 18

WHY WRESTLING

But I say unto you, That ye resist not evil: but whosoever shall smite thee on thy right cheek, turn to him the other also. —Matthew 5:39 (KJV)

(1)

"Fucking faggot!"

When he was in seventh grade, my youngest son started getting picked on, bad. To his credit, he tolerated this. He ignored the verbal jabs, the bump in the hallway, the pinecone lobbed on the playground. He had the confidence to walk away. But he felt it. He felt it all, and it hurt.

One kid teased him relentlessly, mostly gay slurs. The kid was the same size as my son, but he had a reputation as a tough guy and kind of a whacko. He also had a cadre of loyal toadies always in his wake. My son's gregarious nature, his good looks and bright smile, his comfort talking with both girls and adults, infuriated this boy. One April day at recess, the conflict escalated.

Away from the tetherball pole, hopscotch squares, and kickball diamond, my son held court with three girl friends and two boy friends. He guided the group through a discussion of M. Night Shyamalan's thriller *The Sixth Sense*, focusing on the film's subtle foreshadowing and gradual revelations. This was my son's element: theater and film. Did you notice when Bruce Willis said this or Haley Joel Osment did that? He kept the discussion ongoing with and between each individual. A verbal assault shouted across the playground halted the group's analysis of this soon-to-be horror classic.

"Hey faggot. You suck any homo dick today?"

My son's five friends cringed and faltered. Nearby classmates slowed their play to observe without becoming involved. Even the toadies slid back. Today was exceptional. The kid crept forward, his eyes tearing with anger and pain. His glare swept across the three girls in the group before returning to his target. This time he expected an answer.

"Huh? Huh? Faggot! Whose dick?"

My son took a deep breath. He took a small step back, crossing his right foot behind his left, and, like a soldier dismissed from attention, pivoted and turned his back and started to walk away. He moved toward his friends, trying to smile and assure them that this too would pass.

Not this time. No walking away.

The kid stalked on and shoved my son from behind, knocking him a few feet forward. He stumbled and almost righted himself before tumbling to his knees. He bounced up to his feet, in a squat but rising slowly, and turned. The kid kept coming and lunged. He drove both his fists at my son's face like Superman double-punching into flight.

That's when my son's wrestling instincts kicked in.

(2)

MOSTLY TO ENHANCE THEIR development and partially to protect our sanity, my wife and I decided that each of our children would participate in a sport and learn to play an instrument. They would do both at least until they got to high school. Each child could choose the instrument and the sport, but the general principle was not negotiable.

The sports began as early as possible. All my children, when they turned 5, began with soccer in the fall and t-ball in the spring. These are great starter sports. One builds endurance and encourages teamwork; the other develops hand-eye coordination and teaches patience.

Though they all began here, each eventually quit those sports and specialized in activities of their own choosing. My oldest son ran cross country and wrestled. My oldest daughter dove into swimming. My youngest daughter, having climbed to the piano top at 9 months and scaled a two-story ladder at 18 months, gravitated toward gymnastics and has been in the gym, as an athlete or as a coach, ever since.

My youngest son tolerated the soccer and the baseball. However, having been cursed with his father's lack of hand-eye coordination, he excelled at neither. Sports were not his forte. His talents lay elsewhere. He was articulate, demonstrative, and musically gifted. At 5, he had no trouble conversing with and entertaining his aunts, uncles, and grandparents. As my sister often noted, he was a hoot to talk with, not an egocentric child who talks primarily about himself (and is thus completely normal), but an inquisitive listener who complimented her on the pretty blouse she wore and asked how her mutt Desi—part Bull Terrier, part Labrador Retriever—was getting along.

By 8, he played the piano by ear, began acting in community plays, and had more girl friends at school than boy friends. He was a charismatic and good-natured kid, with invitations to every birthday party and Valentines up to his eyeballs. All this, I knew, would eventually make him a target. He was headed toward a difficult stretch, so when he turned 10, I gave him a choice. I told him he could give up both soccer and baseball if he agreed to join his older brother on the wrestling team. He winced.

Wrestling is unlike any other sport. It is one-on-one, it demands strength and endurance, it tests character and will. When you lose in wrestling, you don't just get beat, you get beat-up. Most wrestlers also have to starve themselves to make weight requirements. If you're thinking, "Well, all that is true of boxers." Consider this: even a "busy" amateur boxer will average only one fight every two weeks. Wrestlers can have five matches in one day and forty matches over a ten-week season. Imagine the physical, mental, and emotional toll of a day when you win, lose, win, win, and lose. You went 3-2 overall, but you walk off the mat at the end of that day empty. And there's another tournament next weekend. No sport better tests an individual's resolve.

My son never wanted to wrestle. He was interested in music and theater, not sports. He could meet our family obligation and play soccer in the fall and baseball in the spring without any real commitment. Wrestling meant work. But it also meant only one winter season of sacrifice. He and I discussed the pros and cons of this switch. I reiterated all the standard benefits of being in sports, benefits he was already aware of. Then I cut to the crux of my concern: I told him he needed to wrestle so he could learn how to take care of himself.

"I know you already get teased at school. Not a lot, but it might get worse before it gets better. You need to ignore it, but you also need to not be afraid. Wrestling is going to make you stronger. Teach you some moves.

"I want you to do this, pal. I want you to wrestle. Not so you can fight, but so you can walk away from a fight without being afraid. If you know you can take care of yourself, you never have to prove it to anyone. You can just walk away. But if the moment does arise where you have to ... well ... take care of yourself ... you'll have a plan."

He understood. He started wrestling that year. He got his ass kicked a lot, but he also improved and began advancing further and further in tournaments. He got stronger every day, every season. And he got pretty good at a couple of moves.

(3)

WHEN YOUR OPPONENT GOES high, you go low.

Instead of leaning back to avoid the kid's double punch, my son dropped into his wrestling stance and shot a double-leg takedown. The kid's momentum coming forward helped my son pick him up, pivot him in the air, swing his weight top-heavy, and drive the boy's head and shoulder down into the asphalt.

Stunned but not stopped, the kid fought up to his hands and knees, so my son nailed him with a cross-face, driving his left forearm across the boy's jaw and latching onto the boy's right arm. When the boy lifted his right leg in an effort to stand, my son scooped that leg, locked his hands together in a cradle, and dumped the boy on his back. When the teacher arrived to break things up, my son had the boy locked in a fetal position and every time my son squeezed his arms together, the boy popped himself in the face with his own knee.

The overall results were better than expected. This wasn't Ralphie freaking out on Farkus in *A Christmas Story*. My son looked polished and competent. His reaction was the product of preparation, not luck or emotion. He was a wrestler, and it showed. What he had done, the other kids knew, could easily be repeated. The teasing didn't completely stop, but it quieted and became more distant. My son had earned respect. The father in me was proud of him. He had stood up to a bully and won. More important, he had tried to walk away . . . had, in fact, walked away many times. When pressed, however, he was able to take care of himself.

The teacher in me felt for the other boy. Bullying behavior is learned by example. I can only hope that a subsequent, more empathic "example"—a teacher or coach, perhaps—eventually displaced the cowardly role model this boy had both suffered and aped thus far in his life.

(4)

IN EIGHTH GRADE, MY son won the conference championship at 98 pounds. He finished that season with a 23-8 record. And that was it. He had met his obligation to do a sport at least through eighth grade.

In high school, he turned full bore to theater, jazz band, dance, and journalism. As a senior, out of our district's six high schools and over 10,000 students, he won the Richard W. Calisch Arts Unlimited Award for the student who best exemplifies creative excellence in the arts.

And, as far as I know, he never got into another fight. He never needed to.

CHAPTER 19

VIEWING DEATH

(1)

"You're kidding, right?"

In response to my question—mouthed breathlessly with as much entreaty as my 13-year-old self could muster—my mother gave me *the look* and pincered my shoulder with her bony thumb and index finger to communicate quite succinctly that, No, she was not kidding, and Yes, I better get my butt up to that casket and say goodbye to Mrs. May.

Mrs. May, the ancient—now deceased—widow who lived next door. She had a wispy head of thinning gray hair and a witch's cackle. Too many mornings, I watched from the bus stop across the street as the side door by her garage *eeke*d open, and she gingerly stepped out into the morning sun to fetch the newspaper that invariably landed on her dewy front lawn and not her pocked, concrete strip driveway[73].

---

73 A strip driveway, instead of being a full concrete slab, has two strips of concrete that align with a car's tires. These strips are separated by a grass median. Mrs. May's was the only house in our neighborhood that had this 1920's style of driveway. I thought it was cool, that style, more aesthetically pleasing than a giant slab. Still, you couldn't *play* on such a driveway, so functionally, it didn't make sense.

She always wore a yellowed housecoat (or was it actually yellow?) and slippers speckled a nasty green-brown, the result of continually traversing onto her splotchy grass to retrieve the newspaper boy's errant tosses. Her husband had died years ago—I hardly remembered him—and her two children had grown up and moved out. She lived alone.

One afternoon, a few weeks earlier, I asked my mother why Mrs. May always wore her bathrobe, even in the heat. It was late spring, and I was outside weeding. My mother had come out to check on my progress, to be sure that I was popping the dandelions that spotted our front lawn from the root—Get the whole thing or they'll grow back!—and not just cutting them off at the base.

"It's not a bathrobe," she corrected me. "It's a housecoat. And she wears it whenever she leaves the house because old people get cold. She's very old."

I stopped and glanced over at her house, a two-story brick box with a one-story, one-car, brick box garage. The brick was all painted white, the shingled roof was black, and the only color came from the yellow shutters on the upstairs windows.

"Be nice to her," my mother added. "Mrs. May loves you kids."

She stood over me, the sun behind her, as I squatted on the lawn, one knee down, one knee up. I looked up at my mother when she said this, my eyes veiled by her shadow. Then I turned to look again at the house of our next-door neighbor.

The old lady who pretends to be inspecting her front lawn and then steals our kickball or softball or football—if she can get to it before we do—anytime it misplays onto her property? The one who laughs if she gets it first, and cradles it in her hands, and then retreats into her garage, lowering the door between us, but not before she points a craggy finger to taunt us that she's killed our play for the day?[74]

This lady?

Loves us? Be nice to her? I didn't get it.

Then she died. A few weeks before my graduation from St. Peter's Catholic Grade School.

My mother hadn't heard from her for more than a day. She went to check and found Mrs. May sitting in her living room on one end of a high-backed settee sofa for two. She was still upright, her chin resting against her chest. The couch was turned to face a large picture window that looked out on the front lawn. Mrs. May was wearing both her slippers and her housecoat. In most houses, this couch would have been facing in towards the rest of the living room, maybe toward a television or another couch where company could sit for a conversation. Hers was facing outside, and I can only assume she had been waiting there, watching for us kids.

Now, at her wake, I was being prompted to tell her goodbye.

I'm sure I had attended other wakes in my lifetime, but hers was the first where I remember being conscious of death, of being fully aware that the person lying in the casket at the front of the funeral home (far from where I stood) was dead. I was maturing, <u>trying to. I no</u> longer wanted to be the cowardly little

---

74 I never witnessed the exchange, but somehow the ball always made it into my mother's hands and was returned to me, without explanation or admonition, that evening.

kid who looked away when I got a tetanus shot or insisted on soaking and then slowly peeling off a Band-Aid or yelped and quit when the baseball skimmed off the top of my mitt and doinked me in the forehead. If it's gonna hurt, fine. Stick it in me. Rip that son-of-a-bitch off. Throw another one, harder!

I had no choice but to acquiesce to my mother's behest, so I resolved to embrace the horror, to bear-hug death in both arms and squeeze. I left my mother behind, and with my shoulders square and my head up, I moved into the line of mourners waiting their turns to pray over Mrs. May. I took a few deep breaths as I waited and steeled myself: what would an actual corpse be like?

The kneeler beside the open casket had space for two, but when my turn arrived and the couple before me got up together, I deliberately darted forward and positioned myself in the middle, blocking anyone else from accompanying and thereby distracting me.

I pretended to, but did not pray.

Instead, I took a good, long look into her face. She looked a lot like herself, and I knew that when I had seen her a few days ago she was alive and now she was dead. No air filled her lungs. No blood flowed through her veins. Her house, what I associated most with her, was now empty and would be sold and somebody new would move in. The slippers and housecoat would be thrown in the trash. Every trace of her would soon be gone. I thought about that.

I might have stayed on the kneeler a bit too long, because an usher came forward and tapped me on the shoulder to get me moving. I awoke from my reverie and reflexively made the sign of the cross. I whispered, "Bye," and stood, and turned.

People were watching me.

Two types of eyes met mine as I worked my way back through the parlor to my mother. Half saw a grieving young man who must have really loved this old lady. Half saw an odd little creature with a morbid fixation.

That night, the night of the wake, I lay in my top bunk thinking about Mrs. May and what had transpired that day. I thought about the after-death, more about what it wasn't than what it was. It wasn't all the heaven and hell stuff I'd been told. That just didn't make sense to me. But what it was, I couldn't grasp. Still, I wasn't worried. I gazed up into the plain white ceiling a few feet above my bed and felt at peace.

That night, I dreamt of emptiness.

I knew I was dreaming, or, in a dream state, and yet I lacked the "I know I'm actually lying in my bed sleeping" link to reality. I was conscious only of being present in this dream. And yet the dream had no substance; nothing was happening. I wasn't afraid. I wasn't drifting or drowning or floating in space. This wasn't me *in* the emptiness; I had no corporeal form. And yet, I can't say I *was* the emptiness either. I obviously had to be there somewhere because I was conscious of existing. I felt the emptiness though I myself didn't have any form. I was just there, existing, and yet there was nothing there.

Still, I felt at peace, an exquisite tranquility.

When I awoke, unlike most dreams that disperse like warm breath in winter air, this one remained. The feeling stuck: a serene sense of simultaneously being and not being.

Over the next week, I thought a lot about my dream. I stayed up late most nights, not foregoing sleep, not frightened, but wondering about that emptiness and the nature of my presence in it. Maybe emptiness is the wrong word; maybe somethingness is more accurate. I don't know.

The dream never came back. Eventually, as blessedly happens in youth, my attention shifted and my fixation on death subsided. It's not healthy to think *too* much about what might be next. That sense, however, of there being something totally different—a serenity—after death, remained. And that sense helped the adolescent me, the one transitioning to high school, the one trying to establish an identity, resolve to live some kind of life before that end.

(2)

Hello Reader!

I'm going to make a dramatic shift in voice here. I'm advising you so you don't suddenly feel like a student and wonder how you went from reading anecdotes in your comfy chair to sitting in a desk back in high school.

I loved teaching literature because the experience was so multifaceted for me, and I hope for my students. I'd like to give you just a taste of how one poem can open the door to everything.

Thanks!

(3)

ONE OF THE STAPLES of the Transcendentalism Unit I taught in my American Lit classes was William Cullen Bryant's *Thanatopsis*. The poem is short[75], so I've included all of it here. (Yes, the English teacher in me would like you to read the whole poem. The choice, however, is still yours.) It's beautifully written, a little over 650 words, a roughly four-minute read.

I always recommended that my students read poetry aloud. Poetry needs to be heard, and the speaking only adds to the delight. However, it's essential to treat this poem as prose by pausing only as the punctuation dictates, not at the end of lines. There is no rhyming pattern and no consistent meter. Bryant's diction, syntax, sound, and imagery are what make this passage poetic.[76]

If you want, before you get started, I've provided a quick summary of the poem's content so you can focus more on the language and imagery as you read. That's the most beautiful part. Or you can skip the next paragraph and get right to it. (Or you can skip the whole poem, but that would be like smelling the apple pie cooling on the windowsill, choosing not to eat any, and then discussing how it tasted.)

"Thanatopsis" is a Greek word meaning, literally, a view (opsis) of death (thanatos). This poem is not about dying; this poem is Bryant's take on what comes after

---

[75] I realize short is relative: it's not a haiku poem, but it's not a Homeric epic either.

[76] And the fact that, using line breaks based on length not meaning, he stacked the passage into a column and *called* it a poem. This, of course, is cheating. :<)

death. The first stanza identifies the main speaker of the poem: the still voice of nature, and advises that we listen to this still voice when thoughts of death "make thee to shudder, and grow sick at heart" (13). In the first paragraph of the second stanza, the still voice reminds us how fleeting life is and how we are all destined to "go to mix for ever with the elements" (25), that we shall be "brother to the insensible rock" (27), and how "The oak shalt send his roots abroad, and piece thy mould" (29-30). The second paragraph of that stanza offers a two-part consolation: everyone dies and the earth is a pretty nifty tomb. "Yet not to thine eternal resting-place shalt thou retire alone, nor couldst thou wish couch more magnificent" (31-33). The final stanza advises that we live "sustained and soothed by an unfaltering trust" (78-79) so we can die as one who "lies down to pleasant dreams" (81).

Enjoy!

Thanatopsis

To him who in the love of Nature holds
Communion with her visible forms, she speaks
A various language; for his gayer hours
She has a voice of gladness, and a smile
And eloquence of beauty, and she glides   5
Into his darker musings, with a mild
And healing sympathy, that steals away
Their sharpness, ere he is aware. When thoughts
Of the last bitter hour come like a blight
Over thy spirit, and sad images   10
Of the stern agony, and shroud, and pall,

And breathless darkness, and the narrow house,
Make thee to shudder, and grow sick at heart;—
Go forth, under the open sky, and list
To Nature's teachings, while from all around—   15
Earth and her waters, and the depths of air—
Comes a still voice—

                    Yet a few days, and thee
The all-beholding sun shall see no more
In all his course; nor yet in the cold ground,
Where thy pale form was laid, with many tears,   20
Nor in the embrace of ocean, shall exist
Thy image. Earth, that nourished thee, shall claim
Thy growth, to be resolved to earth again,
And, lost each human trace, surrendering up
Thine individual being, shalt thou go   25
To mix for ever with the elements,
To be a brother to the insensible rock
And to the sluggish clod, which the rude swain
Turns with his share, and treads upon. The oak
Shall send his roots abroad, and pierce thy mould.   30

                Yet not to thine eternal resting-place
Shalt thou retire alone, nor couldst thou wish
Couch more magnificent. Thou shalt lie down
With patriarchs of the infant world—with kings,
The powerful of the earth—the wise, the good,   35
Fair forms, and hoary seers of ages past,
All in one mighty sepulchre. The hills
Rock-ribbed and ancient as the sun,—the vales
Stretching in pensive quietness between;
The venerable woods—rivers that move   40

In majesty, and the complaining brooks
That make the meadows green; and, poured round all,
Old Ocean's gray and melancholy waste,—
Are but the solemn decorations all
Of the great tomb of man. The golden sun,   45
The planets, all the infinite host of heaven,
Are shining on the sad abodes of death,
Through the still lapse of ages. All that tread
The globe are but a handful to the tribes
That slumber in its bosom.—Take the wings   50
Of morning, pierce the Barcan wilderness,
Or lose thyself in the continuous woods
Where rolls the Oregon, and hears no sound,
Save his own dashings—yet the dead are there:
And millions in those solitudes, since first   55
The flight of years began, have laid them down
In their last sleep—the dead reign there alone.
So shalt thou rest, and what if thou withdraw
In silence from the living, and no friend
Take note of thy departure? All that breathe   60
Will share thy destiny. The gay will laugh
When thou art gone, the solemn brood of care
Plod on, and each one as before will chase
His favorite phantom; yet all these shall leave
Their mirth and their employments, and shall come 65
And make their bed with thee. As the long train
Of ages glide away, the sons of men,
The youth in life's green spring, and he who goes
In the full strength of years, matron and maid,
The speechless babe, and the gray-headed man—   70
Shall one by one be gathered to thy side,
By those, who in their turn shall follow them.

> So live, that when thy summons comes to join
> The innumerable caravan, which moves
> To that mysterious realm, where each shall take   75
> His chamber in the silent halls of death,
> Thou go not, like the quarry-slave at night,
> Scourged to his dungeon, but, sustained and soothed
> By an unfaltering trust, approach thy grave,
> Like one who wraps the drapery of his couch   80
> About him, and lies down to pleasant dreams.

(4)

Philosophy

What aspect of human nature is being examined by this work and do we agree or disagree with any conclusions drawn?

THE EXTENSIVE 2ⁿᵈ STANZA, the bulk of the poem, portrays death as inevitable and normal, the great equalizer. All will die and become part of the "great tomb of man" (45). I open our class discussion by focusing on two passages from this second stanza, mostly to mess with my students' heads.

The first is the very existential fear Bryant addresses in lines 58-60, one that I know my students can relate to:

> . . . and what if thou withdraw
> In silence from the living, and no friend
> Take note of thy departure?

Wow. That sucks. What if I die and no one even notices? Ouch.

According to the poem, whether we are forgotten instantly or in ten thousand years makes no difference. To the ages of the earth, it's all the same. Everyone will die and everyone will be forgotten. So, don't worry about it.

Most of my students are not comforted. They live immersed in competition for social status. To be not noticed is not to be at all. I try to inject some humor here. I mock Bryant's irrationally optimistic narrator (It's okay that you'll be forgotten because eventually *everyone* will be forgotten!) by comparing him to the optimist who falls out of a forty-story building; as he passes each floor, the people inside hear him repeating, "So far, so good!"

I realize the connection between Bryant's narrator and this falling guy is a non-sequitur—how exactly do these relate?—but that's good; the comparison adds to the general ambiguity of this lesson. I want my students, to an extent, befuddled. I don't want them trying to find answers to *what if* questions for which there are no answers. For the moment, I only want them reflecting on a common existential fear: *what if I die and no one even notices?*

In class, I wouldn't let this reflection linger too long. I'd probably give an animated shudder, say something like, "Whoa, Dude!" and then move on.

The second passage I stress challenges the common conception most students have of the afterlife.

> Earth, that nourished thee, shall claim
> Thy growth, to be resolved to earth again,
> And, lost each human trace, surrendering up
> Thine individual being, shalt thou go   25
> To mix for ever with the elements...

If death means not only losing "each human trace" (i.e. the body) but also "surrendering up thine individual being" (i.e. the soul) to then "mix forever with the elements," what becomes of *me*, not the physical me, but the conscious me, the thinking me, the only-thing-that-I-can-be-absolutely-sure-exists me?[77]

I let the question hang.

To help my students visualize the contrast between a common conception of the afterlife and Bryant's much more Transcendental conception, I walk through two possible scenarios.

First, I present a linear, concise, loosely Judeo-Christian based mythology of the life and death cycle[78]:

1. a soul descends from the Guf (the Pool of Souls) and is absorbed into a body;
2. that body is now a living person, a blend of body and soul;
3. that person lives a life;
4. when the body dies, the soul is released and, maintaining its individuality, heads to the Well of Souls to await Judgment Day.

---

77   See Descartes: *Cogito ergo sum*. I think; therefore, I am. I introduce my students to this concept earlier in the Transcendentalism Unit.

78   I present this as a "mythology," so I don't threaten anyone's current beliefs. The students know, or should know, that I am making this up, that this is hybrid of my own creation.

5. Judgment Day occurs when the Guf is empty and there are no more souls left to inhabit a body (the Seventh Sign of the apocalypse opens with the silence brought by the birth of a stillborn child, a soulless child).
6. What happens after Judgment Day is anyone's guess, but it's assumed the good souls spend eternity in heavenly bliss while the others are condemned to a seedy Dublin tavern for an eternal "lock in" with all their damned friends.

In either case, after it has been plucked from the Guf, the soul maintains its "me-ness" forever. My individual soul is eternal. I demonstrate this by scooping a soul out of an imaginary Guf with my coffee cup, walking that soul through life (i.e. across the classroom), and then setting the cup on a shelf in the back of the room to await Judgment Day (or summer break . . . whichever comes first).

As simplistic as this demonstration seems, it aligns pretty closely with what most of my students believe. They believe their souls to be individual and eternal. They believe that life and death are linear.

I ask them to contrast that view of death with Bryant's soul scenario. "Instead of setting the cup on the shelf," I tell my students, "what if after death we simply pour it back into the Guf?"

I ask my students to picture the Guf as a giant bathtub. Demonstrating birth, I use a different coffee cup (I keep a supply in my desk) to scoop out a soul. Instead of heading to the shelf in back, however, I walk around the room—life as a circle, not a line—and end up back at the bathtub. At death, I dump my soul back into the tub.

"Picture a glass of water being poured into the ocean," I explain. "The water still exists, but *that exact glass* of water is gone forever. No matter how fast I might try to scoop out another glass, I'll never get *that exact glass* again because the water disperses instantly."

Bryant's poem, I explain, suggests that life and death are cyclical. Body and soul, we are born of the earth and, body and soul, we will return. We surrender up our individual being to again be part of the whole.

I then leave it to my students to *Be a Filter, Not a Funnel*. I have nothing specific to teach, per se. I just want them to consider what Bryant has said and determine if they find any of it useful for understanding their own philosophy and beliefs, or, for understanding the philosophy and beliefs of other people.

I want to emphasize this: I have no interest in influencing what my students believe. I only want them to reflect upon and thus better understand their own beliefs and the beliefs of others. I teach philosophy not to change their minds, but to broaden their perspectives. If I am "teaching" anything in these types of lessons, it is how to be a critical thinker and live an examined life.

(5)

Rhetoric

If everything is an argument, how effectively does this work present its argument?

Bryant originally wrote the poem when he was in his late teens and then published a revised version four years later. The revised version added both the opening seventeen lines (1 To him... a still voice 17) and the closing fifteen+ lines (66 As the long train . . . pleasant dreams 82). In a subsequent lesson focusing on rhetoric, we critique the additions Bryant made and how they impacted his argument.

The revised version of *Thanatopsis* makes two very significant changes to Bryant's argument, changes I note to my students as being essential to getting anyone to listen to what you have to say, especially on controversial, unresolvable, existential subjects such as life after death.

The original, condensed version, begins with this rather nihilistic statement and then reiterates that message for another 40 lines:

> Yet a few days, and thee
> The all-beholding sun shall see no more
> In all his course; nor yet in the cold ground,
> Where thy pale form was laid, with many tears, 20
> Nor in the embrace of ocean, shall exist
> Thy image.

Yeah. Relatively speaking, you're pretty much already dead. Have a nice "few days."

Worse, the narrator is speaking and offering his *own* advice on this subject. And, to be blunt, he sounds like a cocky, invincible teenager. Who is this child to tell me that death just happens and is no big deal? What makes him such an expert? Plus, this is depressing as hell! Great, we're all going to die and become plant food. What's the point, then? I tell my students that I don't know for sure, but I imagine Bryant himself was heavily criticized with just such questions. To his credit, he made some changes. The first introduces a new speaker. The second adds a "point."

The new version, most evident in lines 14-17, shifts the voice of the poem. The authority is now the still voice of nature, not the narrator himself:

> Go forth, under the open sky, and list
> To Nature's teachings, while from all around—   15
> Earth and her waters, and the depths of air—
> Comes a still voice—

Instead of meditating on his own, the narrator is now *listening*—in a very Transcendental way—to the "still voice" of nature. This shift gives Bryant's argument more ethos: this is not *my* view of death; I'm just learning from "Nature's teachings."

One lesson of successful argumentation, then, is to be humble. When offering an opinion on any subject, present that opinion as from a third party, something that you learned and are now considering, not that you *know*. This is most important if you are perceived as inexperienced by the audience you are addressing.

The second rhetorical shift is at the end of the poem. The original version ends with the statement:

> The gay will laugh
> When thou art gone, the solemn brood of care
> Plod on, and each one as before will chase

> His favorite phantom; yet all these shall leave
> Their mirth and their employments, and shall come 65
> And make their bed with thee.

Yeah, there are plenty of pretty images throughout the original poem, but the bottom line is pretty dire: Everyone dies. Deal with it.

By adding the new final stanza, Bryant changes the entire tone of the argument.

> So live, that when thy summons comes to join
> The innumerable caravan, which moves
> To that mysterious realm, where each shall take 75
> His chamber in the silent halls of death,
> Thou go not, like the quarry-slave at night,
> Scourged to his dungeon, but, sustained and soothed
> By an unfaltering trust, approach thy grave,
> Like one who wraps the drapery of his couch 80
> About him, and lies down to pleasant dreams.

Now the advice is to live "sustained and soothed by an unfaltering trust." If I can comfortably accept the inevitability of death, I can live a vigorous and fulfilling life without doubt or fear, knowing always that "pleasant dreams" await.

At this point, I ask my students to picture themselves having a great day, a productive day filled with positive thoughts and good work, not an *easy* day, but the kind of day that leaves you healthily spent, but not exhausted or tapped out. The kind of day that closes with you crawling into bed with a smile on your face, pulling your blankie up to your chin, cuddling your teddy bear in your arms, and letting your eyelids gently close.

Bryant's new ending offers hope, which is the second lesson of his revision. Don't be a Debbie Downer, even if you mean well. Offer some kind of hope at the close of your argument.

Humility and Hope, two very powerful rhetorical devices.

(6)

Introspection

What do I think?

I SAID EARLIER IN this essay that it's not healthy to think *too* much about what might be next. That's true. But it's also not healthy for me to not think about it at all. Bryant's "Thanatopsis" and the bathtub theory I divined from it helped me understand the emptiness and yet somethingness I dreamt about as a child. The emptiness was the loss of my individual soul, my exact self, as I was dumped back into the bathtub. The somethingness was the continued existence of the soul itself as part of the greater whole. I felt like I was gone, but I also wasn't.

Teaching the poem also reminded me to *live*.

This was a primary benefit of my teaching literature. Every lesson became an opportunity for further introspection by me. I wasn't just teaching this stuff; I was learning from it and from my students. I didn't always agree with what the literature argued, but I always found it thought-provoking. And that thought provocation is exactly what I wanted my students to experience as well.

(7)

OKAY, SO LET'S CLOSE with some even further introspection. I'm much older and much closer to what Bryant, in his youth, found so normal and inevitable: Death. Not to be morbid, but it's no longer a *What if?* question for me. It's a *When?* question.

So, where am I?

For now, I believe that death will bring that "exquisite tranquility" I dreamt of after Mrs. May's wake.

For now, I believe that in death I will become part of something more expansive and enlightening than I could possibly imagine. I will gain an awareness of answers more than a specific answer. And yet, I will not be me. I will become something far beyond my current ability to comprehend, and still something else will exist far beyond what can be comprehended at all.

I like an analogy I read using sand in the Sahara to describe this something that cannot, at any time, be fully comprehended: What *I* can comprehend is like one grain of sand in the Sahara desert of what could be comprehended, and what *could be comprehended* is like one grain of sand in a million more Sahara deserts of what actually is.[79]

---

79 I could give this "something" a name such as, "God"; but I don't because, to me, even the word "God" diminishes what I am describing. I agree with Jewish Kabbalists who argue that we should never name that which cannot be named, not because it's disrespectful, but because it's so absurdly inadequate.

I also like the idea of surrendering up my individuality and being part of that something so much more. I don't think I'd want to be just me for eternity.

(8)

I HAVE TO ADD another consideration since I've drifted this far into the ether.

We have a lot of philosophic discussions in my family, usually at night around a fire pit with a few good cigars, some craft beers, and, for those who prefer, a glass or two of Cabernet Sauvignon. I've presented my "Bathtub Theory" to a variety of friends and relatives. The most common challenge I get to this view of death regards punishment. If we all just get dumped back into the bathtub, What about personal responsibility? What about consequences for our actions? What about *Hell*?

What is hell? I maintain that it is the suffering of being unable to love. —Fr. Zossima from Dostoyevsky's *The Brothers Karamazov*

I agree with Dostoyevsky's Father Zossima. Hell is the suffering of being unable to love. That makes sense to me. Hell isn't out there. Hell isn't waiting for me. Hell is right here.

Hell is missing out on getting as close as I can in this mortal coil to experiencing the exquisite tranquility that awaits. Hell is missing out on loving others.

And I need to note that Fr. Zossima makes no mention of *being loved*. I should not concern myself with whether or not I am loved. My only quest should be to love others.[80]

But this is not easy.

Nothing worthwhile is attained easily. Loving others—and this includes loving the "other" that is myself—takes work. This also makes sense. If loving others brings me even a whisper of that unfathomably exquisite tranquility, then it should not be easy. It should be earned.

This takes me to another quote:

> *Nothing in the world is worth having or worth doing unless it means effort, pain, difficulty... I have never in my life envied a human being who led an easy life. I have envied a great many people who led difficult lives and led them well.*—Theodore Roosevelt

I like this. I too admire those who lead difficult lives well.

I especially admire those who love others—putting forth the effort, enduring the pain, overcoming the challenges—and manage to make it *look* easy.

I find it comforting and safe to assume that those who live life this way, those who put in the effort to love others, will eventually, metaphorically, lie down to pleasant dreams.

---

80   I can and should *appreciate* being loved by others, but that should not be my desire.

CHAPTER 20

FOOTBALL AND "THE SCORPION AND THE FROG"

Let every man in mankind's frailty consider his last day; and let none presume on his good fortune until he find life, at his death, a memory without pain. —Sophocles, Oedipus the King

Part One: Football

(1)

I WON'T PREFACE WHAT I did with *before I knew it* or *before I could stop it*, because I both knew it and knew I wouldn't stop it. Not couldn't, *wouldn't*. The football was in my hand, and I was going to throw as hard as I could at Brad "Boomer" deGrom's face, regardless. I wanted to throw it. Fait accompli.

And I hit him. Right square in the chops.

(2)

Evan Leahy and I coached sophomore football at Glenbard South High School. Evan ran the offense; I ran the defense. Evan had coached football for almost 30 years, mostly on the sophomore level. He liked developing talent and teaching the fundamentals without all the bullshit of being a varsity coach.

I was in my second year at Glenbard South, my ninth year teaching overall. I had been hired the previous year as an English teacher, wrestling coach, and football coach. My first year had been passable, but stressful.

I am an emotionally-charged individual. The schools I had taught at prior to Glenbard South had been patient with and tolerant of the near-reckless passion with which I taught and coached. I got positive results, my heart was in the right place, and no one (parents or students) complained. I smashed clipboards, I punched walls, I kicked chairs, I swore. I also was effusive with my praise and encouragement. All of this fell under the umbrella of motivation. As I said, I got results, in both the classroom and on the playing field.

My righteous rage, as I saw it, was at *behavior*, not *individuals*, so that somehow made it not only okay, but necessary.

The first two schools I taught at were Catholic schools; the third school was inner-city. Stereotypes are stereotypes for a reason, and the simple reality was that at those schools, where life is grittier, I could get away with more coarse, bull-in-the-China-shop motivation, as long as I countered it with positive reinforcement. Again, that was key. As long as I balanced attacking the behavior with reinforcing the individual, I was okay. If, of course—note the recurring theme here—I got results, which at these schools, I did.

Glenbard South was neither Catholic nor inner-city. It was an affluent, white kids' school. There were some minorities, but the overall atmosphere screamed refined conservatism. Emotions were to be kept in check; hence, my stressful first year. I had to tone it down. Context matters.

Evan had been an invaluable mentor. Like me, he was an English teacher, so he was able to help me navigate and adapt to the mores of Glenbard South both on the field and in the classroom. I had tremendous respect for him.

Glenbard South, at that time and for myriad reasons, sucked in football. The previous year, with Evan as offensive coordinator and me as defensive coordinator, our sophomore team had gone 1-8. That was typical. Evan couldn't remember the last time his sophomore team had won more than a couple games in a season. (I knew he *could* remember, but didn't want to acknowledge how long it had been.)

This year, however, we had some talent, and we were 4-4 heading into our final game. The school we were playing was 5-3 and, on paper, better than us, but we had a chance. We could finish the season 5-4, the first time over .500 in ages. I wanted to be part of doing that—I'll admit it—for my own ego, but also for Evan.

We were at practice on the Wednesday before our final Friday game. Evan knew we were underdogs, so he decided to add a trick play to the offense, just in case we needed a spark to shift momentum.

In his treatise *The Art of War*, Sun Tzu states: "Wars are won on deception." This principle is universally applicable to any form of combat. The key, though, is timing. I have to establish a pattern that anchors my opponent's expectation and stabilizes his defense. Then, I throw in the deception. I can't just deceive, deceive, deceive; that's not deception. Establish a pattern, break the pattern, re-establish the pattern, break the pattern, and so on. Hence, in baseball, I throw primarily fastballs and mix in some timely change-ups and curve balls. In boxing, I throw primarily jabs and crosses and mix in some hooks and uppercuts. In football, I run predominantly to one area (e.g., between the tackles) and then throw in a reverse run or a bootleg pass.

I won't get too far into Footbology 101. I'll simply note that Evan's trick play—the naked bootleg—was contingent on the defense expecting everyone to go to the right, which should allow a single offensive player to drift back to the left and be wide open. Evan was very worried about introducing any new play the last week of practice because this play would be designed to be run at some crucial point in the game. If it backfired, we'd look like idiots. Still, the other team had surely scouted our offense and knew what to expect, which made the timing prime for deception. He decided to go for it. Only one play, and we'd walk through it carefully to make sure everyone on the offense knew their assignments.

"Walk" is meant literally. I stood off to the side with the defense, and Evan took each offensive player step-by-step through his assignment. On the snap, for example, the quarterback is to take two hard steps—right foot then left foot—to his right, hide the football on his right hip, stick his empty left hand into the running back's belly, and then peel off in the opposite direction with his back to the line of scrimmage, deliberately *not* looking at what is happening behind him. A naked bootleg is "naked" because all the linemen push right to block for the running back, leaving the quarterback alone on the left and very vulnerable. If the deception works, however, when he turns around, he'll be wide open to either run or pass for big yardage.[81]

After several slow repetitions, everyone on the offense seemed to know their responsibilities. So, we decided to run the play at half speed against our defense. I stood on the sidelines next to Evan thinking, "This could be good." I was twitchy, though, so I grabbed an extra football and started tossing it to myself. Just flicking it up a few feet and then snatching it out of the air.

Another caveat. In order to practice a "trick" play, the defense needs to pretend that they don't know what is happening. They need to pretend to be "tricked." Most of the kids on our defense had never played football before high school, so they struggled a teensy bit with this concept.

---

[81] The naked bootleg is a pretty common deception at all levels of football. Our team was excited to try it since it made them feel like real football players.

The quarterback got under center and barked the signals. The center hiked the ball, and the entire offensive line pulled to the right. Instead of following their lead and pretending, all four of the defensive linemen and two of the linebackers failed to be deceived. Instead, they rushed through the gaps left by the offensive line and smothered the quarterback before he could even finish faking the handoff.

Evan looked on the verge of what my mother would have called "a conniption," puffing short breaths to keep from losing it. He never swore, but when he turned to me, every nonverbal gesture in his body screamed, "What the HELL was that?" My defense—they were *my* defense—had failed to play along, and so I had failed him. I was fucking this up.

Okay, I thought, they're sophomores and they're stupid, so try and be patient. It's my fault, I thought, I didn't make the directions explicit enough. I gathered the defense together. "Listen, knuckleheads. This is a TRICK play. TRICK! That means you have to be TRICKED!" I looked around the group and saw a few little lightbulbs twinkle.

"When the ball gets hiked," I continued, "everyone follow the offensive line and flow to the LEFT even though you know the ball will end up going right. Just PRETEND!" I made a demonstrative sweeping motion with both arms. "Goooo LEFT! Try to tackle the running back. Leave the quarterback *alone*. Got it?" They nodded and smiled, bobbing their heads like cocker spaniel puppies. I turned to Evan and humbly mumbled, "We're ready."

He pfiftted, shook his head, and growled out, "Run it again."

The quarterback got under center, called the signals, and we ran the play. Everyone on the defense did exactly as they were supposed to. Everyone except Brad "Boomer" deGrom.

I liked Brad because he was a little loopy and because he had no business playing high school football. A Try-Hard participant, he was skinny, slow, and unathletic. At any other school in our conference, he'd be a manager, but at Glenbard South, he was our second string safety, and he made the highlight play of his career.

As we ran the play, I was still tossing the extra football, trying to relax. When the quarterback peeled back, alone, I spun the ball up in the air, nice and high. I was smiling. The play was working. When I saw Brad break free from the rest of the defense and come racing back on his own, I cringed. The quarterback—our best player—neither saw him nor expected him and got blindsided. Brad drove into the quarterback's lower ribs and spine, blasted him into a sickening back arch, and plastered him into the grass and dirt. Triumphant, Brad sprang to his feet, turned to face Evan and me, and hoisted both fists into the air. His first sack!

At that moment, the football I had been tossing landed in my right hand and as I screamed, "GODDAMMIT!" I fired it at Brad's exultant face.

Bullseye. Thank God he had a helmet on. The football hit him dead between the eyes and knocked him back onto his ass. But it didn't actually make contact with his face. Instead, it wedged between his face mask and the top of his helmet, stopping an inch away from the bridge of his nose. Brad sat stunned, like some wonky alien in a funky spacesuit with a football sticking out of his face. He turned to his teammates for help, for someone to rationalize this absurdity.

No one moved, other than their eyes, which pivoted from Brad to me to Brad.

A nauseating vertigo swelled within me, like I was balancing on a steel beam suspended by cables—nowhere-in-reach—a hundred feet in the air. The wind whirled around me, the beam swayed softly, and I knew that if I even breathed, I'd tumbled off and fall for an eternity. I couldn't move.

Evan saved my ass by shattering the stillness and acting as if nothing extraordinary had happened. He strode over to Brad, extended a hand and snarled, "What are you . . . tired? Get up!" as if Brad had chosen to plop down on the grass in the middle of practice. He pulled Brad to his feet, un-wedged the football—How did this get here?—and sent Brad to get some water from the coolers by the side of the field. Then he turned to the team and yelled, "Run it again!" And they did, four times correctly, just enough time for my dizziness to pass, my hands to stop trembling, and my testicles to drop down out of my throat.

(3)

I LAY AWAKE ON my left side, an extra pillow curled in my arms, staring at the digital clock on my bedside table. 2:58 clicks to 2:59 clicks to 3:00 a.m. The Hour of the Wolf. For most people, this is their hour of deepest sleep, the time when they drift closest to death. For others like me, it is the time we are most often awake, with uncanny precision, haunted by some dilemma. My brain seems to choose this moment to wake me and ask, "Okay, what did you do today?"[82]

I used to fight this untimely perturbation, trying to turn off this cycling of my thoughts. I'd rationalize that whatever I had done that day was not that important. I'd get pissed, cursing myself, "I have to be up in a few hours. I need some fucking sleep! Stop thinking!"

Or, changing tack, I'd lie completely still, regulate my breathing, and try to picture a blank, white screen. Empty all thoughts. Just breathe.

This night, especially this night, neither worked. I couldn't and shouldn't avoid this issue. I *needed* to think on this. This was bad. Over and over a scene looped through my imagination: the football breaks through the face mask and shatters Brad's nose; blood sprays out onto the grass and gushes across his chin and down his jersey as he crumples to the ground. And I? I what? I stand there teetering like a fucking idiot, guilty of smashing this kid's face over a fucking naked bootleg.

One inch. One inch from that happening.

I try to be objective, to step out of myself and assess what I have done. Over and over, I watch that football leave my hand; and, over and over, I realize that a small, dark part of me *likes* it!

What the fuck is wrong with me?

---

82   The Hour of the Wolf is part of Swedish folklore. It's the time between 3:00AM and 4:00AM, when, according to the legend, most people die and most babies are born. I don't recall where I first heard this expression, but I've associated my mind's occasional late night introspective audits with the concept of The Hour of the Wolf for decades.

Part Two: The Scorpion and the Frog

(1)

I FIRST HEARD THE fable of "The Scorpion and The Frog" in the 1992 film, *The Crying Game*. The film won the Academy Award for Best Original Screenplay and was nominated for an additional five awards, including Best Picture.[83] I mention this because the film is outstanding on so many levels. I recommend it, but I've only seen it twice and would not teach this in class. The film is intense and unsettling, a provocative and profound study of human identity. But it is not a re-watchable. I love teaching the fable but have no interest in seeing the movie again.

The fable of "The Scorpion and the Frog" serves as the overarching philosophic motif of the film, and it became one of the cornerstone philosophic lessons of my career and my life. I taught it so frequently—mostly to juniors and seniors in high school—because I thought it worthwhile for my students, but also because I wanted to consistently revisit it myself. 18th Century English scholar Samuel Johnson wrote that people "more frequently require to be reminded than informed." I agree. Teaching the fable was my reminder.

Over the years, I took more license with the film version of the fable, allowing the story to evolve as I saw fit. The overarching theme remained the same, but I added some subtleties to flesh out the story and broaden the message.

---

83 Clint Eastwood's *Unforgiven* won Best Picture that year. I mention this only because I know film buffs (such as my two sons) will wonder what film did win.

Visual aids always help students remember a lesson, so before I told the fable in class, I would amble over to the bookshelf behind my desk and palm the "scorpion in amber" paperweight resting there. The actual scorpion inside, frozen for eternity, is three inches long. Most of my students had never seen a real scorpion. As I held up the paperweight so they could witness this amazing creature, I explained that scorpions are neither reptiles nor insects; they are arachnids, cousins to the spider and the tick.

The scorpion is an aggressive, killing machine, I told my students. While a rattlesnake or other viper will slither off your path, retreating unless surprised or provoked, the scorpion, with its outsized pincers, arched tail, and menacing stinger, will attack if confronted. Scorpions, like sharks—another impressive predator—have survived largely unchanged for over 400 million years due to their singular natures. These two creatures keep it simple. They follow the two most basic and essential biological imperatives: eat and make babies.

After this brief intro, I'd share the story. When I retired in 2018, this is the version of the fable that I taught.

The Scorpion and the Frog.

A TERRIBLE MONSOON STRUCK the Arizona desert and what were normally dry creeks flooded and remained so for days. A scorpion had been separated from her family and searched the banks of a swollen creek for passage across.

She came upon a frog lounging in shallow water. "Mr. Frog, will you help me please? I have been separated from my family, my children. If you will swim me across the creek, I will be forever in your debt."

The frog cringed and backed away. "No. No. I know scorpions. If I let you near, you will sting me."

"Please. I promise I will not harm you. I need to get back to my family. I am not a good swimmer and will be swept away and die if you do not help me. If you *do* help me, I will tell all the scorpions I know to never again harm a frog."

The scorpion's sincerity moved the frog. "Okay," he said, "as long as you promise…"

"I promise!" she interrupted, and she meant it.

The frog allowed the scorpion to crawl onto his back, and together they began swimming across the creek.

The current was strong, and as he swam the frog could feel the scorpion fidgeting. To calm her he said, "Don't worry, Ms. Scorpion; I won't let you drown." The fidgeting stopped.

A few moments later, when they were a little more than halfway across the creek, the frog felt the scorpion tense. She tightened her grip around him and began to tremble. Suddenly, a sharp pain stabbed him in the back, and he realized what the scorpion had done.

As he floundered, both of them helpless and hopeless in the middle of the creek, he said, "Ms.

Scorpion, why have you stung me, for now we both shall die?"

"I couldn't help it," she replied, her tone mournful yet resolute. "It's my nature."

After sharing this fable with my students, I'd read their engagement level and decide how deep to go with our analysis and discussion. I never forced these lessons, and I rarely discussed everything I have written below. I got the basics out and then went wherever the class determined. I didn't look for specific answers. I just wanted the students to think critically about the fable and its possible application to their lives and human nature in general.

So, here's what I had:

- Is the message of the fable simple determinism? We are what we are? How much control do we really have over our behavior, our choices, our personalities?
- Does the scorpion have a choice? Could she have made it all the way across without giving in to her nature?
- Is her predatory nature "bad"? Scorpions kill to survive, and survive they have for millions of years. Yes, that propensity backfired here for both the scorpion and the frog, but does that make this character trait inherently bad?
- Is the frog culpable? Frogs are instinctively laid back and trusting; that's why even little kids can catch them by the pond side. Is the frog equally at fault for agreeing to help the scorpion and not going against his nature, even though

- being laid back and trusting are generally positive characteristics?
- So, why did the scorpion strike? And why when they were *a little more than halfway* over?
- The fable seems to suggest that both free will and fate exist. How does this apply to human nature? Can we be fated to certain inevitabilities and still possess free will? I have a relative who is now twenty-some years sober. Can he ever change his nature? Can he ever stop being an alcoholic?
- What aspects, then, of *my* identity, *my* personality, might be fated? As an example, I scare the shit out of some of my students by telling them that, should they choose to have children, they are fated to be exactly like their parents. And, I add, they will be most like the parent they tend to clash with, since that parent is the one who is most like them. For better or worse, unless I make a conscious effort to be different, I'll end up parenting just like my parents.

I challenge the students to *Be a Filter, Not a Funnel*. These are things *I think* the fable argues. What do you think? Do you buy it? Do we all have scorpions and frogs, characteristics that we are fated to but that can be mitigated by our free will? Or is this all a bunch of horse-hockey?

I introduce this concept very early in the year. Fate versus free will is one of the archetypal themes in literature, and the fable of the scorpion and the frog gives my students something concrete to reference and return to over the course of the year as we consider this fundamental conflict in human nature. We'll never get to the bottom of it all, but we can dive a little deeper each time we examine a new text.

At the end of the year, when we review major concepts from the course, I'll ask students to consider again whether they bought or sold the fable of "The Scorpion and The Frog" and if they've reached any conclusions regarding the interplay of fate and free will in our lives.

Part Three: One of my Scorpions

(1)

THE CRYING GAME WAS released in November of 1992, but I didn't see it until the summer of 1993, the summer after I threw that football at Brad "Boomer" deGrom.

Nothing came of the football incident. That Friday night, we used the trick play to get a key first down on one of our scoring drives, but we lost the game 24-21 on a late interception that was run back for a touchdown. We finished with a 4-5 record, below .500 again. The kids were heart-broken for a moment, but nobody was crushed. This was, after all, sophomore level high school football. Life goes on.

But I was shaken, not by the loss, obviously, but by my behavior, by how close I had come to injuring a student and, quite probably, ending my career in education. I would have had to crawl back to my brothers and beg them to let me return to work for the roofing company. I might, in the long run, have made more money in the family business, but I wouldn't have had a life anything near the life I lived. I was at my best when I was teaching and coaching, and I almost, literally, threw that away.

At the end of the school year, my contract was renewed. As I signed, I felt again the tremors of an earthquake that had passed through my life, but left me, my career, and my family unscathed. The earthquake metaphor seemed to fit. There was a fault line within me that could not be repaired. I had done this before and would do this again because, as I mentioned earlier, a part of me liked it.

In *The Art of War*, Sun Tzu advises that, to win in battle, one should study an opponent's habits, not their mistakes, since mistakes are quickly corrected, but habits are deeply ingrained.[84] I knew my throwing the football at Brad was not a mistake. As summer began, and I had a little more time and a lot more head space, I tried to get a handle on what had happened. During my long Sunday morning runs—some of my deepest moments of introspection—I tried to step outside myself and objectively assess who I was and wanted to be as a teacher and a coach. I tried to understand what my problem was, what the "this" was in "I had done this before and would do this again."

That's about when I saw *The Crying Game*, and the fable of "The Scorpion and the Frog"—a much better metaphor than an earthquake—became part of my philosophic construct. It clicked, and suddenly I had a way of conceptualizing my problem, of seeing the

---

84 A student of mine pointed out that, as far as she could tell, Sun Tzu never says this. "*You* say this, Mr. Burke." Maybe I do, but I'm pretty sure the inspiration came from *The Art of War*.

issue outside of myself, objectively. This bit of distance helped me better work toward a solution.

Before I go on, I need to note that none of this took place quickly. There were epiphanic moments, but no singular, grand epiphany. What I came to understand about myself took time, and I still made mistakes, but I worked to keep them mistakes that could be mitigated by the new habits I sought to adopt.

This, then, is one of my scorpions. I have others, but this is the one that most threatened my career: I am impulsive and explosive. Many of the people who really know me would say, "Well, duh!" because this is so obvious. But I couldn't see it right away. It's hard to admit to myself that a characteristic so foundational to who I am is also a constant, physical threat to myself and others.

I don't see myself as either hateful or malicious. I do not go around looking for conflict. When I explode, I am not the instigator. I am always reacting to some stimulus.

Because I don't see myself as the aggressor, my mind rationalizes that there must be a good reason for me to be doing this, some righteous motive that precipitated my explosion. That's why in the moment, in my mind, I'm justified in throwing the football, or kicking the chair[85], or

---

85   At a home wrestling meet, with the principal sitting in the first row of the bleachers, I got so mad at a wrestler who stalled his way to a 3-2 loss against a very good opponent—instead of taking a risk and going for the win—and then smiled and pumped his fist because he *only lost by a little*, that I turned and kicked the chair I had been coaching in. The chair sailed into the air, did a complete flip, and headed straight at one of my wrestlers who was warming up behind me. Instead of panicking, he caught the chair mid-air, set it down, sat on it, and started fixing his shoelace as if everything that just transpired was completely normal. Out

cracking the clipboard, or punching the wall, or vilifying a family member.[86]

A great injustice has occurred that demands a proportionate response. This rationalization is the real stinger of this scorpion because I'll never convince myself to stop my overreacting if somewhere in my deepest thoughts I think I'm in the right.

And, in a sense, I *am* right. My passion and intensity are essential parts of who I am. I could not have been the teacher or coach I was if I didn't care so much, if I didn't want my students and athletes to succeed. If *I* didn't want to succeed. I CARE! And I should be emotional about the things that matter to me.

I identify with the creature in Stephen Crane's poem, "In the Desert":

In the desert
I saw a creature, naked, bestial,
Who, squatting upon the ground,
Held his heart in his hands,
And ate of it.
I said, "Is it good, friend?"
"It is bitter—bitter," he answered;

"But I like it
Because it is bitter,
And because it is my heart."

---

of the corner of my eye, I saw the principal start to get up, freeze halfway as if his back had locked up, and then plop back down. He never said anything to me about this incident.

86 I so verbally belittled my sister-in-law for betraying an alliance we made while playing the game Risk—but you made a promise!—that she broke down in tears and quit.

I am who I am. (Or, as the sweet potato said, "I yam who I yam.")

My heart is not bitter, but it is passionate, intense, impulsive, and explosive, and I *like* it because it is *my heart*. I don't want to change who I am.

And yet, as with the fable, if I didn't learn to manage what I have accepted as an important part of my nature, I could and would eventually do irreparable harm to myself and others. I needed to enhance and promote my passion and intensity while learning to properly channel the impulsiveness and explosiveness that accompanied it. If I didn't, if I couldn't control my scorpion's strike (I knew I couldn't eliminate it), I too would drown and drag others down with me.

I thought a lot about control that summer, and I think of it now. My scorpion has not changed, but I got through my career without letting it do any fatal damage. How?

The first step was being honest with myself. In the previous paragraphs, I use the words "passionate, intense, impulsive, and explosive" to describe my scorpion. Those words are accurate, but another word snakes in the weeds and is much more concise: Violent. I am a violent person. There is a reason I gravitated toward sports like wrestling and boxing (and it's not just because I have shitty hand-eye coordination). I like the contact; I like the physicality. I like grabbing and hitting things.

I am not a bully, quite the opposite. I was bullied as a child, so, if anything, I respond aggressively to those who try to intimidate or manipulate me or others.

I don't believe in physical discipline. I never spanked my own children; when they misbehaved, my wife and I had a simple rule: if you don't want to listen, that's fine, but then you lose things. They got timeout, or a no-TV night, or the loss of a favorite toy or stuffed animal. (If I really wanted to pile on the punishment, they got the full "behavior modification" lecture: Here's what you do well; here's what you did wrong; here's how to fix it; and here's the benefit you'll reap from this fix.)

And yet, physicality was and is my default response to most confrontations. My first impulse is visceral and predatory. I want to attack the threat, even if that threat is, for example, a fourteen-year-old freshman in my study hall who refuses to take his earbuds out when I asked him to. Why? he whines. Because *That Is The Rule!* I could just rip the ear buds out and throw them in the trash. I don't do this, but I could, I have that urge.

Not being a bully was easy. Not expediting to physicality and escalating to violence in threatening situations (and the biggest threat to my classroom and my teaching is insubordination[87]) took a lot of work.

For all intents and purposes, even though I used a football as broker, I punched Brad deGrom in the face as discipline for not following directions. Under the stress of the moment, I let my scorpion loose, unrestrained by

---

[87] One recurring nightmare I had throughout my teaching career—I'm sure other professions have similar nightmare scenarios that haunt their dreams—was the out-of-control-class scenario where a group of students I really liked would suddenly start behaving in the most bizarrely defiant manner and I could do nothing to either control or stop their aberrant behavior. I'd wake overwhelmed by the realization that I could not teach if the students were not willing to learn, that this was a mutual endeavor. I realize that this nightmare has a good lesson: that my students and I are in this together, but it still scared the shit out of me.

any act of will or intellect. That couldn't happen again. I got lucky that nothing became of it, but I wasn't stupid enough to think my luck would last, or that this type of stressful moment was either singular or anomalous.

However, I couldn't just shut down my emotions, and I didn't want to change who I was. I liked being edgy, unpredictable, and spirited. I liked being the fiery teacher and coach who was establishing a positive reputation for pushing students and athletes beyond what they thought they were capable of. I just needed to temper that scorpion. I needed to be sure that passion and intensity didn't degenerate into impulsiveness and explosiveness.

Fighting this was not easy.

Two things helped: exercise and a change in perspective. I worked to make each into habits; but, more important, I tried to stay ever conscious of how these habits would benefit me not only as a teacher and coach, but also as a human being.

(2)

Exercise.

ON ONE OF MY Sunday morning runs, I either realized or convinced myself that exercise was not just something I did, but something I needed to do. I have to work out; I need that cathartic release of stress and tension.

I rarely sit still. There's always fingers drumming, a foot tapping, or a knee bobbing. I am the chair rocking. Often, unwarranted anxiety—the most frustrating anxiety is when I have no actual reason to be anxious—

builds in me like pus beneath a boil, and it has to be discharged, one way or another, so best for me to pick the means.

Exercise, I remind myself, is essential to my mental and emotional stability. I can channel my violent impulses in a constructive fashion.

I run. I cycle. I train on the elliptical machine. I lift weights. I play sixteen-inch softball. I play basketball (though I would never be considered a basketball player). I've left school staff meetings to use the bathroom, then snuck into some hallway corner to do a few sets of push-ups. I prefer to walk up stairs two or three at a time. I do curls with the shopping bags I carry out of Mariano's grocery store. Anything can become a workout. Everything helps. Any exercise makes me a little less wired.

One workout, however, is critical.

For all the four-plus decades of my teaching career, in every house I've lived in, I've hung a heavy bag and a speed bag (later I added an uppercut bag as well). The speed bags have changed, been broken and replaced, but I've had the same heavy bag. It's an old friend, layered now in duct tape. In the winter, I'd hang it in my basement and work out there. In the spring, I moved it to the garage where it stayed through summer and fall. At least twice a week, if possible, I'd get home from school, change clothes, open the garage door, flip on the boombox (now, slip in the earbuds), and lose myself. Even on days I didn't box, I liked seeing it there in the garage, a forever reminder. Each time I'd walk past, I'd give it a jab or two, a few love taps to promise my pal that I'll be around again soon enough.

Boxing, hitting the bags, was and is a constant.

I need to add a qualifier here. I do not exaggerate when I state that *motivated* exercise, especially boxing, saved my career and made me a better husband and father. I'm in good shape. I know it. But I also know that I don't work out to be in good shape. I work out because I need to, and I have to. The benefit of being in good shape is a very worthwhile residual. But my key motivation is mental and emotional stability. I want to feel like I have some control.

When I head to a workout, I tell myself that this will help. When I finish, I celebrate feeling better. A conscious effort. And it's fun. For me, this constant reinforcement of the positive benefits of my exercise is essential. I do it to feel better and I feel better because I do it.[88] The whole process becomes self-fulfilling.

I quoted Samuel Johnson earlier, that individuals "more frequently require to be reminded than informed." I am one of those individuals. I don't think that I obsess. However, I never want to become complacent. I need to exercise and, just as frequently, to remind myself *why* I need to exercise. My scorpion demands it.

(3)

Perspective.

EXERCISE HELPED QUELL MUCH of the physical anxiety I wrestled with. One big shift in perspective helped put me in a better philosophical frame of mind.

---

88   Now that I'm retired, I also justify a good cigar and a few craft beers with, "I worked out today; I earned this!"

I tried—again, not easy for me to do—to take the focus off winning and place it on fundamentals and execution, attitude and work ethic, emotional content and respect. I can handle a loss—it hurts, but I'll survive[89]—if I know I've been true in the process. Whether in the classroom, at a debate forum, or on an athletic field, I tried to preach process over product. Do the job right and for the right reasons, and the rest will take care of itself. This change was very slow in coming, and I had many relapses because the common goal in most endeavors—and especially in sports—is to win. Why else compete? And yet I try and convince myself that the ultimate end of any competition is not to "win"; the ultimate end is having another human being help me push myself to a better place—physically, mentally, and emotionally—than I could ever have reached on my own.

The boxing program I ran for four years at Wheeling High School was a perfect example of this approach. The boys and girls I coached learned and trained together for ten weeks. At the end of ten weeks, I paired up students of similar size and ability who I thought were ready to box an actual three, one-minute-round match. Each pair fought in an actual boxing ring set up in our high school gym in front of few hundred fans who paid five bucks each to attend. The entire event, our *Contenders for Courage Fight Night*, raised money for the Make-A-Wish Foundation and a local support program for adults with intellectual disabilities. We

---

89 In "A Recovery Run," I wrote about how we remember the wins, but relive the losses. For serious competitors, this is true. Losses have a visceral quality; the memory, even decades later, is a gut punch. But I can live with it, and even become stronger, if I know my process was honest.

had fifteen to twenty fights each year. At the end of each fight, no winner was declared. Instead, the referee raised both boxers' hands and the two fighters hugged (this hugging was not required, but it happened, spontaneously, after each fight). This was ideal competition. The two fighters learned together, trained together, pushed each other, helped each other, and then got into a ring and tried to knock the stuffing out of each other for three rounds. And then they hugged.

I know sports in general could never be like this and should never be like this. Like most fans, I need the sense of closure that comes with knowing who won and who lost. Still, I don't want to lose all perspective and start to think that literally winning is the only acceptable outcome. It's not just about the product. The whole process should matter more.

This shift in perspective carried over into the other facets of my life. When I feel myself getting frustrated or edgy, I try and take a step back and see the bigger picture of process instead of focusing on a specific behavior or outcome. Just yesterday, I stepped out of a coffee shop in downtown Chicago with my café mocha in hand. I passed a street beggar sitting on the corner, and he called out, "Hey Man, I could really use that coffee." I rarely give money to street beggars, but it was cold, and since the coffee couldn't be used for drugs or alcohol, I figured what the heck. I handed the guy the coffee and kept walking. Behind me I heard, "Bitch!" and something clutter and splash. I turned, and the guy had flung the coffee into the street. He sat hunched over grumbling to himself. I urged to go back and kick him in the fucking face. That was a seven-dollar cup of coffee! But I didn't. I kept walking. At first, I thought myself a fool, a sucker, and a raptor claw ripped into my gut and started twisting. I mocked myself: You moron! Then I took a breath, thought a little, and considered two things: first, I didn't do anything wrong giving the guy my coffee and what he did with it was then his choice; second, he probably expected hot coffee, not a fucking *café mocha*. I'm not surprised he threw it in the street. I chilled. A little perspective helped me manage this situation and assuage my initial regret and anger about the outcome.

(4)

I OPENED THIS ESSAY with a quote from the play *Oedipus the King*.[90] I think of that quote often, especially now that I am retired. In a sense, my life as a teacher and a coach is over, and at death, I found my career a memory without pain. In fact, I find it a memory loaded with positives because I know it ended well. In a sense, I won.

However, I won't be doing any victory dances because I am fully aware that I dodged a few bullets along the way. I don't take it for granted that I made it

---

[90] I taught this play for years, and I found it most effective when I taught summer school. First, the play is short and easy to read. Second, there are plenty of twisted elements to keep the plot interesting. Third, summer school students tend to be there because, like Oedipus, the fates have kicked them around a bit; they can empathize with him. I hope they also agreed that Oedipus should have made his own choice *not* to let the fates dictate his path—to take a hand in his destiny—much, much earlier. Perhaps then that choice wouldn't have been so desperate. Don't wait to challenge what is fated.

through almost four decades of teaching and coaching without fucking things up.

An inch. Sometimes winning and losing comes down to one inch. The distance between where the tip of a football stops, and the bridge of a student's nose begins.

Plus, though my teaching career is over, my life is not. The competition continues. I like the imagery and the underlying themes of the fable of "The Scorpion and the Frog." Certain personality traits are fated to me (through nature and nurture). I am these things, for better or worse. To complement that which is fated, I have free will and the choice to exercise that free will. I do this by developing and reinforcing productive, conscious habits that help me toward my better self.

This is not easy, especially over the long haul. But it is possible.

I can make it to the other side of the river.

(5)

Simple versus Easy.

I WANT TO REITERATE something here. Several times in this essay (and others) I have described some task or behavior as being "not easy." This is by design. I often remind myself: That which is simple is not always easy.

Losing weight is simple: just follow the math and consume fewer calories than you expend. Anyone who has tried to lose weight, however, will tell you that this is not easy.

Changing my behavior is simple: do this; don't do that. Following through on these changes, however, is not easy.

I don't want to get frustrated or beat myself up by misinterpreting what is easy, or, by underestimating how much will and work it sometimes takes to do simple things.

CHAPTER 21

TOUGH LOVE AND LATE ESSAYS

(1)

MY DIVISION HEAD AT Glenbard South High School, Maribeth Mohan, was the first to use the phrase "tough love" in one of my evaluations. Describing my teaching style, she wrote, "Mike's tough love approach, while often curt and abrupt, is effective because he truly cares about each student's well-being."

Five years earlier, my division head at Notre Dame High School, Dave Vanden Busch, had written something similar regarding my rapport with students: "Mike may appear abrasive at times, but students note his concern for the development of the total personality, and a mutual respect between teacher and student is evident."

I can't thank the two of them enough. Had either of them focused more on the *curt, abrupt, abrasive* elements of my teaching style instead of the *cares, concern, respect* aspects, I might have been fired from that school. The term is "released" because I had not yet earned tenure, but it means the same thing. I would have been discouraged—okay, devastated—perhaps enough to leave the profession.

Instead, they each not only allowed, but also encouraged me to be authentic. As important, they helped me characterize the type of teacher I wanted to be, the leadership style that would help me toward my better and most sincere self.

Maribeth's phrase resonated, and for the rest of my career, I wanted nothing more than to be a tough love teacher. So, what did that mean? Tough. Love.

The best way for me to explain is by sharing one of my classroom management policies. This policy may seem relevant only to fellow English teachers, but there is a broader application. Every individual in a leadership role—a parent, a flight attendant, a corporate CEO, a cop—has to address some specific, let's say, predictably recurrent misconduct. The same stupid shit, over and over and over again. How that leader addresses that misconduct—what, if any, policies are enacted and how those policies are enforced—says a lot about the individual.

(2)

FROM AN ACADEMIC STANDPOINT, the most frequent and challenging "misconduct" I dealt with as an English teacher concerned late assignments, specifically, late essays.

In my APLAC[91] class, I took a collegiate approach to writing, placing great weight on a few assignments. In a nine-week term, though we would complete

---

91   11th Grade Advanced Placement English Language and Composition at Wheeling High School

numerous non-graded, prep-writing exercises, I would collect and grade only two or three major essays. These essays, including revisions, ended up being 30% to 40% of the student's term grade.

Failing to turn in one of these essays meant almost certain failure for the term, mostly because the few students who skipped such an important assignment weren't doing well in the first place and couldn't afford the substantial deduction of a "0." (Note that even a terrible essay would still earn some points when first submitted, and a few more when revised. If a student made an honest effort and at least turned in the essay, the worst grade he'd start with was a "D," soon to become a "C" with basic revision.)

Very few students want to fail. That meant almost all the students turned in the assignment, eventually.

However, putting so much weight on each essay generated a great deal of pressure on each student and triggered a sort of paralytic timidity. These were good kids who played the due date like the finish line for a casual marathoner: something not to be rushed to and that is best reached only at the very end when one is physically, mentally, and emotionally spent.

Not once in my career did a student turn in one of these essays early. Never did industrious Doug stop at my desk and say, "Here it is, Mr. Burke. I work best when I am organized, timely, and diligent. That's why I'm turning this essay in two days early. Thanks!" Didn't happen. Even the best students—defined by character, not GPA—were prone to procrastination and therefore at risk of not finishing the assignment on time.

Some considered themselves "pressure geniuses" believing, based on habit, not logic, that they did their best work at the last possible moment during the wee hours of the night before the assignment was due. Turning in the assignment, they'd approach my desk either shuffling like stiff-legged zombies from sleep deprivation or skittering like water bugs from all the caffeine they had ingested.

Others lacked the confidence to stick with one idea. Over the three weeks we worked on the assignment, they'd change topics eight times. They reminded me of Rowlf the Dog in *The Muppet Movie* singing, "I hope that something better comes along..." These students suffered a type of commitment phobia; they loved the initial rush of a new idea and the myriad ways they could make that new idea work. So much possibility! They struggled, however, when the actual "work" of making-it-work began because focusing on just one idea meant dropping any other potentially great ways the essay could have progressed. That loss of what could have been (but really never was) paralyzed them.[92]

Still others, the Anal A's, revised ad infinitum, continually identifying some minor flaw in substance or style and magnifying it as a catastrophic misstep that would expose their as yet unmasked ineptitude and plunge their individual grade average off the precarious 98.6% ledge it teetered upon and into the realm of

---

[92] For these students especially, I had a sign hanging in my classroom that read, "Amateurs write; Writers revise." My verbal mantra in this regard was, "Get it done; then make it better." Instead of trying to write their dream essay on the first draft (there is no such thing), the Rowlf the Dog students needed to settle for a "C" first, then revise up to that "B" or "A." Take one idea and just go with it. Make it better by revising, not re-inventing.

Average A students who are destined to graduate, not with *Highest Honors*, but with *High Honors*, or, God forbid, plain old *Honors*. For the Anal A's, the essay is never finished, not because something might be better, but because something is always wrong.

For these reasons and many more, certain students were always clamoring for due-date extensions, to which I invariably responded, "No."

I had a clearly delineated policy on all late assignments: One letter grade deducted per day late for the first four school days; no better than half credit after that. Hence, on a 100-point assignment with a grading scale of 90 (A) 80 (B) 70 (C) 60 (D), a student who turned in a paper two *days* late would lose 20 points off their grade (i.e. an 82 becomes a 62). A student who turned in the essay two *weeks* late could only earn half credit (the 82 becomes a 41).

Strict, but fair.

The biggest challenge of any policy, however, is deciding when to enforce and when to forgo. The answer could be "always and never." I'm always going to enforce the letter of the law, and I'm never going to forgo punishment or consequence. That's not real life, though. Sometimes shit happens and individuals deserve a break. On the other hand—as the saying goes—excuses are like assholes, everyone's got one, and everyone thinks theirs doesn't stink.

Therein lies the issue. How do I separate the wheat from the chaff, the kids with legitimate reasons for being late from those just shoveling horse manure. And what is a legitimate excuse?

If I'm a "pressure genius" and last night's basketball game went to quadruple overtime such that I didn't get home until after midnight and was too totally exhausted to finish my essay (and I had the game-winning assist!), is that a legitimate excuse? Can I get just a one-day extension?

What about Rowlf the Dog's own dog who really did eat the box of Fannie May chocolates I accidentally left on the desk in my room and then carpet bombed our brand-new living room rug such that I spent the entire evening scrubbing shit out of the shag and hustling the dog outside each time his eyes started to bulge? I'll have it to you by the end of the day!

And Anal A, who has the paper finished, but her printer ran out of ink at 4am. She has the essay on a flash drive and will print it in the library during lunch. That's not *really* late, is it? I mean, I have it done, just not . . . on . . . paper.

The problem for me is that I didn't want to hear any bullshit. I don't care about excuses, and I don't give extensions. The due date is the due date. I wanted to keep that firm. But I also didn't want to be a complete asshole. Sometimes life does get in the way of school.

So I thought it through, and I came up with a workable solution, an application of my policy that could be both consistently inflexible and yet compassionately flexible. For all students, the paper is late until it is turned in. No excuses. When you are putting the paper in my hand, then you can explain what happened, but not until the job is finished. Because ultimately, that is what I want. I want the work done. So, get the work done, and then we can talk about consequences for it being late.

(3)

I'M IN MY SEVENTH year teaching APLAC at Wheeling High School. It's mid-September, and our first major essay is due today. Despite my having clearly articulated my policy regarding late essays, four students approach my desk after class, forming a supplicant line.

Teenagers love to negotiate. Each prepares to present his or her case, believing (or deluding themselves) that their unique situation demands an exemption, a suspension of the rules. But before the first can utter a syllable, I lift both hands: Stop.

"I don't want to hear it," I say. One of the boys rounds his lips, a *whuh*-word preparing to escape. I point to the hole, "Close it." He puckers shut. I address the group.

"You all know the late policy. As of right now, your essay is *late*." I roll the "*l*" for effect. "There will be no negotiation." I swipe my hand through the air between us, erasing any possibility. "If you have a legitimate reason for *why* your essay is late, tell it to me *after* you put the essay in my hand. When the essay is in my hand, then we can talk. Until then," I pause, look into the eyes of my students, and stress each word, putting special emphasis on the explosive "d" and "k" sounds, "I . . . don't . . . care."

Two of the students turn, dejected, their arguments dismissed before even being heard. They leave.

A third hangs for a second. She looks to me like a batter perplexed by an umpire who has just called the third strike on a ball well out of the zone. Wait, she seems to say. What just happened? That can't be it. Wait. Let's talk. This isn't fair!!! I turn to the whiteboard, turn my back to her, and begin erasing the scatter of notes from the previous period. She catches on to the reality of this unprecedented rejection. She, too, leaves.

Jennifer remains. She waits for me to finish. I set the eraser back in the rail and turn to her. The classroom is now empty.

"What's up, Jennifer?" My tone intimates that this conversation is not to be about a late essay. That matter has been resolved.

"Mr. Burke," she says, "I just have to tell you why I've been out of it lately…"

She describes a fraction of the chaos she lives with. Her father is moving out—kicked out—on Friday. There is no abuse beyond the alcoholic irresponsibility that drains the financial and emotional resources of the family. Lost wages and lost nights. Her mother has the strength to say enough. Jennifer is the oldest, and she's spent the past few days sheltering her siblings from what is unfathomable to them. They love their father, but he has a problem. How does one explain this to a six-year-old, especially one who has come to accept the aberrant as the norm? That's just dad!

I listen, letting Jennifer vent. She finishes. She never mentions the essay she has not completed.

"Jennifer, thanks for letting me know." I ask her if she's talked with her counselor, the school social worker, her swimming coach. Two out of three. I suggest including the third as well.

She won't say it, she won't ask, so it just hangs there a moment. Other students begin entering the room for my next class. I am a teacher; Jennifer is my student. Regardless of what is happening in life, we have a responsibility to each other. I address that responsibility.

"As far as your paper, it's still late until it's in my hand. Once I have it, we can decide." I reach out to shake her hand, an odd gesture in this context, but necessary here. She takes my hand—a firm, candid grip—and nods.

Over the next two days, each of the other students turns in the essay. Not one gives an excuse. Two just place it on my desk. The other hands it to me in person and says, "Sorry, Mr. Burke." I give her my don't-let-it-happen-again look but also wonder what exactly she is apologizing for. All three lose points per my policy. Funny how that happens. *Before,* they had a thousand excuses ready for why it wasn't finished on time. *After,* there were none.

Jennifer hands me her essay before the start of class the following Wednesday. She's over a week late. That would mean half-credit, a big dent to her grade. She too does not offer an excuse.

"How are you holding up?" I ask.

She shrugs, "I'm managing." The life of too many teenagers: enduring collateral damage from the careless actions of too often oblivious adults.

I nod to her essay. "You're good, Jennifer," I tell her. "You'll earn full credit. No penalty. Good job getting it done." She sort-of-smiles, repressing any emotion, turns, and goes to her desk.

A few weeks later I hear on the school announcements that she and three of her teammates have set a school record in the 200-yard medley relay (she swims the backstroke). I make a point of congratulating her. I also use the moment to ask how things are at home.

"We're adjusting," she says. I nod and smile. And that's it. She's just another student.

(4)

"MIKE'S TOUGH LOVE APPROACH, while often curt and abrupt, is effective because he truly cares about each student's well-being."

"Mike may appear abrasive at times, but students note his concern for the development of the total personality, and a mutual respect between teacher and student is evident."

I took what both Maribeth and Dave had written as encouragement. Again, I credit them with giving me excellent guidance early in my career.[93]

---

[93] I was fortunate to have many excellent mentors over the course of my career. None, however, had the impact that Dave at NDHS and Maribeth at GBS did. They were my direct supervisors for eight of the first eleven years of my career. That being said, I need to give a shout-out to Bill Casey, the Athletic Director while I was at NDHS. He taught me about the power of my presence. Speaking of my cross country runners, he advised me, "These kids look up to you. Recognize that and never take it for granted. Know that you are always being watched. Whether you want it or not, you are a role model." I was 27 years old at the time. Just a fucking kid myself. But I had power, the power of influence over others. That's why I thought a lot about the policies I enacted for my students and athletes.

I *am* curt, abrupt, and abrasive. I also truly care, am concerned with the development of the total personality, and seek mutual respect. I won't get toward being my best as a teacher by being someone else. Authenticity: that's the goal. It sounds so commonsense, but also so damn ridiculous. Doesn't everyone know this? And yet, it's a lot of fucking work.

My "Late Essay" policy in general—and the specific anecdote I share about Jennifer and the other three students—is a good example of what I think Maribeth meant by Tough Love. At the outset, I treated all four students the same—yeah, a little harshly, but that sends an important message: this is not negotiable. And they all finished the essay. Afterwards, I held three students accountable, and I gave one full credit. They all, I hope, learned something. No excuses. No bullshit. Get the job done, and then we'll talk about it.

As I mentioned at the start, late essays were the most frequent and difficult academic discipline issue I dealt with during my career. I held a lot of students accountable, and I gave a few breaks (And I graded a shit-ton of essays). But I tried to be consistent.

I also got occasional pushback, mostly from administrators. Why not allow late essays? Who cares as long as they get it done eventually? Because that's not what I wanted to teach my students. When you have something you need to do, get it done. Don't waste my time (or your energy) on bullshit and excuses. And I don't need "eventually." Sorry, but in life some things have due dates, so learn to get the job done by the date it's due (even if that means now).

(5)

On Authenticity

*A*DOPT THE *P*RINCIPLE; *Adapt the Practice*

It sounds paradoxical to write this, but I wanted to be authentic as a teacher because that's what the teachers I most admired were. They each had bits of practice (how they taught), content (what they taught), and policy (their rules) that were their own. I say "bits" because they taught the same basic class as the teacher next door, they just did it with a little more style and a little more substance.

Most important, the "bits" that made them different didn't seem forced or contrived. Why did Sister Mary Joseph teach history *Jeopardy!* style? No reason. That was Sister Mary Joseph being Sister Mary Joseph. She just taught that way.

And it worked.

CHAPTER 22

THE JOURNEY

(1)

IN HIS ESSAY *EXPERIENCE*, Ralph Waldo Emerson writes, "To finish the moment, to find the journey's end in every step of the road, to live the greatest number of good hours, is wisdom."

Wisdom is realizing that the journey itself is the end. If my journey, every step, is filled with good hours, then I've achieved everything I could desire.

Regarding any competitive endeavor, I want to complete my journey with a victory; but the value of my experience and the worth of my achievement should not be tied only, or even significantly, to that singular end.

The process matters more than the product.

Two examples.

(2)

IN 2003, MY ASSISTANT coach Beth and I guided the varsity girls' softball team at Wheeling High School to a school record 22-win season. No softball or baseball team in Wheeling's history had or has since (as of this writing) won twenty or more games in a season.

Five years earlier, the year before Beth and I took over the team, the program as a whole, including freshman, junior varsity, and varsity levels, had gone a combined 0-86. Not one win at any level. At that time, I was an administrator, the Assistant Principal for Student Activities, and Beth was my administrative assistant. I fired the head coach at the end of that 1999 season—for a variety of reasons that went beyond wins and losses—and set about hiring a new head softball coach. After an intensive three-month search, I had zero candidates. None of the lower-level coaches wanted to move up, and no one from the outside wanted to move in.

Beth and I decided to take over because, basically, no one else wanted the job. It was either us or the vacuous phantom inside the applicant folder. Beth had been an All-Conference softball player at Wheeling, but she had never coached. I had coached a variety of sports, but I had no experience coaching or playing fastpitch softball (or baseball, for that matter.) We were perfect for each other. After a lengthy "Are we sure we want to do this?" discussion in my office, we shook hands, having agreed to learn from each other and do the best we could. We took over the program and coached the varsity team together.[94]

In the spring of 2000, the first year Beth and I ran things, we, the team, finished 4-28. Though small in number, those wins were significant since several of

---

94 As an administrator, I was contractually not allowed to coach, but I did it anyhow by calling myself a volunteer and not getting paid. This was the opening flicker of my eventual realization that I had gotten into education to work with kids, not adults, and that administration might not be a good fit for me.

the girls on our team were three-sport athletes who also played volleyball and basketball. Neither of those varsity teams had won a single game that year. Those athletes, the juniors and seniors, had gone a complete calendar year, from softball in the previous spring through volleyball in the fall and basketball that winter, never having tasted victory. Not one win. When we won our first game—we beat Woodlawn Academy 16-8—the girls, the juniors and seniors, gathered in the dugout in a group hug and wept.

The second year, 2001, we finished 8-24. We doubled our number of victories. That was nice. But more important, we cut our "slaughters" from 18 the previous season to 6 (a slaughter is a loss by ten or more runs). Most of our losses were competitive. And we won three of our final six games. Instead of just playing softball, the girls were becoming softball players. That attitude shift led to more hard work in the off season and some realistic optimism heading into the next year.

The third year, 2002, we won a school record 17 games and finished over .500 for only the second time in school history (17-13). The first time had been Beth's senior year in 1983 when her team went 15-7. Those 15 wins had also been the previous record for wins in a season. Beth was as happy as anyone to see that record finally broken. Together, we had turned the program around.

I admit that scheduling definitely helped. My philosophy was one of thirds: 1/3 of the schedule should be against teams we should beat; 1/3 should be against teams we could beat; 1/3 should be against teams better than us. I was willing to drive any distance to get us a win to fill out that lower third. And it worked. Success builds success. To begin that third year, we lost our first game but then won five in a row. That gave us confidence. We beat all the teams we should have beaten and many of the teams I saw us as "even" with (Though we hadn't beaten any of these teams for several years, I still saw them as teams we could beat). We even beat one of the teams in the top third and put a scare (4-2 loss) into the team that won our conference.

Year number four. 2003.

The journey was rolling along, and I thought we were headed toward another amazing season. We were winning, and the core of freshmen who had helped spark this transformation three years ago was set to be seniors. They would be our leaders.

I felt pretty good about myself, about what Beth and I had accomplished. In high school, I had run cross-country and wrestled, and those are the sports I had found success at as a coach. Now I, we, had led a team that set a school record for wins in Girls Softball, a sport I knew almost nothing about three years earlier. I thought that was pretty cool. Year four would be even better.

Beth and I talked about the upcoming schedule, about the seniors we had returning, about the underclassmen ready to step up. Between ourselves, we set the bar for that 2003 season at 20 wins, a nice round number.

We had a deliberately simple logo printed on all our team apparel:

WHS Softball

20 03

I didn't want to put too much pressure on the girls, so I snuck our goal in without telling them. I put a little extra space in between the 20 and the 03. Our goal was to win 20 games in the '03 season. A number, and I fucked it all up.

We did it. In 2003, we won 22 games and set a new school record, and I've never had a less satisfying three months in my 36 years of coaching. I failed. For selfish reasons, I started counting off the victories, focusing on product instead of process, and somewhere I lost the handle on coaching athletes, mentoring individuals, and building relationships. Instead, I focused on coaching a sport and winning games.

Over the course of the season, though the victories kept stacking up, the team fractured. I don't want to go into all the drama, none of which was earth-shattering. Death by paper cuts. It's just that the longer the season progressed, the less fun the coaching was for me and the playing was for the girls.

The main conflict centered on one of the seniors, probably our best player. She had challenged me from the start, beginning her freshmen year three years earlier, as not being a real softball coach, which, at the time, I readily admitted. But by 2003, I knew what I was doing. I had attended clinics, watched video, and sought advice from other coaches. I now had three years of softball coaching experience. I learned, and we won, which, to me, demonstrated that I knew what I was doing.

However, instead of swallowing my pride and stroking her ego a little, I shut her out. We got more publicity from the local papers the more we won, and I made it a point to always keep the focus on the secondary contributors rather the stars on the team. This could have been a good thing and the right thing to do, if I had given the stars their due as well, especially this one senior. But I didn't, and she became a cancer, and the other seniors were impacted. Two sided with her against me, two just withdrew emotionally. I lost all five.

Pride and ambition are well-masked as virtue. At the time, I told myself I was teaching these seniors about humility and camaraderie and teamwork. Good lessons. That may have been some of it, but a part of me wanted those seniors (and their parents) to recognize what *I* had done to help turn the program around. Instead of building mutual respect about what we had done together, it became a passive-aggressive battle over who had meant more to our success: four years of my coaching and pushing them or four years of their hard work?

A coach never wins this battle. Never. I knew this. I knew better. Earlier in my career, I had helped coach multiple state champions and state medalists in Cross Country, Wrestling, and Track, and also in Debate. Whether as a head coach or assistant, I had always deferred credit to the athletes and my fellow coaches. I never wanted to suggest (as I've seen some coaches do) that *I* had the magic sauce for success. I did this because it was true; there is no magic sauce. As the adage goes, there is a horse and there is water, and though the coach can lead that horse to water, the horse must choose to drink, and that choice supersedes all the leading. I knew this.

However, that year my ego felt threatened,[95] and I needed approbation, I needed someone to see what an amazing job I was doing. So, I fought for that recognition, and I did so by chasing a number, and I lost.

As I mentioned above, nothing significant happened. No big blow-ups. No shouting matches or overt rebellions. We kept winning games as the season progressed, yet every interaction between me and the players and among the players themselves became a little more sterile, which made every moment a little more stressful. There is little worse than walking daily on the eggshells of apathy.

Our 22-14 record at the end of the season might have suggested success, but the journey was a failure.

A decade later, I was at a bar in Wheeling having a few Miller Lites with some guys I played 16" slow-pitch softball with. When I am in a public place, I always try to sit at a table with my back to the wall so I can see the room in front of me. That night, I sat in the shadows against the very back wall. The bar was decent-sized, and a little dark, and crowded. Across the room, I noted four women entering together. They approached a table two away from where our group sat, and as they neared, I recognized that one senior. She didn't see me. I didn't motion or say anything. Eventually, as will happen when consuming Miller Lites, I had to tinkle. At first, I scouted a route where I could avoid her table but soon acknowledged what an ass I was being. Instead, I got up, and, as I passed her table, stopped and

---

[95] The previous year, I had resigned as an administrator and returned to the classroom. I was fortunate to stay at the same school, and quitting administration was the right thing to do, but I still felt like a failure.

said hello. It was a thirty second exchange, and we were both polite, but there was nothing there, nothing between a head coach and a four-year starter, and I couldn't escape the feeling of my having wasted an incredible opportunity so many years ago.

(3)

It's the fall of 2006.

I stand in the grass on the southeast corner of the massive Heritage Park athletic complex in Wheeling. Behind me is a small lake. In front of me, spread out among 83 acres, are softball fields and baseball diamonds and soccer fields and picnic areas and playgrounds. And grass. Lots and lots of grass. Very few paved paths or crosswalks, at least back then, which makes this a perfect setting for our home cross country meets.

I am lingering at the two-mile mark of this three-mile varsity race. All the main runners have already passed. Only the stragglers amble by, trying to maintain enough semblance of body lean, arm swing, and knee lift to sustain the belief that they are, in fact, running. I wait.

Allison approaches; she is the last runner. "Good job," I tell her. There is no need to yell; everyone else is across the field by the finish line. Cross country races have an intimacy most other sports lack. There are no stands, no bleachers. The coaches, the fans, and the spectators are right on the course with the runners. I am a foot or two away from Allison.

"One mile to go. Lift your knees. Use your arms like you're pulling a rope. You're doing great, Allison." She nods and forces a sweaty smile. She does not make eye contact. Instead, she speeds up just a smidge, focusing on the course ahead of her, acknowledging that this is still a competition, a race.

That competition is against our rival, the Bison, in a dual meet. Just two teams. We are three weeks into the fall cross country season, and the girls and I have been figuring each other out.

And I have a decision to make because I am the new head coach, at least for this season.

In cross country meets, the lowest score wins, that total being determined by the sum of each team's top five runners. How fast any individual runs or how far she finishes ahead of the girl behind has no bearing on the team score. Only place matters.

Based on how the runners were spaced when they passed me about six minutes ago at the two-mile mark, we are going to lose this meet, which is why I didn't hustle over to the finish line and instead chose to wait for Allison. After she passes, I look across the field to where the first runner is approaching the finish line. Just as I thought. She is one of mine, and she has a huge lead. Behind her is the first Bison runner, then a gap, another of mine, followed by another gap. After that are three more Bison running shoulder to shoulder. Not far behind that Bison pack, but too far to close the gap in the short distance that is left of this race, are three more of my runners. I do the math. The final score will be Bison 27 (2, 4, 5, 6, 10), Wildcats 28 (1, 3, 7, 8, 9).

There are many other girls in the race, but only these ten will figure in the scoring. We will lose.

Before the race, I sat the whole team down and told our top two runners, the girls who ended up finishing 1st and 3rd, to sit back for the first two miles, to let the top Bison girl lead the race, and to help our other three runners stay close to the main pack of Bison.

"At the two-mile mark," I told the top two runners, "you two can take off. Go get that first girl. But until then, help these girls along. Sit back."

"You three," I pointed to the other scorers, "have to break up their pack of three. Do that, mix in instead of letting them finish as a group, and we win the meet. These two," I point to our top runners, "will help you stay close, but when they take off—at the two-mile mark—you three have to go to work."

I scanned the group, and everyone seemed on board. Nods to me and each other. We had a plan.

At the mile mark everyone was right where they needed to be. The lead Bison girl was out in front by ten or so seconds, but the next nine girls were tightly grouped like a bumble of bees. Our best runner was doing an excellent job in front impeding anyone from moving ahead, and our second girl ran near the back keeping the other girls on our team connected.

I praised them as they passed, "Great job, ladies. Stay together! One pack."

There's an old joke in education that the best place to teach is in an orphanage because there are no parents. That's a bit extreme, but sometimes very accurate. About one hundred yards past the mile mark where I had just encouraged the team, a small cabal of parents wriggled and contorted like inflatable air dancers in a used car lot. As the first Bison girl reached them, several threw up their arms in disgust. They squawked at each other, frustrated and confused. As the pack approached, two of them screamed at their daughters, who happened to be my runners.

"Are you hurt? What's wrong?" our best runner's father shouted. "What's wrong???" He stepped so close to her that she stutter-stepped to avoid hitting him. He pointed ahead to the lead runner. "GO GET HER!" And she did.

"What are you doing in the back?" our second girl's mother screeched. "Get going!" She swung her pointed finger like a sword slicing the air, commanding her daughter to separate from the pack.[96] Her daughter listened. This mother, emboldened by maternal vigor, turned to the other parents behind her, and they astutely provided bullied affirmation.

I was close enough to see and hear the commotion, but helpless to intervene, which was probably a good thing because I might not have been nice.

I could not see the girls' faces; they were running away from me. But I saw the effect their parents had. After our best two girls took off, the next three panicked—abandoned and leaderless—and fell back. The group of three Bison we were trying to break up coalesced, running stride for stride in impressive

---

[96] In fairness, I should note that the top girls from both teams had been running against each other since fifth grade. The families knew each other. The parents had, in their heads, established clear hierarchies of who should beat whom. Our best runner was sixty seconds better than any Bison runner, which is why her father was in such a panic, but also why I knew she could sit back the first two miles and still easily catch and defeat the other girl.

symmetry, and pulled ahead far enough to create an insurmountable gap. All this happened in a span of just two hundred yards, and our plan was sabotaged.

Which is why I now stand at the two-mile mark, having waited for Allison, and watching from a distance as we lose this meet.

I have a decision to make because I am a substitute coach. For the first and only time in my career, I have been hired to be a stopgap, an interim, a temp. As a result, I need not and perhaps should not, make any emotional investment in this team. Why try to build a relationship when I know that relationship will be severed at the end of this one season? Doing so might be most unfair and insincere to these girls.

So, I am puzzling over how to react to what has just occurred. Fire or ice? Passion or apathy? My mind is saying, "Let it go. Do nothing. Do not invest in this team."

My heart, however, has gone arrhythmic, thumping the underside of my ribcage with spastic, sped-up pulses that make the hair on my arms stiffen. I have an obligation to these girls to teach them how to compete.

I think to myself, "Fuh-ck!"

I shake my head, "How did I get myself into this?" and start my walk to where the girls have gathered by the finish line.

(4)

THREE WEEKS BEFORE THE start of that 2006 school year, and five days before the season was set to begin, the head girls' cross country coach at Wheeling had to resign for personal reasons. The current Assistant Principal for Student Activities (APSA)—I had quit that same position a few years earlier and returned, blessedly, to teaching English—was up a creek. The assistant cross country coach, the logical person to move into the head spot, neither desired nor was qualified to be the head coach.

The APSA knew me, knew that I had coached both girls' and boys' cross country earlier in my career and that I had extensive knowledge of the sport. He also knew, however, that I had stepped away from coaching all sports (I still coached debate) and that I, above all, didn't want to coach in the fall because both my oldest son and my oldest daughter attended the University of Notre Dame, and my wife and I didn't want to give up heading to South Bend for football weekends and to visit our kids.

But he was stuck, so he asked anyhow. Having once served the Dark Side[97] and been trapped in that position myself, I sympathized with his predicament. I knew what it was like as an administrator to have a team and no one to coach it. I agreed to help him out, but for only one year. That would give him time to find someone else.

Unlike the softball team I had taken over years before, the girls' cross country program at Wheeling had been a powerhouse for decades, winning four state titles, earning multiple state trophies, and dominating our conference. Only in the last two years had the team fallen on hard times.

---

97 Administration

Girls' cross country programs are dependent on their junior high feeder programs. Without expounding too much on female anatomy, many girls run far better as freshmen than they do as sophomores, juniors, and seniors. Physical maturity doesn't always help an emerging woman's athletic performance.[98]

For years, WHS had the best junior high girls' cross country feeder program in the state. For years, the team had multiple incoming freshmen capable of winning state medals. Couple those girls with the returning place-winners who may have declined a little as they aged but were still pretty darn good, and you have the depth for perennial success. But that feeder coach had retired. And with him went the golden goose.

The team I inherited had some talented runners, but no incoming freshmen capable of contributing on the varsity, and nowhere near the depth necessary to compete for a conference championship, let alone a state trophy. From all I could tell, we would be a solid, middle-of-the-road team, regardless of how well I coached. I couldn't do much good to help the team improve, not without having run a summer program[99], and I couldn't really fuck this thing up. Hell, I didn't even know any of the girls on the team, hadn't had any of them in one

---

[98] In a typical year, half of the top 20 finishers at the IHSA Girls Cross Country State meet are freshmen and sophomores. Contrast that with the IHSA Boys Cross Country State meet where two of the top 20 finishers are typically freshmen or sophomores.

[99] Summer mileage is essential to a successful cross country season. The girls need a 300+ mile base to build on when training for a three-mile race. The previous head coach had resigned for personal reasons, but one of those personal reasons may have been that the girls had been very non-committal to summer running.

of my classes. We were, for all intents and purposes, strangers.

No relationship. No obligation. No expectation.

For the first time in my career, I could relish the opportunity to grab an easy stipend and exert minimal effort because cross country is a very easy sport to coach passably. There are no plays to run, no offense or defense to devise, no positions to coach. There are no time-outs, no half-time speeches, no adjustments to make once the starting pistol has sent everyone on their way. There is very little strategy.

Practice most days is some minor variation of: one-mile warm up, stretch, five-mile run, 10 wind sprints, stretch, see you tomorrow. The competitions are straightforward: each girl runs three miles as fast as she can.

I'd help out the APSA, the girls could have an easy season, and I could collect an easy stipend. All good.

Which is indubitably why my brain was telling me to ignore what had just happened.

(5)

EXCEPT THAT THAT WOULD be no fun, and, more important, a real disservice to these kids. Allison helped me realize that. I coached her up, and she tried a little harder. That's what it's all about, right?

So here we are.

The entire team, all thirty-two girls, freshmen through seniors, is seated on the grass in a semi-circle in front of me. I have pulled them behind a line of bushes that forms the perimeter of the park, that demarcates the border between public space and private residences. We are, in fact, sitting on someone's back lawn.

I have pulled the team behind these bushes, this hedgerow, so we can have some privacy. I don't want the other spectators and parents to see what I am doing. Yes, I know damn well they will hear me—I want them to—but I don't want them to see how the girls are reacting, that is between me and my team.

I have been studying the results on my clipboard, looking down, not because I need to see those results, but because I want to delay any eye contact until I am ready to begin. I shake my head, feigning disgust, and toss the clipboard onto the grass at my feet. I look up, scan the group one time, and start.

"I am your fucking Coach!"[100] I say, a slow, low, assertive statement. I get the shock I want and the girls' full attention.

"In the *future*," I pause letting the emphasis echo, and then gradually raising the volume, "I don't care if GOD HIMSELF screams down from the heavens; you will do what I TELL YOU TO DO!"

"Am I CLEAR?"

The girls, as far as I can tell, react well. Some look up at me and nod. They didn't like losing to our rivals,

---

[100] I describe myself as having stress-induced Tourette Syndrome. In various situations—driving a third consecutive golf ball into the water on the same hole, getting cut-off by some knucklehead playing "find the fastest lane" in bumper-to-bumper traffic, nailing my thumb twice in a row with my hammer while repairing my roof on a frosty Chicago dawn—I have been known to run off poetic strings of profanity eight to ten curses long, never the same swear twice, often having no conscious awareness of what is spewing out of my mouth. This single f-bomb, in this context, was relatively minor.

either. Others bob their heads toward the blades of grass they are picking out of the soil and casting ineffectually into the non-breeze. Everyone has at least gotten the message.

"Ladies," I soften my tone, "we run as a pack, as a team, and I am your coach."

Again, no sign of dissension.

"Good," I say. I point across the hedgerow, "Go."

I cut them loose, back to clean up the course (this is a home meet), and gather their things for the bus ride back to school. The key will be tomorrow morning, if and how many parent phone calls ring into the APSA's office, if anyone calls to complain about the lunatic swearing and screaming at their little girl.

No one does.

(6)

For the rest of the season, I decide to coach as if I have been there ten years and will be there ten years more. In a way, I fake it. I pretend, every day, that I really care about these girls because caring about them makes coaching them more enjoyable. I am not so concerned with wins and losses. I just want to enjoy every day, and to me, that means putting my full effort into the task at hand and demanding the same from the athletes I coach. We even add some 6:00 a.m. four-mile loops (I supply orange juice and bagels afterwards) and long, slow Sunday morning runs (optional) through the local forest preserve.

I still have no intention of staying beyond that one year, but taking this sort of existential "live in the moment" approach helps the time pass both pleasurably and productively.

However, I screw up. By the end of the season, I am not just faking it, I feel it, especially toward the five juniors on the team. I care about them. They aren't simply athletes I coach; they are *my* athletes. And, from their standpoint, I am not just *a* cross country coach, I am *their* cross country coach. We have begun building a relationship. I invested in them, and they invested in me. However, we all know how this will end. The next fall season, I will go back to football weekends and visiting my own kids at Notre Dame, and they will have their fourth head coach in four years. This kinda sucks, but far more for them, because though I am used to the transitory nature of education—how each year there are new students, and the former ones move on—they are not.

After our final meet, the season now officially over, after the bus has taken us back to school and the girls have all been picked up by parents or driven off on their own, I plop down, alone, on a bench outside the building exit closest to the locker room doors. The sun, a respite on this crisp autumn afternoon, sparkles off the asphalt parking lot. I take off my hat and sunglasses, close my eyes, and tilt my head back against the rough brick wall of the school building. I embrace the warmth and resign my future to the deal I had originally made with myself, my family, and the APSA. One season. One and done.

I should have been happy.

(7)

Two weeks after the season ends, I schedule a meeting with those five juniors. I want to know what their plans are for the following summer, how they are going to get ready for the next season, what goals they have as individuals and as a team. I want to ask them about their futures.

To my opening series of considerations for next year, their counter is a collective nonverbal shrug that both tells and asks me, "Why do you care?"

I prod on. "You guys will be seniors; you'll be the captains next year. As you go, so goes the team."

They don't make eye contact, with me or each other. We are meeting in my classroom. I stand at the podium in front, leaning forward, balanced on my elbows. They sit side by side in the front desks of the middle five rows. Each respective desktop has that girl's undivided attention.

"So, what's the plan?" I ask. Nothing. The girls look side-to-side at each other, seeing if anyone has or is willing to offer a response. They are not defiant or sullen or whiney. They just look tired and done with it.

I get it. Senior year, in terms of cross country, is not something they look forward to. They see disarray and further abandonment. Four coaches in four years. Their reaction isn't personal; they know, understand, and accept my situation. Their situation just sorta sucks, in general. All successful athletes are ego-driven. Each has an internal motivation to win. But ego alone isn't enough. To get beyond the limits of what I can do alone, I need others. Ego is important, but relationships are essential. These girls have had little chance to build ones with each other or with a coach because those two things happen simultaneously. And now that they've started to become a team, the same old shit. Yes, it's not personal, but it's hard to feel like it isn't when it's four times in a fucking row.

Seventeen-year-olds shouldn't have to live in despair, not when it can be avoided.

I don't decide until that moment.[101] I'm not a martyr, and I don't feel sorry for these girls. I know how much fun coaching that previous season ended up being, and how much more fun coaching the next one could be. But not if they weren't all in, and I know they are because they all showed up, they all attended this meeting. If they had reacted differently, if they had been okay with everything and not cared, or if they had played the blame-game and wallowed in self-pity, I would have wished them well, and we'd have gone our separate ways. But they didn't.

"I don't think it's fair for you to have four different coaches in four years," I tell them, "so if it's all right with you, I'd like to come back next year, coach for one more season." I look for a reaction, maybe even joy, but they are stoic. They are all intelligent individuals. They know they are not in control of my decision, even though I am pretending to ask their permission. My request is purely rhetorical. They still feel like pawns. Why? Because there's always a catch, and they wait for it. *Under what conditions?* They wonder. *Where's the . . . But . . . ?*

---

[101] I had discussed this possibility with my wife, and she supported me in either regard.

I find out later that much of their reticence and skepticism is because they had resigned themselves to a different fate. Two of the girls had already decided not to run cross country next year. They had had enough. They only showed up for this meeting out of respect for their teammates.

Now, we navigate an awkward silence. They are looking at me, instead of their desktops, and they are waiting. I really don't know what to say. I haven't prepared for this moment. When I made my final decision an instant ago, I thought they'd be content to know I was returning the next year, and we could talk out the details later. I didn't know I'd have to close the deal now.

Inspiration always works out well; otherwise, we'd call it stupidity. Fortunately, I was inspired. A very simple concept pops into my head, and I know to run with it. The girls want to be a team; they want ownership and responsibility; they want conditions that make them a partner in and not an object of this bargain. The solution, I realize, involves basic math: Five girls = Five days of the week.

"But," I say, "I have two conditions. First, you have to be athletes, and you have to be coachable. Do what I say."

I start with this first condition because it is already known and expected. This is not a big deal. They are athletes, especially in terms of mentality. And, over the course of the previous season, they have become more coachable. They have adapted to my training expectations—the types of workouts I prescribe—and my philosophy regarding competition. They are allowed and encouraged to express their opinions, but the final say is mine. They have also embraced my sometimes abrupt and caustic, but caring nature. Still, I need to affirm we are on the same page.

"Second, you five have to run camp next summer."

As I mentioned, I have no idea I am going to require this second condition until just before I start speaking. It turns out to be one of the most profound and rewarding stipulations of my coaching career. The six of us are now both essential and interdependent.

"What does that mean?" Jenny asks. I am not surprised she is the first to speak up. Jenny has no problem advocating for herself and her teammates.

"That means for the six weeks of summer camp, from the middle of June through the end July, each of you takes one day and one workout. For example," I point to Karen, "Karen picks Mondays and the six-mile run around Lake Arlington. Every Monday for the six weeks of camp, she leads that specific workout."

I point to Amber, "On Fridays, Amber picks a track workout, say, 10 x 400m with a 200m jog rest. Every Friday, you all—the five of you and all the underclass ladies who sign up for camp—meet at the track and run that same workout. And so on. This way everyone knows what's happening and who's leading each day of the week. No mystery. No wondering what today's workout is. Every Monday, for example, is the same, and it's that lady's choice. You five can decide who's leading on which days and what that day's workout will be."

"What will you be doing while we're doing your job?" Jenny asks. She has a point. The head coach usually runs (and gets paid for) summer camp. I like the jalapeño in her tone.

"Watching." I smile.

"Can we talk alone?" Julie says, and, with a regal brush of her hand, politely motions for me to leave the room. "And close the door," she adds, a slight grin dimpling her cheeks.

I step out.

After a few minutes, Sammie comes to the door and invites me back in. The other girls are sitting straighter in their desks and their collective eyes track me from the door to the front of the room.

"Okay," Jenny tells me. "You got a deal."

"One condition," Julie jumps in. "On Fridays, after our track workout, we five plus any other girls who want to join us are going to cool down to 7/11 for Slurpees. You buy."

"After a full track workout, you're all going to run a mile-and-a-half to 7/11, drink a belly-full of Slurpee, and then jog back without puking?"

"We'll handle it."

"Then it's a deal."

(8)

I'VE COACHED FOR ALMOST forty years. I've worked with some outstanding individuals and some outstanding leaders. But I've never worked with a group of seniors who led together as well as these ladies did. They fought with each other, and they fought with me; this was not a season void of passion or intensity. We had plenty of both. But there were no destructive explosions. Everything we did was constructive. We built relationships.

These girls wanted to win; they worked their asses off and they deserved to win; but they didn't, not in the actual races, not at the level they wanted.

We didn't achieve any notable success during the 2007 season. We set no school records. We had no significant team accomplishments. Individually, our best girl won the conference championship but then stumbled slightly three weeks later at the State meet.

Our journey's end was unremarkable.

But our journey was exquisite, we lived a great many good hours, and it started with their leadership, their ownership of the program, beginning that summer.

(9)

On Saturday, July 25, 2020, while I was working on an early draft of this essay, in an instance of sublime concurrence, I received, completely unsolicited, a text from Jenny and Karen.

Here's what they wrote: "Hi Coach Burke! We are at the Dunes and reminiscing on the killer workouts you put us through! Hope you're well! 😊" They included a picture of their two smiling faces.

At the start of that 2007 season, I rewarded the varsity team for their hard work over the summer with a trip to the Indiana Dunes just outside Chicago where we ran circuits up and down the sandy hills (the highest being the 126 ft. Mount Baldy) and across the beach alongside Lake Michigan. Each circuit was a little over half a mile; we did five.

I should say, *they* did five, in the sand, under a scorching August afternoon sun, while I stood on top of Mount Baldy, stopwatch in hand, and timed each one. (The actual time to complete each circuit didn't matter; what mattered was that each circuit was being timed.)

I gave them a three-minute, water-and-rest break between each circuit.

The first one was fun, a new experience running in sand amidst the beauty of the dunes, an azure sky domed above us, the sun glinting hints of cool relief off the expanse of Lake Michigan. The second was work. The last three were about survival. Running in sand is difficult; running uphill in sand is a battle of will. Over those last three circuits, steepness and fatigue forced each girl to drop to all fours and bear crawl the last fifty yards to the finish at the top of Mount Baldy.

Those last three reps were a microcosm of our season. The girls talked each other up before each rep. "We can do this." They competed *with* each other and fed off of each other's resolve and determination during each rep. And as each one finished, instead of collapsing on the sand, she stood as tall as her exhaustion allowed and turned to cheer on a teammate fighting up the last few yards. "You got this!"

The text I got from Jenny and Karen: That's the impact I want to have on an athlete or a student, the experience I want us to share. I want them to look back with a sense of pride, fulfillment, and camaraderie while "reminiscing on the killer workouts you put us through." I want them to celebrate the time spent together working toward an end. That literal end is so often just one infinitesimally small part of the whole journey. If it happens, if I win, that's a nice affirmation, but it is by no means the defining achievement.

Process always supersedes product.

To see the journey's end in every step and to celebrate, both during and after, the good hours put into that journey, that is wisdom. Emerson knew this. So did those five very exceptional women I had the honor to coach.

CHAPTER 23

ON ALTRUISM

(1)

"Why do you want to donate your kidney?"

Her question threw me. My chin dipped down and away like a boxer squaring for defense. Is that meant to be rhetorical? After all the questions I've answered, why this one now?

The social worker and I sat across from each other in an examination room at Houston Methodist Hospital in Houston, Texas. We had been talking for almost an hour. There was no desk or barrier between us. We sat directly across from each other, our knees only a few feet apart. The social worker sat posture-perfect with her right leg folded over her left. She had auburn hair pulled back in a tight bun and black-rimmed owl eyeglasses. In her lap she balanced a clipboard. In her hand she held a pen pointed at me in anticipation of a response. I leaned back in my chair, my hands loosely on the arm rests, resisting the urge to grip. I didn't know how to answer this one.

Our setting had an awkward blend of intimacy and sterility. We were sitting close together, discussing some very personal information, in a small room with the door closed. And yet, this was an examination room: a white hospital bed behind me, white curtains draping the walls, white paint, white cabinetry, one stainless steel medical cart, and that smell with all its subliminal associations.

Aware of how nonplussed I had become, Alice—that was her name—set down her pen and note pad, leaned back in her chair, slapped her hands gently on her thighs, and smiled.

I got it. She was giving me the opportunity to be completely honest. I guess that meant we had a relationship, some trust between us. This final question would be off-the-record. "C'mon," her body language suggested, "we're friends now, so give me the simple, straightforward truth."

I continued processing, delaying, so Alice unfolded her legs and leaned forward, elbows to her knees, almost into my bubble. Earlier, her eye contact had been professional, shifting between the list of questions, my face, and the notes she was recording. Now, she tried to see me, honestly. The eyes *are* the windows to the soul. She repeated the question, placing emphasis on the first and third words.

"Why ... do *you* ... want to donate your kidney?"

I can be a wiseass, especially under threat, and she wanted an answer. What popped into my head was a rather crude question of my own: *Why does a dog lick its crotch?* I showed some self-restraint, though, and kept the wisecrack to myself. I didn't want to offend Alice. I knew she wanted what was best for me.

The humorous answer to the dog joke is: Because it *can*. Cue the light bulb. The joke may not have been appropriate, but the punchline was. It fit.

I smiled, shrugged my shoulders, and gave what, to me, was an obvious and completely honest answer to her question: "Because I can."

(2)

IN EARLY FALL OF 2010, my now son-in-law asked my oldest daughter to marry him. They had met as counselors at a camp for adolescents with Type 1 diabetes. There may not be such a thing as love-at-first-sight, but this was close. They shared good hearts, good values, and good looks. They dated long-distance for a while (he was from Houston; my daughter, when not at college at Notre Dame, lived with us in the suburbs just outside of Chicago) to confirm their initial attraction. He eventually asked and she said yes.

Because of the long-distance nature of their relationship, though my wife and I had met him many times, we had never met his parents. "We should all get together," my wife suggested.

Her simple comment initiated a much more complex discussion. Getting together would not be easy.

Jack, my son-in-law's father, had diabetes himself, had had it for years. The disease had taken its toll. He suffered from renal failure that necessitated dialysis three times a week (each a three-to-four-hour session). His only hope was for a transplant. That hope, however, was fading. As I learned after doing some research, the numbers are staggering.

Over 20 million adults in the U.S. suffer from some type of kidney disease. Over 500,000 are on dialysis. Over 100,000 are on the national waiting list for a transplant. At that time (2010), only 15,000 transplants took place each year.

Jack's chances of getting to the top of the list and finding an appropriate match (not a guarantee) weren't good. I went home and gave this all some thought. I talked it over with my wife and decided, what the fuck, let's see if I'm a match. After all, I only need one kidney.

I question the reality, the mundane existence, of miracles or luck. I believe in probability, and that even when the probability is low, there's still a chance. You take the three-quarter court shot as the buzzer sounds, you ask the most beautiful person you've ever met to grab a cup of coffee, and you get a blood and tissue test to at least find out if a total stranger is a match for a kidney transplant.

Sometimes, the one-in-a-million shot goes in, and it's not because you're lucky, it's because you took the shot. Turns out that I was a near-perfect match for Jack, not by some miracle, but because we did the test.

(3)

WHICH IS HOW I wound up talking to a social worker at Houston Methodist Hospital. It was the Tuesday before Thanksgiving. This was day two of the comprehensive physical and psychological examination I had to pass before the surgery itself could be scheduled. If all went well, the surgery would be set one month later, on the Tuesday before Christmas. If this sounds very poetic, aligning with Thanksgiving and Christmas, it wasn't. It was pragmatic. I taught high school English at that time; and since I had to fly to

Houston for these procedures, I wanted them scheduled to overlap my Thanksgiving and winter breaks, so I would not have to miss too much class time.

Day one, Monday, had gone well. A team of doctors reviewed my full medical history. I had more blood and urine tests. I had a full chest X-ray to make sure my heart and lungs were physically fit. I endured a battery of acronym exams: an ECG (electrocardiogram) to monitor heart function; a DRE (digital rectal exam)[102] to check my prostate; an MRI (magnetic resonance imaging) to assess the size, shape, position, and blood vessels of each kidney; and a BMI (body mass index) to measure overall fitness and to help gauge anesthesia. I also had an EGG for breakfast. Everything looked (and felt) great. I passed it all.

Day two. In the morning, I talked with a doctor on the transplant team about the preparation, the procedure, the short-term recovery, the long-term recovery, and the risks. That afternoon, I met with a social worker for the *Psychosocial Live Donor Assessment* interview.

During the first hour of our talk, Alice asked me all sorts of questions about my mental health and well-being. I learned that I was considered a "Good Samaritan Donor." That meant I wanted to donate to a *specific* person, but that I had no relationship with that person. However, despite their biblical reputation for unconditional benevolence, Good Samaritans, it turns out, are suspect. Alice spent a lot of time probing my

---

102 aka The Prostate Poke. Today, a blood test more effectively assesses prostate health, so doctors no longer do the DRE. Though I do not miss the "digit" up my ass, I do miss the running joke I had with my doctor, asking him before the DRE each year if he was going to buy me dinner first. He always smiled and never answered.

overt and covert motives for donating. All her questions, pitched from a dozen different angles and designed to keep me off-balance, sought only one answer: Why?

Was I donating out of a sense of obligation or guilt?

Did I hope to gain something by donating, such as self-respect, public approval or admiration, or even spiritual gifts?

Was I being pressured or coerced in any way?

Had this been an impulsive decision?

Am I having regrets or suffering from anxiety?

Have I suffered from depression or had suicidal thoughts in the past six months?

Alice asked me about alcohol and drug abuse: Was I a heavy drinker? A smoker? Did I ever engage in self-destructive behavior?

She wanted to know if I really understood the risks involved in this type of transplant. Yes, it's a common and safe procedure, but there are always risks, now and later, when I would live the rest of my life with only one kidney.

What about after? How would I feel if Jack's body rejected my kidney, and the transplant failed? What if he died?

Or, after a successful transplant, what if Jack rejected *me* by not showing any appreciation. How would that make me feel?

At first, when all this was being organized a month ago, I questioned why I had to meet with a social worker. After all, this was a *medical* procedure. Why did I have to stick around an extra day to talk about my feelings?

However, the nature of her questions helped me understand the fuller dynamics of this process. There is a darker side to human motivation, a tendency to do good things for questionable reasons. Alice's job was to peek behind the veil, to try and discover if the donor's primary motivation was valid and ethical, and then to probe a little deeper into the secondary and tertiary motivations.

I answered each question, and she took a lot of notes, and eventually the *Psychosocial Live Donor Assessment* portion of our interview concluded. Then, she put away pen and paper, relaxed, and looked me straight in the eye.

Why . . . do you . . . want to donate your kidney?

Looking back now, more than a decade later, I ask myself the same question (except with a slight shift in verb tense) and get the same answer.

Because I could.

I donated a kidney for both cynical[103] and pragmatic reasons. I weighed the costs and benefits, balanced the risks and rewards. I evaluated what was in it for me, and how this could help others as well. I decided that donating was the right thing to do. I am not a martyr. I would not have unwittingly put myself or my family at risk. I was also fifty years old at the time, not thirty. My perspective on life had evolved. I recognized my own mortality as inevitable, out there in the distance, but there, nonetheless. If I could help someone else gain a few bonus spins on the wheel of life, why the hell not?

---

103   I'm using a more classic definition of cynicism: the belief that individuals always act, primarily, in their own self-interest.

(4)

EVERYTHING WENT WELL.

Jack died recently, but my kidney allowed him to attend his son's wedding, travel with his wife, and meet his granddaughter. He carpe diem'd seven good years he would not otherwise have enjoyed.

Other than some time lost to the surgery and recovery, I have had—knock on wood—no consequences.

However, that's not to say there weren't some scares along the way. It's funny, but my most vivid memories of the whole experience weren't about the surgery, or Jack, or even being in Houston. If anyone asks, the stories I tell are about things I might have lost. Three of them. Two indulgences and one necessity. Taken away, almost.

(5)

DURING OUR INTERVIEW, WHEN Alice asked about my alcohol and tobacco consumption, I told the truth. Yes, I drank alcohol and smoked cigars. Then I rationalized that truth.

My parents had been both alcoholics and chain smokers. Neither had lived past sixty years old. I had no desire to follow their example. However, I was no Puritan. I drank—mostly beer—and smoked cigars. I tried to do both in moderation. But, yes, I admitted, I did indulge in each more than the "recommended" amount. Moderation is relative. I take care of myself. I'm in pretty good shape. I work out all the time. I tend to eat well. I allow myself a few vices, I told Alice, but counter that with exercise and diet. I am *not* self-destructive.

This was one of the few answers where I rambled because I worried it might bring a real cost. I feared she would inform me that should I choose to proceed with the donation, I would have to give up both drinking and smoking or risk poisoning my lone kidney. Had that been the case, I would have proceeded with the donation and subsequently abstained (mostly) from drinking and smoking, but this would have been a sacrifice. To my great relief, though Alice jotted down some notes while I babbled my response, she expressed no great concern. She didn't really say anything one way or the other.

Two doctors, however, did say something.

On Tuesday morning, as I was being wheeled to the operating room, the anesthesiologist, a man in his forties, asked me a bunch of routine questions based on the information on my chart. Standard stuff. Just as we got to the final door, however, he nodded to the nurse navigating me down the corridor and stopped the gurney.

"So," he said, tapping the chart, "you smoke cigars?"

I knew the surgery was on—he couldn't disqualify me now—but I was terrified that he would tell me what Alice had not: that I had to give them up. No more smoking!

"Yep," I answered, ready for the cutter to nip this guilty pleasure from my life.

"What are you partial to?" he asked, adding, "I like Hemingways from Arturo Fuente."

"Nice," I smiled. "I smoke CAO Golds and The Edge from Rocky Patel."

He nodded approvingly and patted my shoulder. "Moderation," he advised. "Don't overdo it. And take a month off until after your body recovers. Nothing, for a month."

I could handle that.

(6)

THAT WAS TUESDAY MORNING. As I mentioned, the surgery went well. My recovery also went well, for the most part (more on that in a minute), and by Thursday afternoon I was anticipating my release. However, every time I asked the nurse when the doctor would be coming by to "Bust me out," she told me he was still in surgery.

Now, it was close to five o'clock. "Nobody gets released this late in the day," I said to my wife. "They're going to make me wait until tomorrow." Fuck, I thought. Another night in a hospital bed.

Forty-five minutes later, Dr. Joe Murray, the surgeon who had led the transplant, pushed through my hospital room door. He looked exhausted, but he faked it well. I liked this man. He was older and accomplished. The first time we met, a month earlier during the screening process, he encouraged me to call him Joe or Dr. Joe. His age and experience allowed him to drop the pretension of being "Doctor Murray." Instead, we were all in this together.

"How you doing? Ready to go home?"

"Absolutely."

He held my chart in his hands, humming rhythmically as he flipped through the pages. The melody sounded a little like "The Farmer in the Dell."

Finally, he set the chart down and spoke to me.

"How are you feeling?" he repeated, this time tilting his head forward to read my eyes. No bullshit.

"Good," I said. He nodded.

"What have you been drinking?" His inflection made this seem an accusation, and I immediately felt guilty. My conscience associates "drinking" with alcohol consumption during my teens, as in my mother, herself sloshed, accosting me on a Friday night with *Have you been drinking!* to which I'd whine *I haven't been drinking, I swear!*

"Water and Gatorade," I answered, defensive, having no idea where this was heading.

"Really?" he questioned. I flinched. What had I done wrong?

"That's not gonna help," he frowned. "You need to get that kidney working."

He folded his arms across his chest, puzzling for a second, then raised his right hand up under his chin. He stood posed like Rodin's *The Thinker* and then harrumphed, having weighed several options before reaching a conclusion.[104]

"Do they have a bar in your hotel?" he asked.

I looked at my wife, then back at him. Was this a trick question?

"Yes," I answered.

---

[104] I'm a bullshitter, so I should have known he was bullshitting me from the start, but I didn't. Of course, he knew everything the nurses had given me to drink. He was just messing with me, which was great.

"When you get back, if you feel up to it, go down and have a couple of beers. Just a couple, and none of that *Light* crap, either. Have a Guinness, something with body. Get that kidney working. Give it something to filter."

If I feel up to it? *If?* I fought back tears of exaltation. I loved this man. Way to go, Joe!

"Okay," I nodded. I looked at my wife and shrugged, "Doctor's orders!"

Later that evening, when we got back to the hotel, I didn't have the strength to make it up to our room, so I went right into the bar and settled onto a cushioned stool. My wife, God bless her, brought my stuff upstairs.

I planted my elbows and folded my hands and bent my head in supplication. I allowed a moment for reverence. Then I lifted my eyes and smiled at the bartender.

"Guinness," I whispered.

(7)

I'M STUBBORN AND I'M competitive. I don't like depending on other people. I don't like drugs. In some contexts, these are very admirable traits. In others, not so much.

The third thing I mentioned that I might have lost scared the living shit out of me.

(8)

"WHEN CAN I GET out of here?"

We're back to Tuesday, after the surgery. I have just been moved from post-op to an actual hospital room, a single. I'm still fuzzy with anesthesia but already focusing on my release.

Nurse Violet feigns offense. "But we've only just met!" she chides, tucking in one side of my bedcovers. She smiles, and I like her immediately. She is close to my age, around 50, experienced without being jaded or dispirited. She has a slight, melodious Texas drawl, but her wit is all Irish. "Looking to leave me already?" she adds. She belongs tending bar at a pub in Tipperary.

She stands up straight, at the foot of the bed, puts her hands on her hips, and does her job well. "Two to three days." She reads my mind and adds, "*Not* counting today." She moves to the tray table next to my bed and fills a glass with water. "Thursday at the earliest. Could be Friday. You need to show us you can walk without falling on your face, and you need to make a stool." I want to make some wise-ass comment about not being a carpenter, but she nixes me with a glare.

"When can I start trying to walk?"

"Rest until after lunch, but if you're up to it, you can take a short walk this afternoon."

"Thanks." I immediately make a Thursday exit my goal.

Nurse Violet nods to point. "There's the remote. There's the call button. If you need anything, ring me. Otherwise, get some rest." She leaves.

Pain is there for a reason. Though it sometimes tells us to stop, mostly it reminds us to proceed with caution. It's the body's flashing yellow light: Slow down and be alert. If pain stays the same or gets better, then keep moving forward. If it gets worse, tap the brakes or stop completely. Pain is my guide.

Within reason, I don't mind pain. So, I don't ask Nurse Violet for any pain medication (I was to request as needed). I don't do this to be tough; I do it so I can track my recovery.

The floor I am on, like every other hospital floor I've ever seen, is rectangular with the rooms on the outside and the nurse's stations and utility rooms on the inside. I have a corner room, and on my first walk I make it to the nurse's desk halfway down the hallway before I get a little woozy and have to head back. An hour later, on the second trip, I make it to the end of the hall before turning around. On my third, just before dinner, I take the turn at the end of the hall and resolve to complete the full rectangle of hallways back to my room. I make it. The exercise has generated a healthy appetite, and I finish all my dinner. For the rest of the evening, at ninety-minute intervals, I get up and go for a walk around the square of rooms. I feel proud and know I am at record recovery pace.

That night, an attending physician stops in to check on me and asks if I had made a stool yet. Again, I want to quip about carpentry, but I don't. Doctors lose their sense of humor about halfway through a twelve-hour shift. He is working to be polite and affable, and I don't want to try his patience. I tell him no, and he encourages me to do so in the morning. It sounds like a threat. I had no idea how important it is to poop after surgery. He leaves, and I sleep surprisingly well.

I wake up the next morning, Wednesday, and feel pretty darn good. Not popping a turtle head or prairie dogging yet, but I have no pain and any of the anesthesia-induced spaciness I felt the day before is gone.

"Thursday, my ass!" I think. "I'm getting out of here today." I raise the back of my bed to a sitting position and consider what to do next. I decide to pee.

The bathroom has a large mirror that extends the length of the front wall. In it, I can see myself standing over the toilet. I pause, put my fists on my hips, and puff out my chest. I stand like Superman, admiring this rapidly recovering figure. The blue feather print of my hospital gown brings out my eyes. Fewer than twenty-four hours since donating a kidney, and I look damn good.

Instead of just pulling up the front of the gown to do my business, I untie the back and let the sides hang loose. Now an old west gunfighter, I square off with the figure in the mirror. I reach across to my left hip with my right hand and fling the gown back over my shoulder à la Clint Eastwood in *The Good, The Bad, and The Ugly*. Draw!

My heart stops, and I cannot breathe. I gape, my jaw literally dropping. A swollen, bulbous, purple mass stares back at me from where my genitals should have been. This isn't Barney the Dinosaur soft purple; this is Minnesota Vikings dark purple or *Smoke on the Water* deep purple. This is not good.

I suck in a few breaths and stagger backwards until my bare ass bumps into the bathroom wall. I no longer need to tinkle. "Thisisbadthisisbadthisisbad" hyperventilates through me. I tug my gown down from across my shoulder and cover the offensive area. I need to think.

I shuffle back to my hospital bed, gingerly now, terrified of disturbing whatever alien being has latched onto my crotch. I sit up with my legs stretched out and pull the covers up to my waist. What to do. What to do. I have to call the nurse.

Violet (the nurse, not my genitals) had been on duty the day before. She and I have at least some rapport. She is older and seasoned. Surely, she has seen something like my problem before and can immediately assuage my fears. Yeah, I'd have to endure some witty crack from her, but that would be okay, even welcome. Humor *is* the Lord's panacea.

I buzz for the nurse's station knowing Violet will answer my call. I am frightened and embarrassed. I don't want to turn to a stranger for help. I need her.

No luck.

Instead of Violet, a young, blonde-haired nurse I have not yet met bounces into my room. Her bright, cheery, what-a-beautiful-morning persona petrifies me.

"Hi! How can I help you?" She smiles. I grimace. She waits.

Nurse Annie repeats her question, but with a touch more gravity, "How can I help you?"

"I think I have a problem."

Her smile fades, and she suddenly looks very professional. I feel a little better. She nods her head for me to continue.

Nurse Annie stands near the back of my bed. My hands have been wringing the tops of my bed coverings, tugging them up to my chest. I motion her forward with a nod. She comes closer. I pull aside the sheet and blanket, then reach down to my gown. I hesitate, take a breath, and close my eyes. Slow exhale. I don't want to see her facial expression, but like a teenager at a horror film, I can't help watching through squinted eyelids.

I lift my gown up.

"Whoa!" Annie whispers. I open my eyes a hint more. She looks more amazed than aghast, impressed by this apparent medical marvel. She doesn't exactly say, "See something new every day!" but that's what her body language conveys. Her actual statement, however, though delivered with a casual, yet business-like aplomb, brings me no peace.

"I better get the doctor."

She says this, and, seeking to move quickly without appearing to rush, leaves. I cover up and go back to wringing my bed clothes. Shit!

Nurse Annie soon returns, not with any of the male doctors who might have been on call, but with a female doctor who could have passed for Annie's big sister. They enter like two schoolgirls ready to share a juicy secret; or, at least, that's how I, engulfed by self-consciousness, perceive it.

"I'm Doctor Marina Pisidia." She nods toward my privates. "Let's see what's up."

I am not misogynistic, I am not chauvinistic, I'm not even shy, but c'mon. Forget it, I think, I'm not exposing my mangled frank and beans to these young women. I'll just live with Peter Purple or a purple peter or whatever! Just get me out of here.

Instead, I pull aside the sheet and blanket and, again, lift my gown.

"Whoa," Doctor Pisidia whispers, and Nurse Annie nods in agreement. They are both impressed. (I know we are in Texas, but what's with all the "*whoa*"ing?)

"Am I okay?" I ask, fighting to mask the cracks in my voice.

Dr. Pisidia motions for me to cover up. She has seen enough. "Tell me about yesterday," she asks, "after the surgery, through last night. What have you been up to?"

I tell her about my frequent, progressive walks, how by the last few, I was practically jogging. I brag—though I don't want to sound cocky—about not taking any pain medication. "I didn't need it," I insist. I describe my healthy appetite, how I have eaten well. I confess, however, to having made no stool.

"I *feel* fine," I insist.

She waggles her head, processing.

"I think you overdid it, Mr. Burke, all those walks and no medicine." She sighs, taking a moment to phrase an explanation I can more clearly conceptualize. "In a sense, you locked up your abdomen. Your body was trying to send blood to that area to help you recover from the surgery, but you wouldn't let it get there. So," she nods toward Mulberry Street, "all that blood settled in the lowest spot available."

"The pain medicine isn't just for pain," she teaches me, "it's also a muscle relaxant so your abdomen doesn't lock up and so you can move your bowels. And, the walks are to help get your blood flowing, not to train you for a marathon."

I'm such an idiot.

Dr. Pisidia turns to Nurse Annie, "Be sure he takes his medication, all of it. Limit him to just three walks: one after breakfast, one after lunch, one after dinner." She turns to me. "Stay in bed and let your body do its job. Every now and then, do some breathing exercises to relax. Breathe in through your nose, hold for four-count, purse your lips, and exhale slowly." Back to Nurse Annie, "He *should* be fine by dinner," back to me, "if he listens," back to Annie, "by then, everything should be closer to normal."

"Take it *easy*, Mr. Burke," she assures me, tamping the air with her palm.

"Thanks," I say, nodding to each of them. I am so relieved to have just been stupid. I start puffing spasmodically, my vision blurs, and a few bulbous tears trickle down both cheeks. They politely turn and leave.

(9)

THE WORLD IS A very good place. Yes, there are evil shits who fuck it up and put all of us at risk, but this essay isn't about them. This essay is about altruism, about the vast majority of people being good to each other. Why? Simply because they can.

CHAPTER 24

WHY READ LITERATURE: WHITMAN, "SONG OF MYSELF, 52"

(1)

EVERY POEM ABOUT DEATH should include a reminder about life.

When I die, if circumstances allow and some sort of *Celebration of Life* occurs, I'd like "Song of Myself, 52" by Walt Whitman to be one of the readings. I'd also like, if appropriate, one or even a few of my former students to do that reading.[105] Literature has been a fundamental part of my life, and I'd be remiss if I didn't invite at least one of the authors I've spent decades teaching to speak at my memorial through the conduit of those I taught.

---

105   I say, "if circumstances allow" and "if appropriate" because who knows when and how this death will occur and what will be my status at the time: will I die respected, unknown, disdained? I am working on the first, but don't rule out the second, or third. I try to take nothing for granted; complacency is a crippling vice.

I enjoyed teaching "Song of Myself, 52" to high school juniors because it helped them, for a moment, step out of the chaos of their daily trials and tribulations—the trivial, yet meaningful labors of teenage life—and take a more wholistic view of their existence. Whitman's poem isn't a somber meditation on death; it's a playful tango with everlasting inevitability. The poem's images and diction made my students smile, and the underlying concepts made them think.

I've included Whitman's poem. As with all poetry, I encouraged my students to read it aloud, and with this one, to allow their tongues, teeth, and lips to be especially expressive such that Whitman's unEnglishness and chunky diction bounce around like dice clicking across a craps table. Don't rush. Hear the sounding of his phrases: the alliteration, assonance, and onomatopoeia.[106] Follow the punctuation, and pause at each period to savor the imagery of every sentence.

Finish reading the whole poem, I recommended, then go back and consider what each of these seven sentences suggests on the metaphoric, philosophic, and aesthetic levels.[107]

---

106 Alliteration is repetition of initial consonant sounds: the "f" in *failing to fetch me at first*. Assonance is the repetition of vowels sounds: the "uh" in *the runaway sun*. Onomatopoeia is when the sound is the meaning of the word; while there are no singular examples of onomatopoeia in the poem (though *yawp* probably qualifies), the sound of several phrases clearly mimics what is being described: I can hear the water swirling in the phrase *I effuse my flesh in eddies*.

107 See Burke's website for more on the 4 Level Analysis/Individual Art Assignment.

Song of Myself, 52

The spotted hawk swoops by and accuses me, he complains
    of my gab and my loitering.
I too am not a bit tamed, I too am untranslatable,
    I sound my barbaric yawp over the roofs of the world.
The last scud of day holds back for me,
    It flings my likeness after the rest and true as any on
    the shadow'd wilds, it coaxes me to the vapor and the
    dusk.
I depart as air, I shake my white locks at the runaway sun,
    I effuse my flesh in eddies, and drift it in lacy jags.
I bequeath myself to the dirt to grow from the grass I love,
    If you want me again look for me under your boot-soles.
You will hardly know who I am or what I mean,
    But I shall be good health to you nevertheless,
    And filter and fibre your blood.
Failing to fetch me at first keep encouraged,
    Missing me one place search another,
    I stop somewhere waiting for you.

(2)

THE BELL RINGS, AND I turn and point to a female student sitting in the first row, second seat, over by the windows.

"How old are you?" I ask. She cocks her head, hesitant to answer. The other students are still settling into their seats. She looks to a few of her neighbors to see if anyone knows where this is going, but they are clueless. The question seems harmless enough.

"Sixteen," Dairy[108] answers, smiling. Her voice is just above a whisper, the inflection caught between declarative and interrogative.

I fold my arms across my chest, scrunch my eyebrows, and wait for the rest of the class to come to attention, to cue into this opening to today's lesson. When they quiet and at least appear focused, I continue.

"Are you sure?" I challenge. The class stills and Dairy retreats. Her cheeks involuntarily flush and her smile winces. Everyone sees the pain. Is she wrong? Is *Dairy* wrong? She doesn't mind *being* wrong, but she knows (or at least thinks she knows) that the others have perked up. They're all staring at me!

In this class, she's the AP Alpha, the smartest kid in the room and, likely, the nicest. She's also an intellectual introvert: motivated and diligent, but uneasy with the attention—admiration always tinged with a little jealousy—that her test scores and her grade point average bring. She prefers to stay in the background, to be the unassuming scholar. Now, she is the uneasy center-of-attention, and I am suggesting that she doesn't even know how old she is. I'm messing with her to introduce a central point for today's lesson. This should be harmless banter, but I realize I've struck a chord that goes far deeper than the here and now. This is baggage carried in from elsewhere. However, regardless of the

---

[108] "Dairy" is short for Diarmuid (pronounced DEAR-mwid) which is Irish for "without enemies." Dairy was named after her maternal grandfather, a kind and gentle man who died shortly before she was born. Dairy's parents knew she couldn't be *called* Diarmuid, a masculine name. As a diminutive, they quickly passed on "Diary" and "Deary" and settled on "Dairy," which suggests one who provides or nourishes. Unfortunately, in a wee bit of Irish Irony, Dairy was lactose intolerant. (Not really, but that would be amusing.)

reason, I've embarrassed her. I too am now blushing, and the whole dynamic of the class has become awkward. All in an instant.

To shift the focus, to bail us all out, I pick a pencil off the gutter at the top of her desk and hold it up for the class. "How old is this pencil?"

No one has an answer, and I am definitely off the island. I've embarrassed a student who I—and everyone else—can tell now feels embarrassed over having become embarrassed over something so trivial. Yet here we all are.

I move away from Dairy's desk and to the whiteboard at the front of the classroom. I write, in big red letters, *The Law of Conservation*.

"What's the Law of Conservation?" I ask. "Physics, folks. Not con*vers*ation, con*serv*ation. The Law of Conservation?"

I look to Dairy, wanting to offer her, and me, a way out. I know she is the lone junior taking 12th Grade AP Physics, I know she will answer correctly, and I hope her answering will temper the awkwardness between us, but her head twitches and her deer-in-headlights eyes beg: *Please don't make me.* She will, if I call on her, she will answer correctly and hold no grudge against me. But I don't force her. I call on Jacob instead.

"Jacob, c'mon, what's the Law of Conservation?" He knows the answer, but he doesn't know why I'm asking this question. He is a healthy skeptic, and he doesn't want to be tricked like Dairy appears to have been. Where is this going?

I get him started, "In a closed system, matter and energy..." I beckon with my hand, calling him to complete the statement.

". . . are neither created nor destroyed," he finishes. Perfect. Well done, Jacob. The tension loosens. The class, however, is completely lost. Why is Mr. Burke teaching physics and what does any of this have to do with the Walt Whitman poetry we read last night for homework?

"Good. Thanks. The Law of Conservation states that in a closed system matter and energy are neither created nor destroyed; they are simply redistributed."

I wave the pencil back and forth. "Let's add 'Space' to the mix as well, since without space, nothing could move. Get it? Matter and energy could not act on each other if there were not space for them to do so." I write the three words on the board: Matter. Energy. Space.

"Let's assume that the universe is a closed system. That means all matter, space, and energy are neither created nor destroyed. Everything is constantly being redistributed, but nothing is new. Shapes and forms may change, but the core elements are constant." I pause for an instant and focus again on the pencil.

"So, Jacob, in theory, how old is this pencil?" He thinks for a second.

"As old as the universe," he smiles.

"And . . " I move to Dairy's desk and lay down the pencil. "How old is Dairy?"

"As old as the universe," he laughs.

I turn to Dairy, quipping, "You look pretty good for a few billion years old." She smiles, eased somewhat, and her fellow students laugh with her. Then I leave her alone.

I go on to explain how, if the Law of Conservation is correct, when we die, the matter and energy and space that make up our bodies will simply be redistributed, never lost. "That's part of what Whitman examines in *Song of Myself, 52*," I tell the class, "but in a much more descriptive and poetic fashion."

I break the students into small groups to share key lines and favorite images and to gather questions to ask when we again become whole. The "redistribution" concept has unlocked much of the poem. The fun of our final discussion is calling on different groups who each unravel key phrases that some, but not all, picked up on.

One group notes how the young, *spotted hawk* is telling the old man with *white locks* that his time is over, that he needs to stop *loitering* and just die.

Another group points out how the narrator will become part of the *air*, water (*I effuse my flesh in eddies*), and earth (*I bequeath myself to the dirt*). They laugh at how he suggests that we will eat him and that the nutrients of his corpse will *filter and fibre your blood*.

Another likes the *look for me under your boot-soles* line, and how at the end, the narrator reminds us that we all will meet the same fate: *I stop somewhere waiting for you.*

When we finish, I remind my students to *Be a Filter, Not a Funnel*. "Ask yourself," I say. "Do I buy what Whitman is selling? Does his concept of death fit my experience and my philosophy? Is there anything here I can use?" I want my students to understand what

Whitman's poem suggests, but not to agree. It's up to them.

(3)

BEFORE CLASS ENDS, OVER the last five minutes or so, I tell the students that the poem is not just about death. It's about living life before death. Whitman's narrator is *not a bit tamed* and *untranslatable.* He sounds his *barbaric yawp over the roofs of the world.*

"A *yawp,*" I explain, "is a passionate, audible expression of life. Yawps happen when my emotions well up and explode forth and I don't give a flying-frijole who might be listening. A yawp can be driven by joy, anger, frustration, even relief . . . whatever emotion dominates my being in that moment. A yawp can be shared with others, but it's primarily for me."

And there is the Individual Art[109] challenge. Over the next week, any student can earn up to 10 points of IA credit by sounding their barbaric yawp.[110]

To earn full credit, a student, Jacob, for example, must first ask permission to yawp. "Mr. Burke, I'd like to Yawp today." He then stands alone in front of the class. I tell him to try as best he can to ignore his present surroundings—especially his classmates—and picture the circumstance that is motivating his yawp. Visualize, gather his emotions, and then, when he is ready, let it out. Yawps are sounds, not words, I remind him, so just belt out his passion.

---

109   I didn't give extra-credit per se, but I did allow students to complete Individual Art projects to earn additional credit. See Burke's website for more on the 4 Level Analysis/Individual Art Assignment.
110   Yes, I stole the idea from the film, *Dead Poets' Society.*

Jacob, in fact, is the first to volunteer. His yawp snowballs out over a good seven seconds until his cheeks tomato, his eyes glisten, and his breath is spent. His fellow students flinch at first—he is quite loud— then give him a nice round of applause, and I'm glad I forewarned our security staff that we would be yawping this week and not to be shocked by any boisterous outbursts from room 148.

As simple as this sounds ("You mean all I have to do for 10 points is stand in front of the class and scream?"), it's extremely difficult for most students. Too often we are taught to control our emotions, that self-expression makes us vulnerable, that we should keep a low profile and not draw attention to ourselves. Even in the relatively safe environment of a classroom, we're afraid to cut loose.

By the end of the week, maybe a third of the class has taken advantage of the opportunity. On Friday, as the students enter my class, I call out, "Last day to yawp! Now or never."

Dairy is passing my desk just as I say this, and I add, sotto voce, "Dairy? Yawp?" A reflexive smile—she's so damn polite—but the same wide eyes and tremor of her head. No way. Not today.

But not never.

The Whitman unit is in March. The school year ends in June. On the very last day of class, on that late spring morning when the sky is flawless and the sun sparkles throughout the window glass, Dairy arrives first. She approaches my desk, smiling the same as each day, pleasant and cordial, though today more of her effervescence ripples around her eyes, and her voice has a delightful, mischievous timbre.

"Mr. Burke," she asks, "can I yawp today?" Okay, so it's my turn to be thrown off-guard. I tuck my chin and raise my eyebrows. She's serious.

"I can't give you any credit," I tell her—she doesn't need any, her class average is over 100%—"but you *may*," I correct, always the English teacher, "if you *can*."

"I can," she affirms, then nods and turns to go to her desk.

After the bell has rung and the rest of the students have taken their seats, without any preface or introduction, I call her to the front of the room. "Dairy," I say and wave my hand toward center stage. She takes the spot and stands still. Her classmates silence in anticipation; something is happening here.

She closes her eyes, rolls her shoulders back, and measures out three deep breaths, holding the last one: In. Out. In. Out. In . . .

She *YAWPS* and her complexity bursts out across the room, followed by a blush and a whisper of laughter, and the spontaneous applause of her classmates.

(4)

IN MY CLASS, I define beauty—the aesthetic level—as that which stirs the emotions. That moment with Dairy was one of the most beautiful of my career. She stepped outside her comfort zone, and in that moment connected with one piece of literature we had covered. She did it for herself; her classmates and I were just witnesses.

I would like this poem read at any memorial service I might have for three primary reasons.

First, there's no doubt that Whitman is having fun writing this poem. The subject matter is grave, but his diction dances and struts and taunts and defies. I like that.

Second, the philosophic message of the poem resonates with me. I agree that in death, my body—and perhaps my soul—will be redistributed into the air, water, and earth around me. That's why I would like to be cremated in order to expedite that process. I also appreciate that fundamental need to YAWP at certain seminal moments in my life. I hope to always live with passion, to feel the beauty of the world around me, and to occasionally let those emotions burst forth.

Third, the impact that poem had on one student characterizes, in principle, my relationship with literature over the past five decades of my life. I will never forget Dairy and her demonstration of how literature can be a conduit to reflection, self-assessment, and potential growth.

For her, it was the little "l" literature of one poem.

For me, it has been the all-encompassing capital "L" Literature of books and poetry and music and drama and film and art and everything that addresses some aspect of human nature and challenges me to *Be a Filter, Not a Funnel*, and to ever learn about and feel the beauty of myself and the world around me.

Why read literature?

I might as well ask, "Why live?"

Yawp!

CHAPTER 25

ACKNOWLEDGMENTS

Part One: Admiration

(1)

Above all, be the heroine of your life, not the victim.
—Nora Ephron

ONE OF MY OLDER brothers passed away while I was editing this collection. He is the first of our siblings to die. At his "Celebration of Life" reception, one of my older sisters spoke. In a succinct, matter-of-fact statement, she said, "My father was a beast." She went on to explain that this brother, at a few key moments in her life, had been her protector, her savior, had shielded her from our father.

Some of the stories I've told in this collection are indicative of the violence that was prevalent in our family and the abuse my father inflicted upon each of us; but I, relatively speaking, didn't get anywhere near the worst of it.

My sister's comment triggered something in me, a memory from early adolescence, but also an acknowledgement and a reminder of my tremendous respect for her. I'm going to share this memory to provide just a hint of context for why I opened this section with the quote from Nora Ephron.

(2)

Winter settled heavily that night, a sedate dark snow, massive flakes blanketing everything. I chose to go to bed early. I don't remember anyone else being around. My brothers were gone. I lay awake in bed, staring up at the ceiling, out the window, up at the ceiling. I must have zombied out. A commotion down the hall—a cacophony of mantra-like chants offset by harsh interrogation—raised me from the fog. Voices. Real ones. I sat up and listened.

I got out of bed and followed the sounds down to my sister's room. The door was open, and I stepped in. My sister was curled up on the bed, on her side in a tight fetal position. She had her head buried between her knees. Her arms wrapped tight around her shins and her long hair veiled her face. She made me think of a roly-poly, one of those little bugs that when touched, snaps into a defensive shell. She twitched as she begged, "pleaseletmediepleaseletmediepleaseletmediepleaseletmediepleaseletmedie."

My mother sat on the bed, both hands trying to pry my sister open, barraging her with questions: *Where were you?* Tug an arm. *What did you take?* Twist a wrist. *What did you do?* Slap on the shoulder. *WHAT DID YOU DO?* Shake. Shake. Shake.

Neither of them saw me. I couldn't take it. "Don't!" I screamed. My sister's mantra diminished to a whisper.

My mother's hands flattened on my sister's back, and she turned to me in slow motion, her face ashen. "Go to your room," she said, low, flat. She added, nodding behind me, "Close the door."

"Now."

As I turned to leave, now trembling violently enough to make my voice quaver, I yelled to my sister, both plea and command, "DON'T DIE!"

She didn't.

(3)

But she had some rough years ahead. Not my story to tell.

However—and it's a significant however—she eventually got her feet under her and became a nurse. For over three decades her vocation has been caring for others, putting others before herself. I know she's good at what she does. Kindness in tiny packages delivered continuously. Hard work, too. Hard work to love others and to love yourself loving others.

We are not close; we live a long way away. There is no animosity, just too much baggage for that train to make it cross country. I've never told her this, but I admire her. Instead of being the victim of her life, she's become the hero. That takes tremendous courage and a shit-ton of introspection about and acceptance of what we can and can't control in our lives. She is not perfect—we're all fallible human beings—but I think she works at it. I think she works at being her better self.

"Jimmy, some of it's tragic, and some it's magic, but I've had a good life all the way."—Jimmy Buffett, "He Went to Paris"

My wish for her is that she looks back on her life with the stoic positivity of the old man in this song. I hope she focuses on the good hours of her journey and celebrates the person she is. Most of all, I thank her for being a positive role model.

Part Two: Thanks

THIS HAS BEEN A years-long journey, and I've had quite a few beta readers along the way. I'm guilty of a bit of redundancy in these acknowledgments because I use the word "perspective" multiple times. That's by design because that's what I sought.

- Alexis Quiterio, the first person to read my essays. Thanks for the early feedback and sharing your always positive energy.
- Meg Files and the members of the 2023 Tucson Festival of Books Masters Workshop. Thanks for recognizing one of my essays and providing invaluable feedback on balancing my narrative voice with my teacher voice.
- Julie Ruzkowski. Thanks for providing an elementary teacher's perspective on several of my essays.
- Darren Pierre. Thanks for reading my full collection from the perspective of a collegiate professor and published author, and for suggesting that I eliminate some of the randomness and provide more of a narrative arc to this collection.

This final product would not have been possible without that adjustment.

- John Uhrik and Laura Johnson, my colleagues and friends. You both provided a high school English teacher's perspective on my essays and excellent suggestions regarding both content and structure. More important, you've both been enthusiastic encouragers for me to keep going and finish this journey. You are both outstanding educators, and I hope the day comes when you too can tell your stories.
- Kayla Kennedy, my former student and current friend and mitts partner. The smartest move I've made since retiring was bartering boxing lessons for your critique of my writing. You read each essay multiple times and provided layered, constructive criticism from a non-teacher perspective. You also progressed from being a boxing student to the best mitts partner I could imagine. You are awesome.
- Jacob Sweetow, my former student and current friend and book club partner. Our philosophic discussions and basic life musings helped keep me mindful of life as a product of the present even though I was spending so much time writing about the past. The lessons we learn evolve, but don't age. You are my constant reminder of this.
- John Kading, Len Sitko, Kevin Campbell, Jenny Giron, and Karen Segura. You each read essays in which you were central characters and provided crucial feedback to help me get those stories

right. You and Kayla and Jacob are each emblematic of the individuals I have taught and coached over the years who have inspired me and helped me toward my better self. Good students make good teachers. If I was a good teacher, it was only because you and thousands of individuals like you motivated me to be so.

I mention above that "thousands of individuals" have motivated me. That is not an exaggeration. Over my career, I figure I have taught and coached over four thousand young women and men. I have also worked with hundreds of colleagues. Thank you all for being a part of my life, my career, and my stories.

I want to thank JuLee Brand for taking a chance on this collection. I hope these words matter.

Finally, I want to thank my wife, children, sons-in-law, daughter-in-law, and grandchildren for the work they do every day to be their better selves. I will never take this work for granted because you constantly remind me how important and ultimately rewarding it is. To my children, especially, I am so grateful and honored to be a part of your lives. Mike, you are my favorite oldest son. Ben, you are my favorite youngest son. Kristin, you are my favorite oldest daughter. Amy, you are my favorite youngest daughter. I love you all beyond measure.

Mike Jr, I do need to give you a special shout-out for doing multiple critiques of all my essays and giving me excellent advice on which to choose for the final edition. You and Jenna also gave me a beautiful gift that I cherish: a leather-bound copy of my full collection.

Kathy, we've been married for over forty years now. These essays are about me as a teacher, but I could not have been the teacher I was without your love and support. I've always kidded that the acronym that should follow my name to designate my "profession" is HFTC. Husband, Father, Teacher, Coach. I've always tried to keep that order as my priority (though I admit the time allotment to those roles sometimes gets skewed). We joked when we got married that a commitment for "life" was a bit much, so we agreed to renegotiate after fifty years. I look forward to that renewal of our commitment to each other.

CHAPTER 26

DISCUSSION QUESTIONS: LESSONS LEARNED

IN ALL REGARDS, THE goal here is to *Be a Filter, Not a Funnel*. Think about what Burke has written and then decide for yourself if his point is valid and useful, or if he's full of bean dip. In the questions below, I use the word "teacher." However, as noted in Chapter Two, I mean teacher as one who teaches, not necessarily the professional educator. To me, every leader in every role is a teacher.

These questions are meant as starters for thought and discussion.

1. Burke argues that "All that is not tragedy is comedy" and that we shouldn't "obsess over an outcome that didn't occur." Do you agree? Do any of your personal experiences or family stories align with this philosophy? Did potential tragedy ever become comedy because the worst didn't happen? (Moonshine)

2. Take a look back at the five types of ethos presented in Section 8, paragraph 2. Burke states that the best teachers, such as Fr. Francisco, establish ethos in a variety of ways. Who are the best teachers you've known and how did they establish ethos? Who were some of the weakest and what did they lack? What is your plan? How do you intend to establish ethos in the various leadership roles you fill? (Ethos and Titular Power)

3. Burke opens this essay by stating that his "teaching career began with a lie." What did he learn about teaching in general, but especially about himself, from his experience with Sergio's mom? (Ethos and Titular Power)

4. Critique the final word of this essay. What does that "Maybe" suggest? (Hot Lava)

5. The crux of this essay is about how difficult it is to be both empathic and humble, to walk in another's shoes without judging and to learn without presuming to know. Why is this so difficult, and why is it so important for a teacher to try and be both empathic and humble? (Soldier's Work)

6. "My life is defined more by subtle gestures than by Hallmark Moments." To what extent is this true? Is a quiet evening on the couch with my wife watching our favorite TV series more indicative of our relationship than our actual wedding day? (The Sneeze).

7. Are certain aspects of our character and personality, in a sense, inherited? To what extent are

we fated, for better or worse, to becoming our parents and/or childhood role models? (Love Taps)
8. Burke writes that "Intellect annuls fate, but only through introspection and then action." Analyze and evaluate this statement. (Love Taps)
9. Why the aside in Section 3? Does Burke's aunt offer valid advice regarding how to support someone who is grieving? (A Recovery Run)
10. "An unfortunate reality of sports is that we remember the wins and relive the losses." Do serious athletes ever fully recover from the pain of a dramatic loss? (A Recovery Run)
11. As a teacher, what are the "grains of sand" that most wear on you? What de-escalation strategies work best for you? (Escalation)
12. Regardless of where you are in the arc of your career, how concerned are you with your legacy? How would you like to be remembered by the (possibly thousands of) students you taught? (Escalation)
13. The best positive role models "aren't trying to do anything more than set a good example." How did Miss Portier set a good example while also maintaining distance? Why would it be "dangerous" for Burke to imagine that Miss Portier actually liked him? (Righteous Indignation)
14. Students need and want discipline. True? What, for a teacher, are the implications of accepting this adage? (The Olive Tree)
15. Burke refers to Clarissa, by name, 23 times in this essay. And yet, he prefers no one talk about

what happened to her or about "it." Why? (Ought versus Actual: Clarissa)
16. Discipline is, arguably, the most challenging aspect of a teacher's job. The previous five essays, from "Escalation" through "The Double Bird," have all dealt with some aspect of discipline. Are there four or five takeaways from these essays that seem most practical and applicable, at least in principle, to any teacher-student relationship?
17. How much do good manners matter in effective discipline, i.e. discipline that impacts behavior beyond the singular incident being addressed? (Note: Not taking things personally is an essential aspect of good manners.)
18. Are co-curricular activities as fundamental to an individual's education as any academic class? (Wrestling with an Existential Crisis)
19. Critique Burke's advice to "simplify things" in order to survive to the end of a career. What are the potential drawbacks to this approach? (Survival)
20. What are the dangers of "being, at times, *that* guy"? What are the rewards? What equity needs to have been built into a relationship before one can get away with this type of joking around? (A Healthy Dose of Skepticism)
21. Many great athletes have overcome dramatic adversity at some point in their careers. What character traits and outside influences most help these individuals persevere? (The Mask)
22. Evaluate Burke's advice: "I want you to wrestle. Not so you can fight, but so you can walk away

from a fight without being afraid. If you know you can take care of yourself, you never have to prove it to anyone. You can just walk away. But if the moment does arise where you have to . . . well . . . take care of yourself . . . you'll have a plan." Is this advice practical for everyone? (Why Wrestling)
23. Burke claims he has "no interest in influencing what my students believe." He only wants to "broaden their perspectives." And yet, doesn't broadening one's perspective, by the fact itself, influence one's beliefs? To what extent is broadening one's perspective a fundamental part of an individual's education? (Viewing Death)
24. This is the most personal and introspective essay Burke has shared. Could this essay have been written prior to Burke's retirement from teaching? (Football and "The Scorpion and the Frog")
25. Who are the most authentic teachers and coaches you've met during your educational career? What "bits" of practice, content, and style made them exceptional? (Tough Love and Late Essays)
26. Process over product. Relationships over wins. How practical is this approach given our often hyper-competitive atmosphere? (The Journey)
27. Critique Burke's final assessment. Is the world "a very good place"? (On Altruism)
28. When is the last time you *Yawped*? (Why Read Literature: Whitman, "Song of Myself, 52")

ABOUT THE AUTHOR

OVER THE COURSE OF his career, **Mike Burke** taught English and coached a variety of men's and women's sports and activities at five different high schools in the suburbs of Chicago. (He was also on the Dark Side for seven years.) Now retired, his debut memoir-in-essays looks back on the lessons learned through a lifetime in education. Married for over 40 years, he and his wife have four adult children and seven grandchildren. Aside from enjoying plenty of family time, he complements his new "career" as an author by giving boxing lessons, announcing high school basketball games, and facilitating a local Writers Workshop. A dynamic speaker, Burke has presented at state and local conferences on leadership, athletics, and classroom pedagogy. His experiences as a teacher and coach continue to inspire his writing and his message. His next book, *Run*, is currently under construction.

coachmfburke.com

www.ingramcontent.com/pod-product-compliance
Lightning Source LLC
Chambersburg PA
CBHW021139160426
43194CB00007B/631